Systems Software

Systems Software

Essential Concepts

First Edition

Eurípides Montagne
University of Central Florida

Bassim Hamadeh, CEO and Publisher
Amy Smith, Senior Project Editor
Alia Bales, Production Editor
Jess Estrella, Senior Graphic Designer
Natalie Piccotti, Director of Marketing
Kassie Graves, Senior Vice President of Editorial
Jamie Giganti, Director of Academic Publishing

Copyright © 2022 by Eurípides Montagne. All rights reserved. No part of this publication may be reprinted, reproduced, transmitted, or utilized in any form or by any electronic, mechanical, or other means, now known or hereafter invented, including photocopying, microfilming, and recording, or in any information retrieval system without the written permission of Cognella, Inc. For inquiries regarding permissions, translations, foreign rights, audio rights, and any other forms of reproduction, please contact the Cognella Licensing Department at rights@cognella.com.

Trademark Notice: Product or corporate names may be trademarks or registered trademarks and are used only for identification and explanation without intent to infringe.

Cover image copyright © 2018 iStockphoto LP/GeorgePeters.

Printed in the United States of America.

To my family.

Brief Contents

Preface — xiii

Chapter 1. Systems Software — 1

Chapter 2. The Processor as an Instruction Interpreter — 11

Chapter 3. Stacks, Recursion, and Nested Programs — 43

Chapter 4. The Heap — 65

Chapter 5. Lexical Analyzers and Symbol Tables — 81

Chapter 6. Syntax Analysis and Code Generation — 103

Chapter 7. Assemblers, Linkers, and Loaders — 129

Chapter 8. Understanding the Interrupt Mechanism — 151

Chapter 9. Processes and Threads — 177

Chapter 10. Process Synchronization — 191

Detailed Contents

Preface	xiii
Chapter 1. Systems Software	**1**
Activating Prior Knowledge 2	
What Is Systems Software?	3
Software Tools for Program Development	4
Software to Create Runtime Environments	6
Outline of the Book	7
Summary 9	
Exercises 9	
Bibliographical Notes	10
Bibliography	10
Chapter 2. The Processor as an Instruction Interpreter	**11**
Activating Prior Knowledge 12	
On Naming and Data Representation	13
A P-code Register Machine	16
Computer Organization	17
Memory Organization	19
Fetch Execute Cycle	22
Assembly Language Programming	25
Assembler Directives	30
Instruction Set Architecture	32
Process Address Space	36
Some Remarks on VM/0	38
On Word Length and Byte Addressable Memories	38
On Condition Codes	39
On Increasing VM/0 Word Length	39
Summary 39	
Exercises 40	
Bibliographical Notes	41
Bibliography	41
Chapter 3. Stacks, Recursion, and Nested Programs	**43**
Activating Prior Knowledge 44	
Stack Mechanism	45
VM/0 Stack Architecture	47
Activation Records and Procedure Calls	48

Introduction to PL/0   53
Recursive Programs   57
Lexicographical Levels and Nested Programs   59
Summary 62
Exercises 62
Bibliographical Notes   63
Bibliography   64

Chapter 4. The Heap   65

Activating Prior Knowledge 66
Programming Constructs for Handling Memory Dynamically   67
Requesting Storage Dynamically   69
Why We Must Return Allocated Memory   74
Garbage Collection   76
Summary 79
Exercises 79
Bibliographical Notes   80
Bibliography   80

Chapter 5. Lexical Analyzers and Symbol Tables   81

Activating Prior Knowledge 82
On Programs and Compilers   83
On Alphabets   84
Lexical Analysis   87
Regular Expressions   89
Transition Diagrams   91
Symbol Table   91
Summary 99
Exercises 99
Bibliographical Notes   101
Bibliography   101

Chapter 6. Syntax Analysis and Code Generation   103

Activating Prior Knowledge 104
Syntax Analysis   105
Top-Down Parsing   114
Intermediate Code Generation   117
Summary 125
Exercises 126
Bibliographical Notes   127
Bibliography   128

Chapter 7. Assemblers, Linkers, and Loaders   129

Activating Prior Knowledge 130

Translating Assembly Language to Object Code	131
A Note on Static Linking	140
Loaders	142
Absolute Loader	142
Bootstrap Loader	143
Relocating Loaders	145
Summary 147	
Exercises 148	
Bibliographical Notes	148
Bibliography	149

Chapter 8. Understanding the Interrupt Mechanism — 151

Activating Prior Knowledge 152	
From Fetch-Execute to Fetch-Execute-Interrupt	153
Traps	157
The Program Status Word	165
I/O Interrupt	166
Timer Interrupt	168
System Calls	169
Summary 174	
Exercises 174	
Bibliographical Notes	175
Bibliography	175

Chapter 9. Processes and Threads — 177

Activating Prior Knowledge 178	
Process Concept	179
Process Control Block	181
Process Address Space	181
Process States	182
Transforming a Program into a Process	184
Thread Control Block	185
On Threads and Multicores	186
Summary 189	
Exercises 189	
Bibliographical Notes	190
Bibliography	190

Chapter 10. Process Synchronization — 191

Activating Prior Knowledge 192	
Concurrent Execution	193
Critical Sections, Mutual Exclusion, and Race Condition	194
Low-Level Synchronization Mechanisms	200
The Bounded-Buffer Producer-Consumer Problem	203

Monitors	205
Guarded Commands	212
Message Passing	215
Summary 218	
Exercises 219	
Bibliographical Notes	220
Bibliography	220

Preface

Systems Software: Essential Concepts has evolved from a set of course notes used in COP 3402, a course on systems software for computer science majors at the University of Central Florida (UCF). This course provides students' first incursion in a domain of knowledge that studies the interrelation among computer organization, programming languages, assemblers, compilers, linkers, loaders, and operating systems. The prerequisites for COP 3402 at UCF are a course in computer programming and a course in computer logic and organization, in which students get acquainted with the MIPS processor and its assembly language.

The aim of this book is to give students a basic knowledge of timeless concepts and mechanisms in the systems software area and to show students how the seminal ideas that gave birth to systems software have evolved and adapted to technological changes without losing their essence. Every now and then new ideas in computer architecture have been used to design faster computers. As in the early days of computing, an assembler and a loader are needed, and compilers and operating systems are the eternal companions of a computer system. Whenever possible, we have tried to present the concepts without neglecting their history. We, as many others, believe that in science and technology we must always take a look to the past to have a better understanding of the present in order to move forward to the future.

How to Use the Book

This book can be used as a stand-alone introduction of the fundamental concepts required for students planning to enroll in more advanced courses in compilers and operating systems or as a complementary book for students taking courses in compilers and operating systems. The book divides its pages mainly into two main subjects: compiler fundamentals and the basic mechanisms and data structures required to support operating systems. In the compiler arena, students must implement a small compiler, and in the operating system domain, students gain an understanding of the interrupt mechanism, process and thread implementation, and process synchronization. A programming project in which students implement a virtual machine and a compiler is a backbone for this course.

Fundamental concepts on compilers:

Students will gain an understanding of the runtime environment by being exposed to a virtual machine and the stack mechanism.

Students will learn to implement a scanner and the management of symbol tables.

Students will learn to implement parsing and code generation for a virtual machine.

Compiler programming project:

In COP 3402, students acquire hands-on experience by implementing a virtual machine and developing a small compiler that generates code for the virtual machine. The project is divided into four steps:

HW1: Implement a virtual machine.

HW2: Implement a scanner.

HW3: Implement a parser/code generator for a tiny language (PL/0), whose grammar does not support functions.

HW4: The grammar of the compiler implemented in Homework 3 (HW3) is extended to support function calls.

Operating systems fundamentals:

Students learn how an interrupt mechanism is created and the relevance of interrupts to implement protection mechanisms and to serve as a means to communicate user programs with the operating system.

Students gain an understanding of the interrelation among the process control block, the process address space, and the CPU.

Students gain an understanding of low-level synchronization mechanisms, such as test-and-set and semaphores. They also will learn high-level synchronization through monitors and communicating sequential processes (CSP).

I hope the readers of this first edition enjoy the reading, and as the textbook is a work in progress, I welcome all your comments and criticisms. You can reach me by email at euripides.montagne@ucf.edu.

Acknowledgments

My deepest gratitude goes to all the students who have taken COP 3402 Systems Software and provided feedback. They have contributed to improving the course continuously from one semester to the next. I am also grateful to all the teaching assistants who worked with me in the systems software course for their enthusiasm and involvement in helping students learn. The students who took the class in Fall 2020 and Spring 2021, and the teaching assistants who worked with me in those two semesters, deserve special recognition because they helped me test the preliminary edition of this book.

I am also grateful to my colleagues and to the administrative and technical staff in the Computer Science Department at UCF for creating such a productive environment.

I would like to thank the reviewers of the preliminary edition. Their feedback is greatly appreciated.

It has been a pleasure to work with the Cognella staff, who contributed to supporting this project. My thanks to Jennifer McCarthy, field acquisition editor, who contacted me and enthusiastically encouraged me to initiate this endeavor of transforming my class notes into a textbook; Susana Christie, developmental editor, who with patience and good humor provided me with the guidelines to create a manuscript and gave me some pedagogical tips to insert into each chapter; Abbey Hastings and Alia Bales, who kindly helped me in the production stage; Jess Estrella, who did excellent work in designing the book cover; and Amy Smith, project editor, whose professionalism made this endless writing and revising process enjoyable.

Most importantly, my infinite gratitude to my wife, Mireya, for her patience, support, and encouragement throughout the course of this long project. Luna, our cat, was also of great help in this project to reinforce the concept of interrupts. She frequently jumped onto the keyboard as a way of reminding me that I had to play with her.

Chapter 1

Systems Software

A journey of a thousand miles begins with a single step.
—Lao Tzu
  Tao Te Ching, chapter 64

INTRODUCTION

When someone wants to solve a problem using a computer, an algorithm to solve it is required, and that algorithm must be expressed in a programming language. In general, people think programming languages were created to instruct the computer to carry out a specific task or application. This is partially true, because programming languages were created mainly, as Donald Knuth says in his work Literate Programming, "to explain to human beings what we want the computer to do." A series of transformations is needed to convert the program written by the programmer into its executable version, and all those transformations are carried out using different programs classified as systems software. When the executable version is ready for execution, once again, systems software programs are required to create the environment where the executable version will run. Systems software programs will interact with programmers from the moment the program is first written until the moment the executable version of the program runs to completion.

In this chapter we show the landscape of what this book is about. We initiate the chapter by defining systems software. Then we present a classification of systems software programs, basically in two groups. The first group encompasses programs to help programmers develop

CHAPTER OBJECTIVES

- To introduce the concept of systems software.
- To understand the difference between systems software programs used for program development and systems software programs required for program execution.
- To explore all transformations a program passes through from the moment it is written to the moment the program is executed.

applications, and the second set includes programs that create an environment that allows the execution of application programs. We show all steps required to transform a program written in high-level language into a program in execution or process, and for each step, we identify which one of the systems software programs is used. Finally, we present an outline of the content of each chapter.

VOCABULARY

This is a list of keywords that herald the concepts we will study in this chapter. They are organized in chronological order and will appear in the text in bold. We invite you to take a look at these keywords to find out which ones you are familiar with.

Systems software
Text editors
Compilers
Assemblers
Linker
Operating systems
Loaders
Dynamic linkers
Program libraries
Executable program
Assembly language
Electronic Delay Storage Automatic Calculator (EDSAC)

Fortran
Screen editors
Object code
Linking
Text section
Data section
Relocation section
Symbol table
Executable and Linkable Format (ELF)
Process
Runtime environment
Command interpreter

Process address space
Text
Data
Heap
Stack
Process control block (PCB)
Process ID
Program counter (PC)
Stack pointer (SP)
State
CPU registers
Dispatching

ACTIVATING PRIOR KNOWLEDGE

In this section we will present a series of activities. In some of them you can choose one or more options. Sometimes, if you do not agree with the given answers to choose from, you will be allowed to give your own answer. By the way, this is not a test.

1. Which one of these programs can be classified as systems software?

    Text editor ☐
    A program to compute factorial ☐
    Compiler ☐
    Loader ☐

2. Mark the words denoting the same concept.

   Assembler ☐   Compiler ☐   Translator ☐

3. Mark the programs you have used.

   Compiler ☐   Text editor ☐   Command interpreter ☐

4. Is it true that Program = Process?

   Yes   ☐
   No   ☐
   Sometimes ☐

5. Skim the chapter and pay attention to the words written in **bold**. Count the number of words you are familiar with.

6. To execute a program, the Operating System (OS) must load the program from hard disk. Where does the operating system load programs in the computer?

   In the CPU   ☐
   In memory   ☐
   50 percent in memory and 50 percent in the CPU ☐

7. Have you used any of the following programs?

   Linker   ☐
   Loader   ☐
   Debugger   ☐
   Assembler   ☐
   Text editor ☐

What Is Systems Software?

When you ask someone what systems software is, there is a tendency to answer by naming one or two of the programs considered as systems software. Therefore, we will start out with Leland L. Beck's definition of systems software:

> **Systems software** consists of a set of programs that support the operation of a computer system
>
> —Leland L. Beck, *System Software: An Introduction to Systems Programming*, 3rd ed. Reading, MA: Addison Wesley, 1997. page 1

Beck's definition is clear and encompasses all programs considered as systems software, such as compilers, loaders, assemblers, text editors, operating systems, and many others. We can classify systems software in two groups: programs to create a software development environment and programs to create a runtime environment. Examples of programs in each group are mentioned below.

1. Development environment: Some programs that assist programmers in writing application programs are:

   Text editor
   Compilers
   Assemblers
   Linkers

2. Runtime environment: Some programs that create a runtime environment are:

   Operating systems
   Loaders
   Dynamic linkers
   Program libraries

Assemblers and loaders could be considered as the first two pieces of systems software developed to help human beings write programs in a symbolic language and load the **executable program** in the computer memory for execution. **Assembly language** has been in use since the late 1940s; for example, the **Electronic Delay Storage Automatic Calculator (EDSAC)** was a computer built in 1949 at Cambridge University by a team led by Maurice Wilkes. This computer had an assembly language whose operations (opcodes) were encoded using a single letter, a significant step compared to writing programs directly in binary. The assembler and loader were combined into an "assemble-and-go" program that translated the program written in assembly language into executable code and immediately loaded the executable version of the program in memory for execution. The **Fortran** programming language can be considered the first high-level notation for writing programs. Fortran (short for "formula translation") was designed in the late 1950s by John Backus and his team at IBM, and the first compiler was delivered in 1957. With the invention of computer monitors, the necessity of a text editor (full **screen editors**) was a natural challenge, and by the late 1960s, the Control Data Corporation (CDC) had developed a text editor for the operator console. Text editors and compilers made the programming process easier. From the standpoint of creating a runtime environment with a friendly interface, operating systems are the ones that characterize this functionality the most. General Motors implemented the first operating system on an IBM 701 in 1955.

Software Tools for Program Development

In the program developing process, the programmer should focus on solving a problem and expressing the solution of the problem in a programming language. If we provide programmers with the appropriate tools to ease their work, they will be more productive and less distracted by solving secondary problems. In this section we will briefly present some systems software programs to support programmers in the program development process.

We will assume that programmers understand the syntax of the programming language that they are using to write programs. Then, to write a program, the first tool we have to provide programmers is a text editor. With a text editor, programmers can create and edit their programs at ease. Once they are able to write programs using the text editor, the next systems software program they need to get acquainted with is a compiler. They need to know how to invoke the compiler to translate the program into assembly language or **object code** (binary). If the program is translated into assembly language or if the program was written in assembly language, then programmers need to know what step to follow next to translate the assembly version of their program into object code. This means they need to know how to invoke the assembler. Now you have an idea of how the source program written in a high-level language is translated into an executable version (object code) by using different systems software programs.

In the early days, when they used a "translate-and-go" approach, object code could be loaded into memory and executed. Nowadays, we are able to combine several object codes together into a single module and then load this combined object code for execution. This step, called **linking**, is carried out by the linker or linkage editor. The object code is an executable file that has a header with the program ID and information about the different sections within the file. These sections include the **text section** (code), the **data section**, the **relocation section**, and the **symbol table**, to name a few. The executable file is known nowadays as the **Executable and Linkable Format (ELF)**. When the ELF is loaded into memory for execution, a **process** is created by the operating system and the program is allowed to run. Figure 1.1 illustrates different systems software programs and the way they are related.

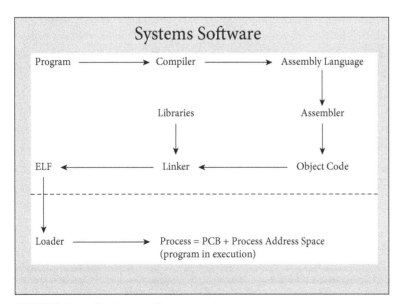

FIGURE 1.1 Systems software road map.

Software to Create Runtime Environments

When thinking about **runtime environments**, the program or set of programs that characterize a runtime environment is the operating system. Operating systems are event-driven programs that create a friendly interface between the user and the computer system. They also handle all system resources efficiently. The **command interpreter** is the layer of the operating system that allows the user to interact with the computer system. A user can type in a command using a command-line interpreter (CLI) or a graphical user interface (GUI), and the operating system will take the appropriate actions. For instance, to invoke a compiler to compile a program, a command must be given to the operating system, and the operating system will load the compiler and allow the compiler to read the user program as a text file. The compiler will translate the program into assembly language, then the operating system might invoke the assembler and allow the assembler to read in the assembly language program, and the assembler will translate the program into object code. To execute the program, we can interact with the operating system and type in a command to tell the operating system to load and execute the program.

To carry out the execution of a program, the operating system has to create two objects in memory per program. One of them is the **process address space**, which is a memory segment divided into four sections:

- **Text** section
- **Data** section
- **Heap** section
- **Stack** section

The text section is used to store the executable program starting at memory address zero in the process address space. The data section is located right after the text section, and it is used to store global data. Next you will find the heap, which is used to support programming languages that allow the handling of memory dynamically. Finally, the stack, which begins at the highest memory address in the process address space, is used to control the calling and returning from subroutines and also to save temporary space for local variables and parameters when functions are called. The other object is the **process control block (PCB)**, a data structure containing information about the state of the process. A program in execution (a process) can be in different states while running. For example, if a process is using the CPU, we can say that the process is in the "running state"; if the process is waiting for the completion of an I/O operation, we can say that the process is in the "waiting for I/O state." The process could be also in the "ready state," which means waiting for the CPU. In the process control block, we can find the following:

- The **process ID**
- The **program counter (PC)**
- The **stack pointer (SP)**

- The **state** of the process (for instance, running or ready)
- Contents of the **CPU registers** at the moment the process left the CPU
- And some other relevant information that allows the operating system to keep track of each process. All the information stored in the PCB is called the context.

Figure 1.2 illustrates the relationship among the object code, the process address space, and the process control block. Observing the figure in detail, you will find that the text and data sections of the object code (executable file) are copied from the object code into the process address space.

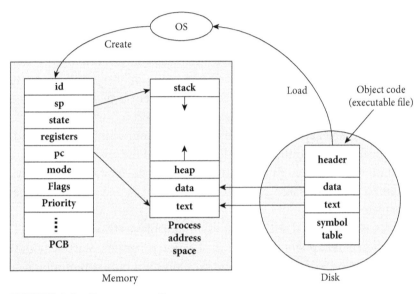

FIGURE 1.2 Process creation.

When there are several processes in memory, they are competing for CPU time, and the operating system will choose one of them to use the CPU. The selected process is dispatched (CPU assigned). **Dispatching** means copying information from the PCB into the CPU; for instance, copying the PCB program counter into the CPU program counter or copying the PCB stack pointer into the CPU stack pointer. This way the CPU program counter will be pointing in memory to the program (text section) and the CPU stack pointer will pointing to the stack of the selected process.

Outline of the Book

This book aims to provide a basic knowledge of systems software to computer science and information technology students to allow them a smooth transition toward more specialized courses in compiler and operating systems. We will equip students with a background sufficient to delve into those areas with little difficulty. The book is organized as follows.

Chapter 2 presents the processor as an instruction interpreter of assembly language. Computer organization concepts are given, and the repertoire of instructions, or instruction set architecture (ISA), of a virtual machine is explored in detail. We start out the chapter with a review of positional number systems and data representation. Then we present the architecture of a register virtual machine, which we call VM/0, to show students the relationship between assembly language and computer organization, which is fundamental to writing assemblers and compilers. Toward the end of the chapter, we give a smooth introduction to the process address space.

Chapter 3 deals with the stack concept as a mechanism to implement the invocation of subroutines or functions and to control the return from the subroutine to the caller environment. We start the chapter with a description of the stack mechanism and then present two new registers in the VM/0 machine to handle the stack. The instructions call, increment, and return are described in detail. Then we present the activation record as a fundamental data structure for subroutine linkage. In the second part of the chapter, we illustrate the handling of recursion using the stack mechanism. Then we present lexicographical levels and the handling of nested programs.

Chapter 4 is about the heap and its usage to support programming languages that handle memory dynamically. We describe the implementation of the heap mechanism, then give a brief introduction to best fit and first fit as techniques for memory management. The problem of fragmented memory is also presented, and the mark-and-sweep garbage collection approach is explained.

Chapter 5 presents the lexical analyzer and symbol tables as two fundamental elements in the implementation of compilers and other application programs. Starting with the concept of alphabet, we move on to describe how the symbols used in programming languages can be converted into an internal representation or tokens. Then the implementation of symbol tables is explained in detail.

Chapter 6 gives you a basic knowledge of parsing and code generation. These two concepts are central to the development of compilers, and understanding them will allow you to delve into the compiler arena in a comfortable way. Examples of parsing and generating code for different programming statements are given.

Chapter 7 is about assemblers and loaders. Assemblers allow you to understand how assembly language is translated into an executable file, and by knowing about loaders, you will be able to understand the way the operating system loads programs for execution. Linkers as programs that create an executable linkable file from several object files are briefly presented.

Chapter 8 presents the interrupt mechanism as a fundamental concept to help readers understand the way user programs communicate with the operating system to request service. The interrupt mechanism also provides a protection mechanism to assist the operating system in detecting and stopping malicious or careless user programs from invading other user address spaces or even the operating system itself. The interrupt mechanism also provides an interface between user programs and the operating system, which allows user programs to request service from the operating system.

Chapter 9 presents the concept of process as a program in execution. Process and thread implementation issues are described. We also present the support required to implement a multithreading environment. A brief introduction to handling multiples treads on a multicore is also given.

Chapter 10 deals with implementation issues of concurrent execution of sequential programs and process synchronization. Hardware and software mechanisms are studied in detail. We conclude the chapter with an introduction to the message passing mechanism.

SUMMARY

In this chapter we began by defining systems software as a set of programs that support the operation of a computer system. Then we classified systems software in two categories: programs to support programmers in the development of applications programs, and another set of programs, basically put together under the single name operating system. These programs create what we know as a runtime environment to execute application programs. Operating systems create a friendly interface for the user and the computer system and handle all computer system resources efficiently. We illustrated, using a block diagram, the road map that we will follow in this book.

EXERCISES

1. What is an algorithm?
2. What is a program?
3. What is a compiler?
4. What is a text editor?
5. What is an assembler?
6. What is assembly language?
7. Does object code = assembly language?
8. When the operating system dispatches a process, name two fields of the PCB that are copied in the CPU.
9. What is an operating system?
10. What is a loader?
11. Are assemblers and compilers translators?
12. We can refer to all the information stored in the PCB by a single name. What is that name?

13. Fortran is considered the first implementation of a high-level language. Is it still in use?
14. Name five programs that are considered to be system software.
15. What is a system programmer?

Bibliographical Notes

An interesting work on the benefits of programming methodology is described by Donald Knuth in.[1] Programs considered to be systems software have been around since the late 1940s as tools to ease the programming process.[2,3] David Barron presents a good monograph describing assemblers and loaders.[4] An in-depth source for implementing assemblers and loaders is presented by David Salomon.[5] Leland L. Beck gives a very good and in-depth description of various types of systems software in his system software book.[6] The book could be considered the first on systems software as we know it nowadays. The Fortran compiler was a major step in the development of systems software to ease the programming process by allowing programmers to write programs in a high-level language.[7] Another valuable tool to help programmers write programs was the full-screen editor developed by the Control Data Corporation in the late 1960s for the operator console. The General Motors–North American Aviation input/output system (GM-NAA I/O), also known as GM OS, was the first operating system developed, and it was implemented on an IBM 701.[8] It was a batch system, which allowed a program to run as soon as the one being executed had run to completion.

Bibliography

1. D. E. Knuth, *Literate Programming*, The Computer Journal, Vol. 27, No. 2, 1984.
2. M. V. Wilkes and W. Renwick, "The EDSAC, an Electronic Calculating Machine," *Journal of Science and Instrumentation* 26 (1949), p. 385.
3. M. M. Wilkes, "The EDSAC Computer," in *Joint AIEE-IRE Computer Conference Review of Electronic Digital Computers*, 1951.
4. D. W. Barron, *Assemblers and Loaders*, 3rd ed. Elsevier North-Holland, 1978.
5. D. Salomon, *Assemblers and Loaders*. Ellis Horwood, 1993.
6. L. L. Beck, *System Software: An Introduction to Systems Programming*, 3rd ed. Reading, MA: Addison Wesley, 1996.
7. J. W. Backus et al., "The FORTRAN Automatic Coding System," in *Western Joint Computer Conference*. Los Angeles, 1957.
8. R. L. Patrick, *General Motors/North American Monitor for the IBM 704 Computer*. Chicago, IL: RAND Corporation, 1987.

Chapter 2

The Processor as an Instruction Interpreter

The world was so recent that many things lacked names, and in order to indicate them it was necessary to point.
—Gabriel Garcia Márquez
  One Hundred Years of Solitude

CHAPTER OBJECTIVES

- To review positional number systems used by programmers and computers to represent data and instruction.
- To discuss the necessity of knowing computer organization to understand assembly language.
- To explore how assembly language works.
- To describe the concept of process address space.

INTRODUCTION

The role of a processor (CPU) in any computer system is to execute programs stored in memory. These programs are represented as a sequence of zeros and ones. The processor must discern program instructions from data values. Human beings have developed programming notations, known as programming languages, to write programs to instruct computers to follow a series of commands to solve problems using a computer. One of these programming languages is assembly language, also known as symbolic language.

The processor is basically an interpreter of assembly language instructions, and in this chapter we will present the organization of a tiny computer and a set of assembly language instructions that our tiny processor accepts. This repertoire of instructions is called the instruction set architecture (ISA). For each instruction, we will discuss its instruction format and how it is encoded in binary. Finally, we present the concept of process address space to visualize the way the operating system assigns and organizes memory space for program execution.

VOCABULARY

This is a list of keywords that herald the concepts we will study in this chapter. They are organized in chronological order and will appear in the text in bold. We invite you to take a look at these keywords to find out which ones you are familiar with.

Decimal number	Condition code (CC)	System call
Hexadecimal number	Flags	Operating system (OS)
Binary number	Bit	Standard input (stdin)
P-code	Byte	Standard output (stdout)
Algorithm	Half byte	Assembler directives
Program	Word	Text
Programming language	Random access memory (RAM)	Data
Memory	Memory address register (MAR)	End
Input/output devices		Instruction format
Processing element (PE)	Memory data register (MDR)	Global data pointer (GDP)
Central processing unit (CPU)	Program counter (PC)	Object code
Instruction set architecture (ISA)	Instruction cycle	Process
	Fetch	Program in execution
Assembly language	Decode	Process address space
Register	Execute	Stack segment
Register file (RF)	Identifier	Heap segment
Instruction register (IR)	Memory location	Data segment
Control unit (CU)	Variable	Text segment
Arithmetic logic unit (ALU)	Assembler	

ACTIVATING PRIOR KNOWLEDGE

In this section we will present a series of activities. In some of them you can choose one or more options. Sometimes, if you do not agree with the given answers to choose from, you will be allowed to give your own answer. By the way, this is not a test.

1. The number 10 is:

    A decimal number ☐
    A binary number ☐
    A hexadecimal number ☐
    All are valid answers ☐

2. What is the language that computers execute?

    Python ☐   Go ☐   Java ☐   Assembler ☐   Binary ☐

3. Assume that ADD can be encoded as 0001 and we can use three registers identified as A, B, and C. If A is encoded as 0011, B as 0010, and C as 0001, write the instruction ADD C B A using zeros and ones.

4. What is the highest value that can be expressed with 8 bits?

   8 ☐
   64 ☐
   16 ☐
   If the answer is not given above, please give yours. _____

5. A compiler is a program that translates:

   From C++ to binary ☐
   From C++ to machine language ☐
   From C++ to assembly language ☐
   From C++ to object code ☐

6. To execute a program, the OS must load the program from disk. Where does the operating system load the program?

   In the CPU ☐
   In memory ☐
   50 percent in memory and 50 percent in the CPU ☐

7. Skim the chapter and pay attention to the words in **bold**. Count how many of those words you are familiar with.

On Naming and Data Representation

Naming is a gift that allows human beings to identify real and abstract objects. Furthermore, naming permits us to synthesize a concept or a definition of a complex concept in a single word. Without a naming scheme only ostensive references would be possible, which would make the handling of information in any knowledge domain extremely difficult. Therefore, we need to use a naming scheme to identify the information units and mechanisms to store and handle objects in a computer system.

Probably, the first abstract objects or symbols we assign names to are the **decimal numbers**. The decimal number system is a positional system that uses ten symbols to represent numbers. They are **0, 1, 2, 3, 4, 5, 6, 7, 8, and 9**. Each one of these digits has a name that we use for human communication. For example, the symbol **3** is called **three**. These basic decimal digits can be grouped into a string of digits to construct other numbers. As the decimal system is a positional number system, the same digit has a different value depending on its position in the string. For instance, in the number 777 the seven on the right has a value of 7, the one in the middle has a value of 70, and the one in the left has a value of 700.

TABLE 2.1 REPRESENTING A NUMBER IN THE DECIMAL SYSTEM

Position in the string	5	4	3	2	1	0
Position value in power of 10	10^5	10^4	10^3	10^2	10^1	10^0
Position value	100,000	10,000	1,000	100	10	1
Decimal number	0	0	0	7	7	7

From Table 2.1 we can deduce the value of a decimal number. It can be obtained by multiplying each symbol in the string by its position value and then adding up all the multiplication carried out, as shown below:

$$777_{10} = (7 \times 100) + (7 \times 10) + (7 \times 1) = 777_{10}$$

This can be rewritten using the power notation using 10 as the base of the system (ten symbols), where the exponent indicates the digit position:

$$777_{10} = (7 \times 10^2) + (7 \times 10^1) + (7 \times 10^0) = 777_{10}$$

Similarly, we could define another set of 16 symbols and create the **hexadecimal number system**. This system has 16 symbols. For the first ten symbols we will borrow the ten symbols of the decimal system. For the others six symbols needed, any symbol could be selected, but the first six letters of the alphabet will do the job. Let us say then our symbols will be **0, 1, 2, 3, 4, 5, 6, 7, 8, 9, A, B, C, D, E, and F**. Since we are used to working with numbers, numerical values are given to each letter symbol A, B, C, D, E, and F, as presented in Table 2.2.

TABLE 2.2 REPRESENTING SYMBOLS AND VALUES IN THE HEXADECIMAL SYSTEM

Symbol	0	1	2	3	4	5	6	7	8	9	A	B	C	D	E	F
Value	0	1	2	3	4	5	6	7	8	9	10	11	12	13	14	15

As the hexadecimal system is a positional system as well, each symbol will have a different value depending on its position in the string. In this case the base of the system is 16; therefore, powers of 16 will be used. Applying the same rules we used for decimal symbols, we can calculate, using Table 2.3, the decimal value of the hexadecimal number 1AF.

$$\begin{aligned}1AF_{16} &= (1 \times 16^2) + (10 \times 16^1) + (15 \times 16^0) \\ &= (1 \times 256) + (A \times 16) + (F \times 1) = 431_{10}\end{aligned}$$

TABLE 2.3 **REPRESENTING A NUMBER IN THE HEXADECIMAL SYSTEM**

Position in the string	5	4	3	2	1	0
Position value in power of 10	16^5	16^4	16^3	16^2	16^1	16^0
Position value	1,048,576	65,536	4,096	256	16	1
Hexadecimal number	0	0	0	1	A	F

You can use the prefix **0x** to indicate that the number is in hexadecimal notation. Therefore, you can write down 0x1AF instead of $1AF_{16}$ in the above equation, and it has the same meaning.

$$0x1AF = (1 \times 16^2) + (10 \times 16^1) + (15 \times 16^0)$$
$$= (1 \times 256) + (A \times 16) + (F \times 1) = 431_{10}$$

We could define another positional system involving only two symbols, say **0** and **1**, and create a **binary number** system. Binary numbers are central to computer systems because that is the language computers use. The first evidence of the usage of binary numbers is found in China circa 2500 BCE, in the *I Ching,* or *Book of Changes.* The *I Ching* uses an unbroken line to represent "heaven" and a broken line to represent "void." The two symbols are grouped into trigrams. A trigram is a set of three lines in which any one of the three lines could be broken or unbroken. An example of a trigram is ☰. In 1703 the German philosopher and mathematician Gottfried Wilhelm von Leibniz (1646–1716) presented his work to the European scientific community to show the correspondence between the unbroken line and the digit 1 and the broken line and the digit 0. In his work he also showed formally that trigrams represented a positional binary number system and illustrated the development of binary arithmetic operation. However, there is evidence that the British mathematician Thomas Heriot (1560–1621) had experimented with binary arithmetic before Leibniz. By the way, Heriot invented the symbols for the relational operators "greater than" (>) and "less than" (<).

The binary system only supports two symbols, making its base 2. Following a similar argument as the one used for the hexadecimal system, we can figure out that the decimal number 5 is represented in binary as **101**. You can verify this by using Table 2.4 and observing that each binary number is multiplied by its positional value:

$$101_2 = (1 \times 2^2) + (0 \times 2^1) + (1 \times 2^0)$$
$$= (1 \times 4) + (0 \times 2) + (1 \times 1) = 5_{10}$$

The three positional systems described above are central to information technology and computer science because decimal numbers are used by human beings, binary is used by computers, and hexadecimals can be thought of as a short notation to deal with strings

TABLE 2.4 REPRESENTING A NUMBER IN THE BINARY SYSTEM

Position in the string	5	4	3	2	1	0
Position value in power of 10	2^5	2^4	2^3	2^2	2^1	2^0
Position value	32	16	8	4	2	1
Binary number	0	0	0	1	0	1

of binary numbers. Let us illustrate this by expressing the number 431 using 16 binary digits and 4 hexadecimals digits.

$$431_{10} = 0000\ 0001\ 1010\ 1111_2 = 0x01AF$$

TABLE 2.5 REPRESENTING 16 DISTINCT MEMORY ADDRESSES IN BINARY (HALF BYTE), HEXADECIMAL, AND DECIMAL

Binary	hexadecimal	decimal
0000	0x0	0
0001	0x1	1
0010	0x2	2
0011	0x3	3
0100	0x4	4
0101	0x5	5
0110	0x6	6
0111	0x7	7
1000	0x8	8
1001	0x9	9
1010	0xA	10
1011	0xB	11
1100	0xC	12
1101	0xD	13
1110	0xE	14
1111	0xF	15

If you observe carefully, you will realize that each hexadecimal digit can be represented in binary using 4 binary digits. Table 2.5 can be used to translate from binary to hexadecimal and vice versa any time we are dealing with memory locations or need to observe the contents of a specific memory location. It is recommended to work with hexadecimal digits instead of binary digits.

$$
\begin{array}{cccc}
0000 & 0001 & 1010 & 1111 \\
\downarrow & \downarrow & \downarrow & \downarrow \\
0 & 1 & A & F
\end{array}
$$

A P-code Register Machine

P-code, or pseudo code, is the name given to the instruction set of a virtual machine or software interpreter. In this chapter we will present VM/0, a p-code architecture based on the interpreter proposed by Niklaus Wirth in the implementation of PL/0. The main difference between VM/0 and Wirth's p-code is that in VM/0, a register file is used to carry out arithmetic and relational operations. A subset of the VM/0 assembly language will be presented in this chapter and will be extended in chapter 3.

The words **algorithm**, **program**, and **programming language** are used quite often when we try to solve a problem using a computer. We will define them to set up a common understanding of the meaning of these words. An **algorithm** is a set of steps to be performed to solve a specific problem. If you intend to solve a problem using a computer, you will need to instruct the computer, and to do this, you have to write a program. Therefore, we can define a **program** as an algorithm expressed in a programming language. A **programming language** is a notation (or "artificial language") created to instruct the computer and to allow programmers to understand each other's program.

Computer Organization

Since John von Neumann conceived the idea of a stored-program computer in 1945, a computer consists basically of three units: **memory**, **input/output devices**, and a **processing element (PE)**, also known as a **central processing unit (CPU)**. Nowadays, there are other types of processing elements designed for specific purposes, such as **graphic processing unit (GPU)**, **tensor processing unit (TPU), and quantum processing unit (QPU)**. When designing a CPU, we are creating an instruction interpreter capable of executing a set of instructions or commands generally known as the **instruction set architecture (ISA)**. You can look at the ISA from two different perspectives: from the hardware standpoint, the CPU uses zeros and ones; and from the programmer standpoint, without an ISA, programmers would be doomed to program the computer in binary. **Assembly language**, or symbolic language, was created, as any other programming language, to allow programmers to understand each other's program and to instruct the computer to executed programs. To give you an idea of programming in assembly language, let us start describing VM/0 CPU. There are several **registers** in VM/0 CPU. Each register is a small, high-speed logic circuit capable of storing a binary number, and we can think of it as a container. Some of these registers are grouped together under the name **register file (RF)**, and these are the sole registers programmers can use, through assembly language instruction, to manipulate data. For a register file of four registers, we can denote them as R[0], R[1], R[2], and R[3], where R stands for a register and the number in square brackets identifies a register in the register file. For example, let us assume that we need to add two numbers, say 17 and 23, and the two numbers are stored in register R[0] and R[3] respectively, and the resulting value of the arithmetic operation will be stored in R[2]. We can carry out the operation R[2] = R[0] + R[3] using the assembly language instruction ADD this way:

ADD R[2], R[0], R[3]   ; **programmer level**

Note: The ";" is used to indicate the beginning of a comment.

This instruction should be read as follows: take the contents of register zero (whose value is 17) and register three (whose value is 23), add them up, and store the resulting value (40) in register two. It is worth noting, that R[0] and R[3] are the source registers, and R[2] is the target or destination register. For encoding R[2] = R[0] + R[3] in binary using 16 binary digits, we can expect something like:

$$0000\ 1000\ 1100\ 0001 \quad ; \text{computer level}$$
$$0x08C1 \quad ; \text{in hexadecimal}$$

Similarly, the numbers stored in R[0] and R[3] could be used to compute R[2] = R[0] − R[3] using the assembly language instruction SUB as follows:

$$\text{SUB R[2], R[0], R[3]} \quad ; \text{programmer level}$$

Another register in the CPU is the **instruction register (IR)**. Programs written in assembly language do not allow programmers to manipulate IR—only the CPU hardware can do that. When the IR receives an instruction, such as ADD R[2], R[0], R[3] from memory, it forwards the opcode, ADD, to the **control unit (CU)**, and the CU decodes the opcode (identifies the instruction) and initiates the necessary steps to execute that instruction. The CPU control unit is hardwired to decode and execute all instructions of the ISA. The operation R[2] = R[0] + R[3] is carried out in the **arithmetic logic unit (ALU)**; this unit is commanded by the control unit to execute all types of arithmetic, relational, and logic operations the computer supports. Figure 2.1 depicts VM/0 executing the operation ADD R[2], R[0], R[3].

We just gave an example of an arithmetic operation, but the CU is able to execute other types of operations, such as relational operations; for instance, comparing two numbers to find out if they are *equal*. To explain the way this can be carried out, we need to introduce the instruction **EQ** (test for equality) and show how it works using **condition codes (CCs)**. Condition codes are associated with the ALU and they can be tested after execution of an arithmetic, relational, or logical operation, for knowing their status, which can change as a side effect of the execution of the instruction. There are three **flags** in the CC register in VM/0-CPU (a flag can be thought of as a single-bit register): N (negative), Z (equal to zero), and P (positive). They are extremely useful for changing the control flow of a

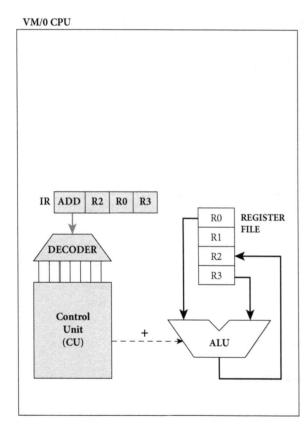

FIGURE 2.1 PM/0 CPU executing instruction ADD.

program. A condition code is set to 1 if a condition is met; otherwise, its value is zero. Assuming R[0] = 21 and R[3] = 21, we can figure out that condition code Z is set to 1, once the compare register instruction (EQ) has been executed because the condition R[0] = R[3] holds. Figure 2.2 illustrate the execution of the instruction EQ.

EQ R[0], R[3]   ; programmer's level

The way relational operations work is by subtracting the contents of the two registers involved in the instruction, and depending on the resulting value, condition codes are set out. In the former example, as both registers have the same value, then R[0] − R[3] = 0, and therefore condition code Z is set to 1. These relational instructions affect condition code flags. Table 2.6 shows the way CCs are set depending on the relational or arithmetic operation executed.

Memory Organization

The storing and handling of information in memory can be carried out at different levels. In VM/0, as in any other computer system, the basic information unit is the **bi**nary dig**it**, widely known as a **bit**, which allows us to represent the two symbols of the binary number system (0 and 1). Bits can be grouped together to form other information units that convey more information, like **bytes**, **half bytes**, and **words**. A byte is a sequence of 8 bits capable of storing $2^8 = 256$ different values, and a half byte is represented with a sequence of 4 bits. A word could have variable length, say 16, 32, or 64 bits, depending on technology, and it gives us information about the size of each memory location. In VM/0 a word consists of a sequence of 16 bits. Each memory location contains either an instruction or a data value, and the interpretation of those 16 bits (the word)

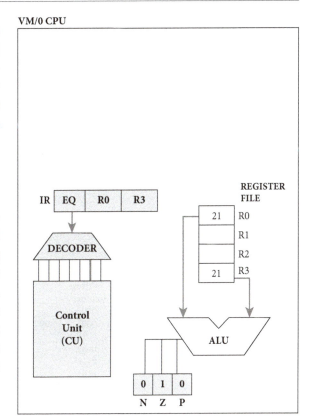

FIGURE 2.2 VM/0 CC executing instruction EQ.

TABLE 2.6 **CONDITION CODES SETTINGS**

Description	Condition codes
Test for equality	Set Z = 1
Not equal	Set Z = 0
Less than	Set N = 1
Less than or equal to	Set Z =1 or N = 1
Greater than	Set P = 1
Greater than or equal to	Set Z =1 or P = 1

as instructions or data values will be carried out by the CPU or processor. For example, in a 16-bit word the number 431 and the instruction ADD R[2], R[0], R[3] can be represented as:

    0000 0001 1010 1111   ; this is the data value 431 in binary
    0000 1000 1100 0001   ; this is instruction ADD in binary

The memory (**MEM**) unit of VM/0, also known as **random access memory (RAM)**, can be thought of as a linear array where each memory location or word has a label called its address. We denote the access to a specific memory location by using the following notation MEM [*address*], where MEM stand for memory and *address*, a number, indicates the memory location we are referring to. For instance, to access the content of memory location 0001 we write MEM [0001]. We depict this arrangement in Figure 2.3. Notice that the content of memory location 0001 is 5 (in binary) and the content of MEM [1101] is 431 (in binary).

Address in binary	Memory RAM	Address hexadecimal	Address decimal
0000		0x0	0
0001	0000 0000 0000 0101	**0x1**	**1**
0010		0x2	2
0011		0x3	3
0100		0x4	4
0101		0x5	5
0110		0x6	6
0111		0x7	7
1000		0x8	8
1001		0x9	9
1010		0xA	10
1011		0xB	11
1100		0xC	12
1101	0000 0001 1010 1111	**0xD**	**13**
1110		0xE	14
1111		0xF	15

FIGURE 2.3 Representing 16 distinct memory addresses in binary (half byte), hexadecimal, and decimal.

There are two CPU registers used to access memory; they are known as **memory address register (MAR)** and **memory data register (MDR)**. For selecting a memory location, MAR is used. MDR has a bidirectional connection with main memory, and this allows it to receive in a CPU register the contents of a specific memory location selected by MAR or to store a value from a register into a memory location pointed to by MAR. These two registers allow us, using assembly language instruction, to move data and instructions back and forth between the CPU and memory. This occurs at the CPU level, and programmers do not have to bother about these details. Figure 2.4 shows a detailed view of the execution of the instruction **LOD R[0], 0, M**. In this instruction, LOD means load or copy data from memory into a CPU register; the first operand indicates the register receiving the data; the second value, a zero, means unused (n/a), but it is mandatory to use it (you will find out why in chapter 3), and **M** stands for a memory address (identifies a memory location). Before explaining how the instruction is executed, we must clarify some details about the notation to refer to a specific field in a VM/0 instruction once the instruction resides in the IR. We will use a dot (".") as a selector. For example, the IR has four fields, and to refer to the opcode we will use IR.OP. Likewise, to refer to the address M we will write IR.M.

Once the instruction **LOD R[0], 0, M** reaches the IR, it is decoded, and the control unit carries out three steps to execute the instruction.

1. Memory address **M** is copied in **MAR**.   // MAR ← IR.M
2. **MAR** selects memory location **M**   // MDR ← MEM [MAR]
   and sends its content to **MDR**.
3. The content of **MDR** is copied in **R[0]**.   // R[0] ← MDR
4. Back to Fetch

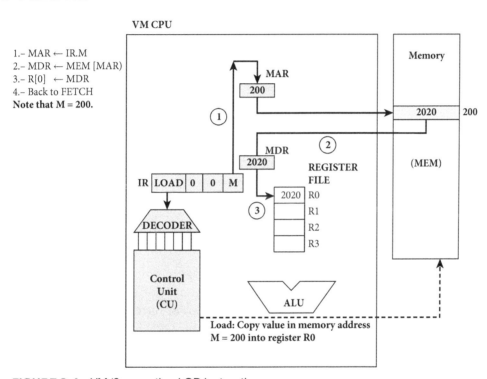

FIGURE 2.4 VM/0 executing LOD instruction.

Sometimes we need to store the content of a register, say R[0], in a memory location, in which case we must use the instruction store (**STO**). When instruction **STO R[0], 0, M** reaches the IR, it is decoded, and the control unit will carry out the following steps:

1. The content of memory address **M** is copied in **MAR**.   // MAR ← IR.M
2. The content of R[0] is copied in **MDR**.   // MDR ← R[0]
3. **The content of MDR is copied into memory address M.**   // MEM[MAR] ← MDR
4. Back to Fetch

Figure 2.5 shows the execution of the store instruction. Observe in the figure that the encircled numbers match steps 1, 2, and 3 of the execution of the instruction STO as described above.

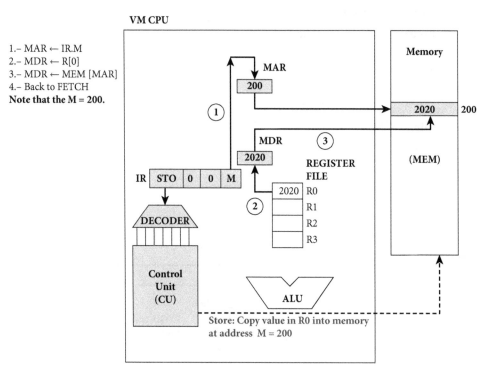

FIGURE 2.5 VM/0 MEM executing STO instruction.

Fetch Execute Cycle

We can think of a program as a sequence of commands or instructions stored in memory that flow sequentially, one at a time, from memory to the CPU for execution. Each time an instruction is executed, the CPU needs to know where to find the next instruction to be executed. There is a register for this purpose in the CPU called the **program counter (PC)**, which points to the next instruction to be fetched for execution. The reason we call it PC is because instructions in memory are stored sequentially in contiguous memory locations; therefore, each time an instruction is retrieved from memory and sent to the CPU for execution, the PC is incremented by "one" to point to the next instruction in the sequence, which is stored in the next memory location. Thus, the PC behaves just like a counter. This is in general how the CPU controls the flow of instructions from memory to the CPU. The three steps required to execute an instruction or **instruction cycle** are **fetch, decode,** and **execute.** In **fetch**, an instruction is copied from memory into the CPU instruction register, and the PC is incremented by one to point to the memory location where the next instruction to be executed resides. Figure 2.6 illustrates the fetch cycle at the machine level. These are the steps carried out in Fetch:

FETCH: MAR ← PC
         PC ← PC + 1
         MDR ← MEM[MAR]
         IR ← MDR

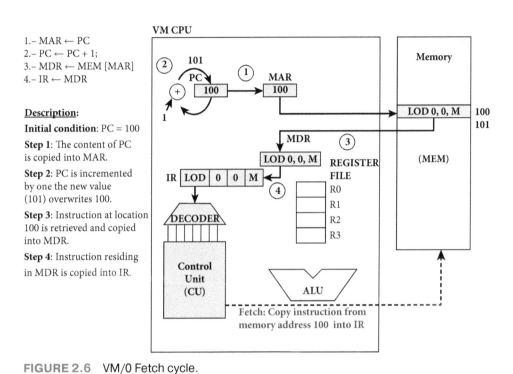

FIGURE 2.6   VM/0 Fetch cycle.

Then in the **decode** step, the control unit uses the opcode (IR.OP) and identifies the instruction.

DECODE: Control Unit ← IR.OP

Once the instruction has been identified, the CU immediately initiates all required actions to execute the identified instruction. For example, for the instructions ADD, EQ, and LOD, we have:

If IR.OP = ADD   Then   ALU ← R[y]
                         ALU ← R[z]
                         R[x] ← R[y] + R[z]
                         Back to FETCH

If IR.OP = EQ   Then   ALU ← R[x]
                          ALU ← R[y]
                          If R[x] = R[y] then set Z ← 1
                          Back to FETCH

If IR.OP = LOD   Then   MAR ← IR.M
                          MDR ← MEM [MAR]
                          R[x] ← MDR
                          Back to FETCH

Where x, y, and z can take the values 0, 1, 2, and 3 depending on the registers you are using. Figure 2.7 illustrates the instruction cycle (fetch-decode-execute).

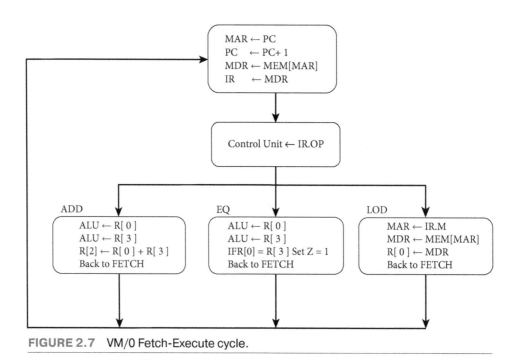

FIGURE 2.7 VM/0 Fetch-Execute cycle.

As you can observe in the fetch cycle, each time an instruction is retrieved from memory, the PC is incremented by one to point to the instruction that resides in the next memory location. Nevertheless, there are some instructions that allow the disruption of sequential execution by overwriting the PC before the next instruction cycle begins, and in this way different and more interesting ways to control the flow of instructions toward the CPU can be implemented.

Assembly Language Programming

A good example of an instruction that overrides the program counter thanks to the use of condition codes is **JumP** on **C**ondition (JPC). Another instruction that overwrites the PC but without checking out condition code flags is jump unconditional (JMP). We will put together some of the instruction already explained to write a small program in assembly language to illustrate the usage of JPC 0, 0, M, where M is a memory address. This instruction checks on condition code flags, and if any one of them is equal to 1 then the PC is overwritten by copying IR.M into the PC (PC ← IR.M). Note that in the next example, memory addresses are given in hexadecimal

```
0x0    0
0x1    5
0x2    3
0x3    1
0x4
0x5
0x6    LOD R[ 0 ], 0, 0x2      ; Number 3 is loaded in register R[0]
0x7    LOD R[ 1 ], 0, 0x3      ; Number 1 is loaded in register R[1]
0x8    LOD R[ 2 ], 0, 0x0      ; Number 0 is loaded in register R[2]
0x9    LOD R[ 3 ], 0, 0x1      ; Number 5 is loaded in register R[3]
0xA    ADD R[2], R[2], R[3]    ; Successive sums accumulated in R[2]
0xB    SUB R[0], R[0], R[1]    ; If (R[ 0 ] - R[ 1 ] = 0) then set Z ← 1
0xC    JPC 0, 0, 0xE           ; If Z = 1 then PC ← 0xE
0xD    JMP 0, 0, 0xA           ; PC ← 0xA
0xE    STO R[2], 0, 0x4        ; Store resulting value in location 0x4
```

In this program, the number before the instruction indicates the memory location where the instruction resides. The PC points to the first instruction (PC = 0x6), and a single 0 in any instruction field means that the operand is not used by the CPU. This program multiplies two numbers (5 x 3) using successive additions. In instructions 0x6 to 0x9, registers are loaded with the initial values stored in locations 0x0 to 0x3. The initial value of register R[2] is zero. The instruction at address 0xA will add 5 to register R[2] each time it is executed, and the resulting value is stored back in R[2]. The value 3 stored initially in R[0] will be used to control the loop. Each time the SUB instruction is executed, R[0] is decremented by one, and eventually R[0] will reach the value zero and will set condition code Z to one (Z ← 1). Instruction JPC checks whether Z is equal to one, and if it is, address 0xE is copied into the PC, and the next instruction to be executed will be the one at location 0xE. But if the condition is not met (Z ≠ 1), the address 0xA is copied into the PC, and the program remains in the loop.

In the next example you can observe the usage of JPC after using the instruction EQ. As the two registers have the same value, EQ will set Z to one. Then JPC realizes that Z = 1 and makes PC ← 0x9, in this way skipping any instruction stored in location 0x8.

Memory Address	Memory (RAM)	
0x0		
0x1	8	DATA
0x2	8	
0x3		
0x4	LOD R[0], 0, 0x1	TEXT (code)
0x5	LOD R[1], 0, 0x2	
0x6	EQ R[0], R[1], 0	
0x7	JPC 0, 0, 0x9	
0x8	ADD R[0], R[0], R[1]	
0x9		

Equipped with this set of assembly language instructions, you can command the CPU to execute them. But what about the handling of data? We will introduce a pseudo-instruction **WORD** that will help you handle data in VM/0 assembly language. We will start out with an example to show you the usefulness of this pseudo-instruction. Imagine you have two values stored in two different memory locations (or cells)—and as you know, inside a computer everything is represented in binary. For example:

memory address	memory contents (variables)
000000000001	000000000001001
000000000010	000000000011000

WORD permits the association of names or labels with a memory location. These names are also known as **identifiers**. An identifier allows programmers to refer to a **memory location** using a name instead of strings of 0s and 1s. As the content of memory locations might change as the program runs, memory locations are also known as **variables**. WORD allows programmers to reserve a memory word and define the initial value for that specific memory location. In summary, we could say that WORD is used for variable declarations. It is worth mentioning that **assembler** is the name of the program that makes the mapping between identifiers and memory locations to ease the handling of data in assembly language. Now we can show you how to use WORD to work with integers instead of using binary numbers. In the following example, variables a, b, and c are declared, and their initial values are 9, 24, and 0 respectively.

Label	Operation	Initial value
a	WORD	9
b	WORD	24
c	WORD	0

We can now write a program to add a couple of numbers, say 24 and 9, and forget about memory addresses.

Program 1

Line number	Label	Operation	Operands (or data values)	
1	a	WORD	9	**DATA (data segment)**
2	b	WORD	24	
3	c	WORD	0	
4		LOD	R[0], 0, a	**TEXT (program segment)**
5		LOD	R[2], 0, b	
6		ADD	R[3], R[1], R[2]	
7		STO	R[3], 0, c	

Now that you are familiar with some VM/0 assembly instruction and data declarations, we could introduce some special instructions to carry out input/output (I/O) operations. These special instructions known as **supervisor calls (SVC)**, or **system calls**, allow a user program to request service from the **operating system (OS)**. The only thing we need to know about the OS at this moment is that the operating system is a program that manages computer system resources efficiently and provides an environment for programs to run. As I/O operations are handled by the operating system, when a program needs to input or output data, a call must be made to the OS, and the operating system will execute the I/O operation on its behalf. The way to write down these system calls in VM/0 assembly language is:

SYS 0, 0, 0   ; Program stops, waits for user input.
SYS 0, 0, 1   ; Displays a value on the monitor screen.

Although the way I/O is handled by the OS is hidden from the user program, we will give you an idea of how it occurs. In memory-mapped I/O (MMIO) there is, in the OS area, a memory location or I/O buffer associated with each device. VM/0 has only two I/O devices: a keyboard and a monitor. The keyboard is considered the **standard input (stdin)** and is identified with the number 0. The monitor is the **standard output (stdout)** and is identified with the number 1. The I/O buffer for the keyboard will be denoted as INBUF and the one for the monitor OUTBUF.

As for SYS 0, 0, 0 (input) this is what occurs:

1. The program stops momentarily and waits until the user types in a value on the keyboard and presses the return key.
2. The operating system moves the input value from the keyboard port to INBUF and then from INBUF to the register with a higher denomination; in VM/0 it would be R[3].

R[3] ← INBUF ← Keyboard

Note: We will need an STO instruction right after SYS 0, 0, 0 to move the input value from the R[3] register to a memory location.

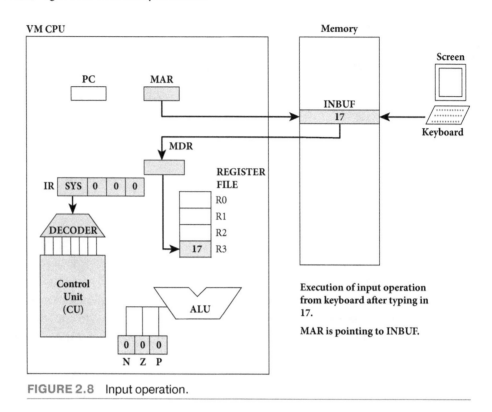

FIGURE 2.8 Input operation.

As for **SYS 0, 0, 1 (output)** this is what occurs:

1. The operating system stores the content of R[3] into the OUTBUF and then sends the contents of the OUTBUF to the monitor port.
2. The monitor displays the content of the monitor port on the screen.

Note: We will need an LOD instruction before SYS 0, 0, 1 to move a data value from a memory location to the R[3] register.

These two instructions used back to back allow the program to accept data from the keyboard and display it on the screen (echo). Figures 2.8 and 2.9 depict the input/output devices connected to memory.

Another system call you need to know at this point is **end of program (EOP)**. This system call tells the operating system that the program has run to completion properly. The operating system will take the appropriate actions to collect the resources the program was using.

SYS 0, 0, 2   ; End of program (EOP)

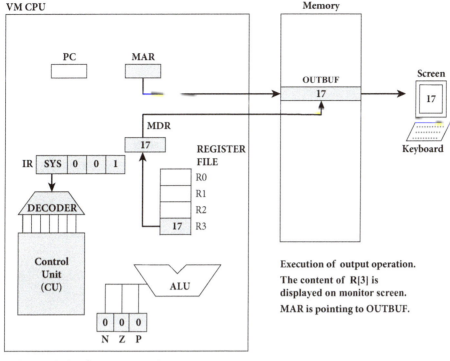

FIGURE 2.9 Output operation.

Let us proceed to make a list of all VM/0 instructions we have described thus far. In this list we will use x, y, and z to refer to register numbers, and they can take any value from zero to three. M is a modifier that has different interpretations depending on the instruction:

Mnemonic	Meaning	
LOD Rx, 0, M	Rx ← Mem [M]	(Copy the content of memory location M into Rx)
STO Rx, 0, M	Mem [M] ← Rx	(Copy the content of Rx into memory location M)
ADD Rx, Ry, Rz	Rx ← Ry + Rz	
SUB Rx, Ry, Rz	Rx ← Ry − Rz	
EQ Rx, Ry, 0	Set Z to 1 if Rx = Ry	
JPC 0, 0, M	Set PC to M (PC ← M), if Z = 1 or N = 1 or P = 1 (here M is an address)	
JMP 0, 0, M	Set PC to M (PC ← M)	

SYS 0, 0, 0   INPUT   (Accept value from keyboard)

SYS 0, 0, 1   OUTPUT (Display value on monitor screen)

SYS 0, 0, 2   HALT   (Tells OS that the program ended properly)

Equipped with this set of VM/0 instructions, we could write a program that reads in two values, displays the two values on the monitor screen, add them up, and finally displays the result on the monitor screen (c ← a + b).

Program 2

Line number	Label	Opcode	Operands	Comments
1	a	WORD	0	; Declaration a = 0
2	b	WORD	0	; Declaration b = 0
3	c	WORD	0	; Declaration c = 0
4		SYS	0, 0, 0	; R[3] ← keyboard
5		STO	R[3], 0, a	; a ← R[3]
6		SYS	0, 0, 1	; Display R[3] content on monitor
7		SYS	0, 0, 0	; Input from keyboard into R[3]
8		STO	R[3], 0, b	; b ← R[3]
9		SYS	0, 0, 1	; Display R[3] content on monitor
10		LOD	R[0], 0, a	; R[0] ← a
11		LOD	R[1], 0, b	; R[1] ← b
12		ADD	R[0], R[0], R[1]	; R[0] ← R[0] + R[1]
13		STO	R[0], 0, c	; c ← R[0]
14		LOD	R[3], c	; R[3] ← c
15		SYS	0, 0, 1	; Display R[3] content on monitor
16		SYS	0, 0, 2	HALT: Tells OS that the program ended

Assembler Directives

The next step to improve VM/0 assembly language is the incorporation of **assembler directives** to assist the assembler in translating the program into binary (executable code). It is important to know that directives do not generate code. Directives tell the assembler where the data section begins, where the text section (program) begins, and where it ends. We will introduce three directives to be used with our assembly language:

.text	(This directive tells the assembler where the programs section begins)
.data	(This directive tells the assembler where the data section begins)
.end	(This directive tells the assembler where the program ends)

To show you the usage of directives, we will place them into program 2, and the program will be explicitly divided in two segments: a DATA segment and TEXT segment.

Line number	Label	Opcode	Operands	Comments
1		.data		
2	a	WORD	0	; Declaration a = 0
3	b	WORD	0	; Declaration b = 0
4	c	WORD	0	; Declaration c = 0
5		.text	main	; Program begins at main (line 6)
6	main	SYS	0, 0, 0	; R[3] ← INBUF ← keyboard
7		STO	R[3], 0, a	; a ← R[3]
8		SYS	0, 0, 1	; Display (R[3] → OUTBUF → Screen)
9		SYS	0, 0, 0	; Input from keyboard into IOB
10		STO	R[3], 0, b	; b ← R[3]
11		SYS	0, 0, 1	; Display (R[3] → OUTBUF → Screen)
12		LOD	R[0], 0, a	; R[0] ← a
13		LOD	R[1], 0, b	; R[1] ← b
14		ADD	R[0], R[0], R[1]	; R[0] ← R[0] + R[1]
15		STO	R[0], 0, c	; c ← R[0]
16		LOD	R[3], c	; R[3] ← c
17		SYS	0, 0, 1	; Display (R[3] → OUTBUF → Screen)
18		SYS	0, 0, 3	; HALT: Tells OS that program ended
19		.end		

Note: Label main indicates where the program begins.

Instruction Set Architecture

The **instruction format** of VM/0 has four components, which we will refer to as fields. The CPU will handle each field differently depending on the opcode. The ISA of the VM/0 has 20 instructions divided in two groups. Instructions beginning with opcode 0000 are used for arithmetic and relational operations, and all other instruction have an opcode not equal to 0000. We will show how they are encoded using the following instruction format.

OP	Rx or n/a	Ry or n/a	Rz or memory address or a number or n/a

VM/0 Instruction Format

Where,

- **OP** Is the operation code (for example: LOD)
- **Rx** Unused or refers to a register in the register file (**destination register**)
- **Ry** Unused or refers to a register in the register file (**source register**)
- **Rz** Depending of the opcode it indicates:
  A register in arithmetic instructions (**source register**)
  (e.g. ADD R[1], R[2], R[3])
  A constant value, or literal (instruction: LIT)
  A program address (instruction JMP)
  A data address (instructions: LOD, STO)

There are 11 arithmetic/relational operations that manipulate the data within the register file. These operations will be explained after some basic VM/0 instructions. Rx, Ry, and Rz can be replaced by 0, 1, 2, and 3 depending what register of the register file you want to use.

(Opcode)			
01 – **LIT**	**Rx, 0, M**		Load a constant value (literal) **M** into register **Rx**
02 – **LOD**	**Rx, 0, M**		Load value into Rx from memory location **M**
03 – **STO**	**Rx, 0, M**		Store value from Rx into memory location **M**
04 – **JMP**	**0, 0, M**		Jump unconditionally to memory location **M (PC ← M)**
05 – **JPC**	**0, 0, M**		Jump on condition: if any CC equals 1, then PC ← **M**
15 – **SYS**	**0, 0, 0**		Read in input from keyboard and store it in register R3
SYS	**0, 0, 1**		Display content of register R3 to the screen
SYS	**0, 0, 2**		End of program (program stops running)

In the table below we will present the opcode in binary of the instructions explained so far. All arithmetic operations have the same opcode **OPR** (OPR = 0000) and a function code to select the appropriate arithmetic operation, as shown below.

Opcode in binary	Mnemonic	Function in binary	Arithmetic/relational operation
0000	OPR	0001 →	ADD
0000	OPR	0010 →	SUB
0000	OPR	0110 →	EQL
0001	LIT		
0010	LOD		
0011	STO		
0100	JMP		
0101	JPC		
1111	SYS		

Now let us take a look at the encoding of these instructions in 16-bit words:

LIT Rx, 0, M

15	14	13	12	11	10	9	8	7	6	5	4	3	2	1	0
0	0	0	1	R	x	M	M	M	M	M	M	M	M	M	M

OPCODE   Register   Constant value (literal)

LOD Rx, 0, M

15	14	13	12	11	10	9	8	7	6	5	4	3	2	1	0
0	0	1	0	R	x			M	M	M	M	M	M	M	M

OPCODE   Register   Memory location

STO Rx, 0, M

15	14	13	12	11	10	9	8	7	6	5	4	3	2	1	0
0	0	1	1	R	x			M	M	M	M	M	M	M	M

OPCODE   Register   Memory location

ADD Rx, Ry, Rz

15	14	13	12	11	10	9	8	7	6	5	4	3	2	1	0
0	0	0	0	R	x	R	y	R	z			0	0	0	1

OPCODE — **Registers** — **Function**

SUB Rx, Ry, Rz

15	14	13	12	11	10	9	8	7	6	5	4	3	2	1	0
0	0	0	0	R	x	R	y	R	z		0	0	0	1	0

OPCODE — **Registers** — **Function**

EQ Rx, Ry, 0

15	14	13	12	11	10	9	8	7	6	5	4	3	2	1	0
0	0	0	0	R	x	R	y				0	0	1	1	0

OPCODE — **Registers** — **Function**

JPC 0, 0, M

15	14	13	12	11	10	9	8	7	6	5	4	3	2	1	0
0	0	0	0	M	M	M	M	M	M	M	M	M	M	M	M

OPCODE — **Memory address**

JMP 0, 0, M

15	14	13	12	11	10	9	8	7	6	5	4	3	2	1	0
0	0	0	0	M	M	M	M	M	M	M	M	M	M	M	M

OPCODE — **Memory address**

SYS 0, 0, 0

15	14	13	12	11	10	9	8	7	6	5	4	3	2	1	0
1	1	1	1											0	0

OPCODE — **STDIN**

SYS 0, 0, 1

15	14	13	12	11	10	9	8	7	6	5	4	3	2	1	0
1	1	1	1											0	1

OPCODE — **STDOUT**

SYS 0, 0, 2

15	14	13	12	11	10	9	8	7	6	5	4	3	2	1	0
1	1	1	1											1	0

OPCODE   EOP

The function values for all arithmetic and relational operations and the description of the actions taken by each instruction are shown below:

Opcode in binary	Mnemonic	Function in binary	Arithmetic/ relational operation	Description
0000	OPR	0001 →	ADD	Rx ← Ry + Rz
0000	OPR	0010 →	SUB	Rx ← Ry − Rz
0000	OPR	0011 →	MUL	Rx ← Ry * Rz
0000	OPR	0100 →	DIV	Rx ← Ry / Rz
0000	OPR	0101 →	MOD	Rx ← Ry mod Rz
0000	OPR	0110 →	EQ	If Rx = = Ry then Z = 1
0000	OPR	0111 →	NE	If Rx ! = Ry then Z = 0
0000	OPR	1000 →	LT	If Rx < Ry then N = 1
0000	OPR	1001 →	LE	If Rx = < Ry then N = 1 or Z = 1
0000	OPR	1010 →	GT	If Rx > Ry then P = 1
0000	OPR	1011 →	GE	If Rx > = Ry then P = 1 or Z = 1

Now that you have a better understanding of the VM/0 instruction set architecture, let us take a look at program 2 translated into binary and hexadecimal. By the way, from now on we will use the notation R3 instead of R[3] to make the writing of programs less cumbersome. Also, we need to justify the usage of line numbers as memory addresses for variables a, b, and c to make the example easy to follow, but we will repair this inaccuracy right now. As DATA and TEXT are two separate segments, the data is loaded from the beginning of the data segment and the instructions are loaded at the beginning in the TEXT segment. All variable addresses are accessed as a displacement from the beginning of the data segment. A **global data pointer (GDP)** register in the CPU points to the beginning of the DATA segment.

Memory location	Label	Opcode	Operands	Binary	Hexadecimal
		.data		; no code generated	
0x0	a	WORD	0	0000000000000000	0x0000 ← GDP

0x1	b	WORD	0	0000000000000000	0x0000
0x2	c	WORD	0	0000000000000000	0x0000
		.text main		; no code generated	
0x0	main	SYS	0, 0, 0	1111000000000000	0xF000 ← PC
0x1		STO	R3, 0, a	0011110000000000	0x3C00
0x2		SYS	0, 0, 1	1111000000000001	0xF001
0x3		SYS	0, 0, 0	1111000000000000	0xF000
0x4		STO	R3, 0, b	0011110000000001	0x3C01
0x5		SYS	0, 0, 1	1111000000000001	0xF001
0x6		LDO	R0, 0, a	0010000000000000	0x2000
0x7		LDO	R1, 0, b	0010010000000001	0x2401
0x8		ADD	R0, R0, R1	0000000001000001	0x0041
0x9		STO	R0, 0, c	0011000000000010	0x3002
0xA		LOD	R3, 0, c	0010110000000010	0x2C02
0xB		SYS	0, 0, 1	1111000000000001	0xF001
0xC		SYS	0, 0, 3	1111000000000010	0xF002
		.end		; no code generated	

Process Address Space

Once an assembler translates a program into binary, we refer to it as **object code**. In order to run the object code, we need to load it into memory. When the program is running, we call it a **process**; hence, we define a process as a **program in execution**. To run a program, the operating system must assign to the program a memory area called the **process address space** (or user address space). This process address space is divided into four segments: **stack segment**, **heap segment**, **data segment**, and **text segment**. In this chapter, we have been dealing with the text segment and data segment. The stack segment, which will be discussed in chapter 3, is used to manage the calling and returning from subroutines. The heap segment, which will be discussed in chapter 4, is used to provide memory on demand to allow some programming languages to handle memory dynamically. Figure 2.10 depicts the process address space; you can observe that the text segment begins at location 0x0000, followed by the data segment beginning at memory location 0x2000. You will find the heap segment starting at location 0x4000 and the stack segment beginning at location 0x6000. The user address space ends at location 0x7FFF. The operating system area or kernel address space uses all memory locations from 0x8000 to 0xFFFF. The size of every segment in the user address space is based on the ones proposed by Knuth in his MMIX computer.

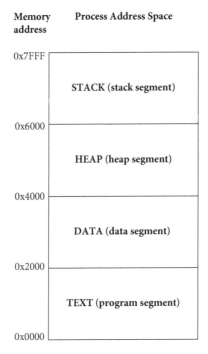

FIGURE 2.10 Process address space.

We are now ready to load the assembled object code for program 2 into the process address space. We will use hexadecimal next to each line in TEXT and variable names next to each line in DATA to make the understanding of the object code easier.

Memory address	Process Address space		
	0000 0000 0000 0000	c	**DATA (data segment)**
	0000 0000 0000 0000	b	
GDP → 0x2000	0000 0000 0000 0000	a	
	1111 0000 0000 0010	0xF002	**TEXT (program segment)**
	1111 0000 0000 0001	0xF001	
	0010 1100 0000 0010	0x2C02	
	0011 0000 0100 0010	0x3002	
	0000 0000 0100 0001	0x0041	
	0010 0100 0100 0001	0x2401	
	0010 0000 0100 0000	0x2000	
	1111 0000 0000 0001	0xF001	
	0011 1100 0100 0001	0x3C01	
	1111 0000 0000 0000	0xF000	
	1111 0000 0000 0001	0xF001	
	0011 1100 0000 0000	0x3C00	
PC → 0x0000	1111 0000 0000 0000	0xF000	

This example might have made you realize how useful it could be to have a hexadecimal representation of the program. For instance, you might notice that each instruction starting with a 0xF is a system call, and if the instruction begins with 0x0, it is an arithmetic or relational instruction. As we are currently dealing with the data and text segments, the stack and heap segments are omitted in this example. Once the program is loaded in the text segment at location 0x0, the PC is set to point to that address (PC ← 0x0000). The global data pointer is set up to 0x2000 (GDP ← 0x2000), and all variables are accessed as a displacement from the GDP. If you observe carefully, you will notice that memory location zero is at the bottom of the process address space, which means you have to follow the program from the bottom up. Similarly, variables are accessed from the bottom up in the data segment. For instance, variable **c** is encoded in instruction as address **0x2** because that is the distance (displacement) from the GDP.

Some Remarks on VM/0

When reading about assembly language for other architectures, you will find that the PC is incremented by four to move the program counter from one memory address to the next, and the word length is 32 bits. Below, you will find some comments to help you better understand the assembly language of architectures like MIPS, Intel, and ARM.

On Word Length and Byte Addressable Memories

VM/0 word length is 16 bits, which means that to move from one memory location to the next, a jump of 16 bits must be done. We will use the VM/0 fetch cycle presented in section 2.3 to explain:

$$\begin{aligned}
\text{FETCH:} \quad & \text{MAR} \leftarrow \text{PC} \\
& \text{PC} \leftarrow \text{PC} + 1 \\
& \text{MDR} \leftarrow \text{MEM[MAR]} \\
& \text{IR} \leftarrow \text{MDR}
\end{aligned}$$

As you can see, the PC is incremented by one because VM/0 is word addressable. There are current architectures like MIPS and ARM that are byte addressable, which means they can move from one byte to the next. Then if we have a 32-bit word and memory is byte addressable, the PC must be incremented by four to move from one word to the next. Hence, FETCH will be executed this way:

$$\begin{aligned}
\text{FETCH:} \quad & \text{MAR} \leftarrow \text{PC} \\
& \text{PC} \leftarrow \text{PC} + 4 \\
& \text{MDR} \leftarrow \text{MEM[MAR]} \\
& \text{IR} \leftarrow \text{MDR}
\end{aligned}$$

If VM/0 were byte addressable, the PC would have to be incremented by two in the Fetch cycle.

On Condition Codes

There are three condition code flags in the VM/0-CPU: N, Z, and P. We included the P flag because it was more intuitive working with the three conditions separately. However, only with flags N and Z can all conditions be tested, as shown in the following table.

Description	Condition Codes
Test for equality	Set Z = 1
Not equal	Set ~Z = 1
Less than	N = 1
Less than or equal to	Set Z = 1 or N = 1
Greater than	Set ~Z = 1 and ~N = 1
Greater than or equal to	~N = 1

As you know, VM/0 is a virtual machine, and therefore we do not need to implement all the condition codes of an actual processor. In CPUs such as MIPS or Intel, there are other flags to detect overflow (V flag) or carry (C flag).

On Increasing VM/0 Word Length

We have described VM/0 using a 16-bit word to keep it simple. However, all concepts presented so far can be implemented in a 32- or 64-bit word. For instance, using 32 bits we can do the following:

a. Use 6 bits for the opcode, which will allow us to represent $2^6 = 64$ different opcodes.
b. Use 4 bits to represent registers and increase the numbers of registers in the register file to 16.

SUMMARY

In this chapter, we reviewed the concepts of positional number systems and highlighted the importance of binary numbers because that is the language computers use. Then we introduced an assembly language (the ISA) for a virtual machine (VM/0) and explained how each instruction was executed. This ISA allowed us to write simple programs for VM/0. Then we introduce a system program called the assembler, which translates assembly language into binary to allow the CPU to execute the user program. Finally, we introduced the concept of process as a program in execution and explained that each time we need to run a program, the operating system creates a process address space for the program.

EXERCISES

1. Write down the numbers from 0 to 20 in decimal, binary (use 8 bits), and hexadecimal.

2. Convert the followings numbers to decimal:
   a) 00010001
   b) 10010111
   c) 0xFA
   d) 0xABC

   Hint: Use $\sum_{k=0}^{n-1} d_i b^i$ where **b** stands for base and **d** stands for digit. For example, in 10101010_2, n = 8 and the b = 2:

1	0	1	0	1	0	1	0
↓	↓	↓	↓	↓	↓	↓	↓
d_7	d_6	d_5	d_4	d_3	d_2	d_1	d_0
×	×	×	×	×	×	×	×
b^7	b^6	b^5	b^4	b^3	b^2	b^1	b^0

3. Convert the following binary numbers into hexadecimal:
   a) 1111000000000001
   b) 0000000001000001
   c) 0000110100000110
   d) 0000100111000011

4. Convert the following hexadecimal numbers into binary:
   a) 0x0D41
   b) 0xF001
   c) 0x200A
   d) 0x3C03

5. The binary strings in question 3 represent the encoding of four VM/0 instructions. Convert the strings into assembly language.

6. Write down the steps carried out in VM/0 fetch cycle assuming memory is byte addressable.

7. What operation executes the VM/0 control unit to find out which one of the condition codes might be set to one?

8. Write down the steps the VM/0 control unit must execute for the instructions:
   a) STO R2, 0, 10
   b) LOD R3, 0, 5
   c) JMP 0, 0, 7

Bibliographical Notes

A tiny p-code interpreter was proposed by Wirth[1] as the target machine to implement the PL/0 compiler. MIXAL assembly language for a hypothetical computer was proposed by Knuth[2] in his book series *The Art of Computer Programming* as a tool to teach algorithm, data structures, and programming. Wirth's RISC interpreter[3] was proposed as a virtual machine to be used as the target machine for the Oberon Compiler. MMIX, a RISC hypothetical computer, and its assembly language[4] were proposed to replace MIX architecture. A good introduction to Intel x86 CPU is presented by Bryant and O'Hallaron,[5] and for an in-depth understanding of MIPS processors, we refer readers to Patterson and Hennessy.[6] There is also an excellent description of the ARM architecture presented by Patterson and Hennessy.[7] About the origins of binary numbers and binary arithmetic, we refer readers to Leibnitz.[8]

Bibliography

1. N. Wirth, *Algorithm + Data Structures = Programs*. Upper Saddle River, NJ: Prentice Hall, 1976.
2. D. E. Knuth, *The Art of Computer Programming: Fundamental Algorithms*, 3rd ed., vol. 1. Upper Saddle River, NJ: Addison-Wesley, 1973.
3. N. Wirth, *Compiler Constructions*. Redwood City, CA: Addison-Wesley, 1996.
4. D. E. Knuth, *The Art of Computer Programming, Volume 1, Fascicle 1: MMIX a Risc Computer for the NEW Millennium*. Upper Saddle River, NJ: Addison-Wesley, 2005.
5. R. E. Bryant and D. R. O'Hallaron, *Computer Systems: A Programmer's Perspective*, 3rd ed. Boston, MA: Prentice Hall, 2016.
6. D. A. Patterson and J. L. Hennessy, *Computer Organization and Design: The Hardware/Software Interface*. Cambridge, MA: Morgan Kaufmann, 2013.
7. D. A. Petterson and J. L. Hennessy, *Computer Organization and Design: The Hardware/Software Interface ARM Edition*. Cambridge, MA: Morgan Kaufmann, 2017.
8. G. G. Leibnitz, "Explication de l'arithmétique binaire," *Mémoires de mathématique et de physique de l'Académie royale des sciences* (1703), pp. 85–89.

Chapter 3

Stacks, Recursion, and Nested Programs

So the last shall be first, and the first last.
Matthew 20:16
—The Bible

INTRODUCTION

The stack principle, or last-in-first-out storage method, was initially developed to evaluate expressions written using the parenthesis-free notation known as reverse Polish notation. The beauty of this method attracted the attention of many researchers, and almost immediately the stack concept was used to implement recursive procedures in programming languages, developing compilers, and building stack organized computers. Nowadays, the stack principle is used in computer systems mainly for subroutine linkage.

We initiate this chapter with a detailed explanation of the stack mechanism, or pushdown storage. Then glancing backward to the process address space, we remind you that the base of the stack is at the top of the process address space, and therefore the stack pointer has to be decremented by one for the stack to grow and incremented by one to shrink. Then we present the concept of activation record as a means for subroutine linkage. Finally, the implementation of recursion and nested procedures is described.

CHAPTER OBJECTIVES

- To review the concept of pushdown storage, or stack mechanism.
- To discuss the usage of the stack and activation records to control subroutine linkage.
- To explore the implementation of recursive functions using several instances of the same activation record.
- To understand the implementation of nested procedures.

VOCABULARY

This is a list of keywords that herald the concepts we will study in this chapter. They are organized in chronological order and will appear in the text in bold. We invite you to take a look at these keywords to find out which ones you are familiar with.

Last in first out (LIFO)	Return address (RA)	End
SP	Parameters	Subroutine declaration
Push (data value)	Local variables	Procedure
Pop ( )	Increment (INC)	Function
Text	Call (CAL)	If-statement
Data	Return (RTN)	If-then
Heap	Reserved word	If-then-else
Stack (run-time stack)	PL/0	While-do
Activation record (AR)	Var	Recursion
Stack frame	Statement	Lexicographical level
Base pointer (BP)	Assignment statement	Static link (SL)
Stack pointer (SP)	Constant	Static chain
Functional value (FV)	Main	
Dynamic link (DL)	Begin	

ACTIVATING PRIOR KNOWLEDGE

In this section we will present a series of activities. In some of them you can choose one or more options. Sometimes, if you do not agree with the given answers to choose from, you will be allowed to give your own answer. By the way, this is not a test.

1. Is there anything that looks familiar to you in these three options?

    a. 6
    b. 3!
    c. 3 × 2 × 1

2. Assume you have three boxes and a container. The boxes are placed in the container as shown below: First box 1, then box 2, and finally box 3.

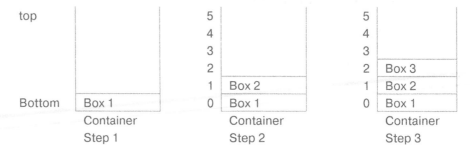

If placing a box into the container is considered a push step and getting a box out of the container is considered a pop step and boxes can only move in and out through the container top:

   a. Find out how many push steps are necessary to put box 1 inside the container.
   b. Find out how many pop steps are necessary to got box 1 out of the container in step 3.

3. Skim the chapter and pay attention to the words written in **bold**. Count the number of words you are familiar with.

4. Does LIFO = FILO?

5. The following expression 3 4 * 5 6 * + is expressed in reverse Polish notation. Rewrite this expression using infix notation.

6. Observe the following picture. Each level in the three is called a lexicographical level, and the root is level zero:

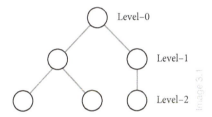

   a. How many steps are necessary to move from level 2 to level 0?
   b. How many steps are necessary to move from level 1 to level 0?
   c. How many steps are necessary to move from level 2 to level 1?

Stack Mechanism

The stack is a data structure that could be implemented using an array, and its management follows the **last in first out (LIFO)** behavior. In the CPU there is a register called the stack pointer (**SP**), which points to the top of the stack, and two operations are used to insert data values into or remove them from the top of the stack.

1. To place a value on top of the stack, we can use the operation push, whose format is: **PUSH (*data value*)**. This operation increments the SP by one and inserts a data value on top of the stack. These are the steps for the PUSH operation:

   PUSH (a), means → SP = SP + 1
   Stack [SP] = a

2. To remove a value from top of the stack and store it in a variable, say b, we can use the operation **POP( )**. This operation removes whatever data value is found on top of the stack and decrements the stack pointer by one, as described below:

b = **POP ( )**, means →   b = Stack [SP]
                                       SP = SP - 1

An illustration will help illustrate the effects of these operations. In figure 3.1 the top row shows three stack states: In the initial state, the SP points to stack location zero, whose content is the value 7. Then we show the stack after executing PUSH (23), and finally on the right-hand side, we present the stack after executing PUSH (29). It is worth mentioning that at these stages, the values in the shaded area are unreachable with a single application of POP ( ). In the second row of stacks in figure 3.1, observe the three stack states after applying the following operations to the stack in the right-hand side in the top row:

b = POP ( )
PUSH (5)
PUSH (31)

It is worth noticing that after executing b = POP ( ), the number 29 is in stack location 2 but is unreachable and is considered to be garbage. If another PUSH operation is executed, for

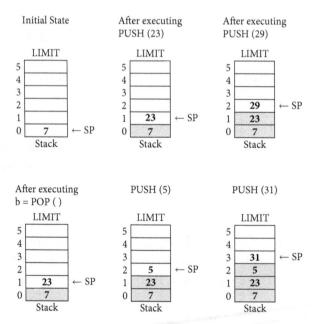

FIGURE 3.1 Stack states after using PUSH ( ) and POP ( ) operations.

example PUSH (5), the 29 will be overwritten with the value 5. The stack state after executing PUSH (31) can be seen in the right-hand side of the second row of stacks.

VM/0 Stack Architecture

VM/0 is a stack machine that provides a process address space for programs to run. Recall from chapter 2 that the process address space is a memory area organized in four segments: the **text** or code segment, which contains a list of instructions; the **data** segment, which stores global variables declared in the main program; the **heap**, which provides memory to the program on demand; and the **stack (run-time stack)**, which stores local variables and manages the changing of environments by keeping track of subroutine calls and returns.

Let us bring back an image of the process address space as a reminder that the stack is placed at the top of the address space.

Memory address	Process address space	
0x7FFF	STACK (stack segment)	←Bottom
0x6000		← Limit
0x4000	HEAP (heap segment)	
0x2000	DATA (data segment)	
0x0000	TEXT (program segment)	

As the stack bottom is located at the top of the process address space, the stack grows downward and shrinks upward. Therefore, we must redefine the way PUSH and POP work in the VM/0 computer system as follows:

PUSH (data value)   b = **POP ( )**
   SP = SP − 1   b = Stack [SP]
   Stack [SP] = a SP = SP + 1

Figure 3.2 shows the example illustrated in figure 3.1 using the new version of the PUSH and POP operations.

When a program is running, it frequently changes from the execution of one function to another. Each time a function is called, some information from the caller and called function

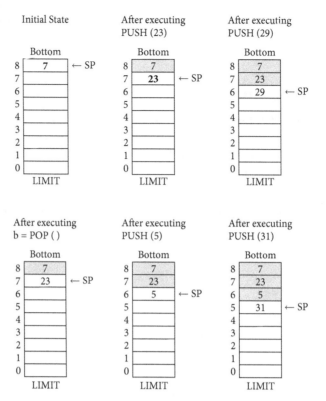

FIGURE 3.2 Stack states using standard PUSH ( ) and POP ( ) operations as they are carried out in actual computer systems.

must be saved in the stack to restore the caller environment upon completion of the called function. This information is stored in an **activation record (AR)** or **stack frame**. Activation records are data structures inserted into the run-time stack each time a function is called in and popped out upon completion of the called function. To manage the stack in VM/0, we need to add three more registers to the VM/0 CPU. These registers are the global data pointer (GP), which points to the data area; the **base pointer (BP)**, which points to the base of the current activation record; and the **stack pointer (SP)**, which points to the top of the stack. Figure 3.3 depicts the BP and SP pointing to an AR in the stack and the GP pointing to the data area.

Note: The words *procedure*, *function*, *method*, and *subroutine* will be used interchangeably.

Activation Records and Procedure Calls

There is an activation record associated with each function or procedure, and each time a function is called, its activation record is inserted on the stack. The data stored in the AR is a mix of caller and called function information. From the caller we need to store the contents

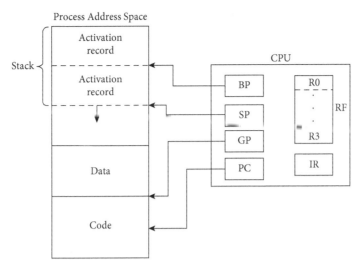

FIGURE 3.3 The GP, SP, and BP pointing to the stack in the process address space.

of the PC register, BP register, and reserve space for **parameters** passed on from the caller function to the called function. From the called function standpoint, we have to reserve space for the **local variables** declared in the function.

The AR layout consists of the following parts: **functional value**, **dynamic link**, **return address**, **parameters**, and **local variables**. Each one of these fields is described as follows:

- **Functional value (FV):** Location to store the function returned value.
- **Dynamic link (DL):** Points to the base of the previous activation record. This address is copied back from the DL to the CPU base pointer when the called function ends to restore the caller environment.
- **Return address (RA):** Points, in the code segment, to the instruction located right after the **call** instruction executed by the caller. This address is copied from the RA to the CPU program counter after termination of the current function or procedure (called function) to restore the caller environment.
- **Parameters:** Space reserved to store the actual parameters the caller function is passing on to the called function.
- **Local variables:** Space reserved to store local variables declared within the called function.

Let us explore and find out where the above mentioned information is stored in the AR. Figure 3.4 presents the data structure of called AR and shows where each field is placed.

To understand the way ARs are inserted on the stack, we need to add three new instructions to the VM/0 ISA. These new instructions will be used by a program to **increment (INC)** the stack pointer to accommodate the activation record, to **call (CAL)** a function, and to **return**

Activation Records (AR)

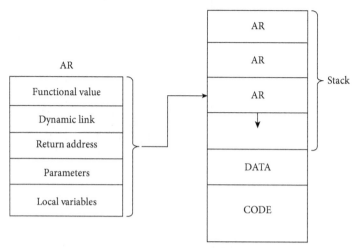

FIGURE 3.4 Activation record description and their placement in the stack.

(RTN) from a subroutine to the caller function once the called function ends. These new instructions are described below:

(Opcode)
07 – **INC**   0, 0, **M**   sp ← sp – M;   Reserve space for AR

The instruction INC reserves space in the stack to place an AR each time a function is called. The **M** field in the instructions indicates the number of words to be reserved. This is carried out by subtracting the value **M** from the **SP (remember that the stack grows downward)**. The number of words reserved includes space for FV, DL, RA, parameters, and local variables. The instruction INC is always placed at the beginning of each function, including the main function, and its instruction format is given below:

INC 0, 0, M

OPCODE   **Numeral**

The second instruction, CAL, is used to call a subroutine in a program. The description of the actions taken by this instruction is shown below:

(Opcode)
06 – **CAL**   0, 0, **M**   stack[sp – 1] ← 0;   FV ← 0
                                stack[sp – 2] ← bp;   DL ← CPU.BP
                                stack[sp – 3] ← pc;   RA ← CPU.PC
                                bp ← sp – 1;   Set BP for callee
                                pc ← M;   Points to subroutine

The first action taken by this instruction is to store a zero in the functional value field. Then, to save the environment of the caller, the content of the CPU register BP is stored in the dynamic link field, and the CPU PC register is saved in the return address field. These two values will allow the environment of the caller to be restored when the called function ends. In figure 3.5 you will find a graphical interpretation of this instruction. On the left-hand side, you will see the stack before the execution of the call instruction (CAL) and then in the center the state of the stack once the CAL instruction is executed. Finally, on the left-hand side, we illustrate the state of the stack once the called function executes the instruction INC.

The format of the instruction CAL is similar to the instruction jump (JMP), but CAL takes many more actions than JMP because JMP only overwrites the PC.

CAL 0, 0, M

15	14	13	12	11	10	9	8	7	6	5	4	3	2	1	0
0	1	1	0	M	M	M	M	M	M	M	M	M	M	M	M

OPCODE   **Memory address**

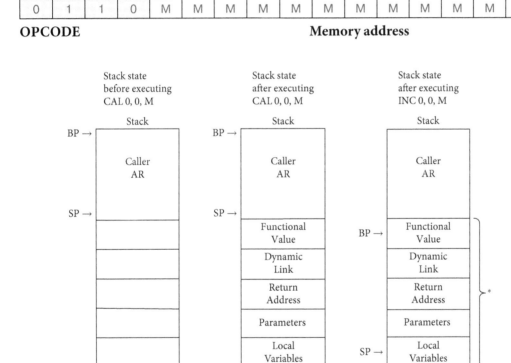

FIGURE 3.5 Insertion of an activation record in the stack.

The third instruction is return. Each time a subroutine ends, the caller must take control of the CPU. Placing the instruction return (RTN) as the last instruction of the subroutine will accomplish this task.

(Opcode)
0000 – RTN   0, 0, 0   sp ← bp + 1;
                                    bp ← stack[sp - 2];   CPU.BP ← DL
                                    pc ← stack[sp - 3];   CPU.PC ← RA

As you can see in the instruction format RTN, the opcode is the same one use in arithmetic and relational operations (OPCODE = 0000), and the function value is 00000.

Opcode in binary	Mnemonic	Function in binary	Operation return
0000	OPR	0000 →	RTN

RTN 0, 0, 0

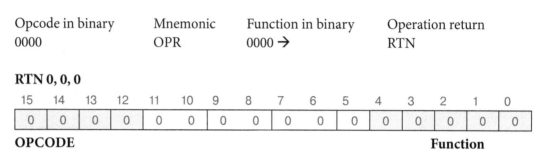

The following illustration shows how the three instructions are placed in a program:

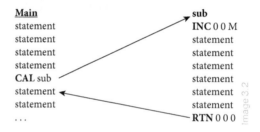

Now we will present a program written in VM/0 assembly language where you will see the usage of the instructions INC, CAL, and RTN.

0	JMP	0 0 10		Jump to address "10" (main program begins)
1	JMP	0 0 2		Jump to address "2" (subroutine begins)
2	INC	0 0 6	Sub	Increment SP by 6
3	LIT	0 0 13		Load constant value 13 on register R0
4	STO	0 0 4		Store the contents of R0 in memory location 4
5	LIT	0 0 1		Load constant value 1 on register R0
6	STO	0 0 5		Store the contents of R0 in memory location 5
7	LIT	0 0 7		Load constant value 7 on register R0
8	STO	0 0 5		Store the contents of R0 in memory location 5
9	RTN	0 0 0		Return from subroutine
10	INC	0 0 6	Main	Increment SP by 6

11	LIT	0 0 3	Load constant value 3 on register R0
12	STO	0 0 4	Store the contents of R0 in memory location 4
13	LIT	0 0 9	Load constant value 9 on register R0
14	STO	0 0 5	Store the contents of R0 in memory location 5
15	CAL	0 0 2	Call subroutine
16	SIO	0 0 2	End of program

The order of execution of these instructions in VM/0 and the stack state after the execution of each instruction is illustrated in figure 3.6. You can see that after the execution of instruction 11 (LIT 0, 0, 3), the contents of the register file is shown ($R0 = 3$, $R1 = 0$, $R2 = 0$, etc.)

Program running on VM/0

	pc	bp	sp	registers	stack	code
Initial values	0	1	0	0 0 0 0 0 0 0 0 0	0 0 0 0 0	0 jmp 0 0 10
						1 jmp 0 0 2
0 jmp 0, 0, 10	10	1	0	0 0 0 0 0 0 0 0 0	0 0 0 0 0	2 inc 0 0 4
10 inc 0, 0, 6	11	1	6	0 0 0 0 0 0 0 0 0	0 0 0 0 0	3 lit 0 0 13
11 lit 0, 0, 3	12	1	6	3 0 0 0 0 0 0 0 0	0 0 0 0 0	4 sto 0 0 4
12 sto 0, 0, 4	13	1	6	3 0 0 0 0 0 0 0 0	0 0 0 0 3	5 lit 0 0 1
13 lit 0, 0, 9	14	1	6	9 0 0 0 0 0 0 0 0	0 0 0 0 3	6 sto 0 0 5
14 sto 0, 0, 5	15	1	6	9 0 0 0 0 0 0 0 0	0 0 0 3 9	7 lit 0 0 7
15 cal 0, 0, 2	2	7	6	9 0 0 0 0 0 0 0 0	0 0 0 3 9	8 sto 0 0 5
2 inc 0, 0, 4	3	7	12	9 0 0 0 0 0 0 0 0	0 0 0 0 3 9 | 0 1 1 16	9 rtn 0 0 0
3 lit 0, 0, 13	4	7	12	13 0 0 0 0 0 0 0 0	0 0 0 0 3 9 | 0 1 1 16	10 inc 0 0 6
4 sto 0, 0, 4	5	7	12	13 0 0 0 0 0 0 0 0	0 0 0 0 3 9 | 0 1 1 16 13	11 lit 0 0 3
5 lit 0, 0, 1	6	7	12	1 0 0 0 0 0 0 0 0	0 0 0 0 3 9 | 0 1 1 16 13	12 sto 0 0 4
6 sto 0, 0, 5	7	7	12	1 0 0 0 0 0 0 0 0	0 0 0 0 3 9 | 0 1 1 16 13 1	13 lit 0 0 9
7 lit 0, 0, 7	8	7	12	7 0 0 0 0 0 0 0 0	0 0 0 0 3 9 | 0 1 1 16 13 1	14 sto 0 0 5
8 sto 0, 0, 5	9	7	12	7 0 0 0 0 0 0 0 0	0 0 0 0 3 9 | 0 1 1 16 13 7	15 cal 0 0 2
9 rtn 0, 0, 0	16	1	6	7 0 0 0 0 0 0 0 0	0 0 0 0 3 9	16 sio 0 0 2
16 sio 0, 0, 2	17	1	6	7 0 0 0 0 0 0 0 0	0 0 0 0 3 9	

FIGURE 3.6 Program in assembly language executing on VM/0.

Let us explore now the way the stack changes state from the perspective of high-level languages.

Introduction to PL/0

Programming languages provide us with a notation to write programs to solve problems using a computer. They give us a series of rigid rules (syntax) to be followed and some words, called **reserved words**, which are part of the language. In addition, the languages provide us with a series of special symbols such as plus, period, semicolon, and many others, which are also part of the languages. These reserved words and special symbols must be used solely as stated in the language grammar. Although programming languages look very rigid in their structure, they are flexible enough to allow a programmer to insert external names and numbers chosen by the programmer. These external names, known as identifiers, can be used to name constants, variables, functions, procedures, and methods.

PL/0 is a small programming language proposed by Niklaus Wirth, and it could be considered a tiny subset of Pascal. We present here a variant of PL/0 with some added programming constructs that will help us explain some concepts. A program in PL/0 consists of two parts: declarations and statements. Each variable declaration reserves a memory location and associates a name (aka identifier) with that memory location. The way to declare a variable in PL/0 is by using the reserved word **var** follow by an identifier; for example, to declare the variables a, b, and c, we have to write:

var a, b, c;

Statements are used to tell the computer what has to be done. For instance, the **assignment statement**

a:= b + c;

instructs VM/0 to execute an arithmetic operation by adding the contents of variables b and c. The assignment symbol ":=" tells the computer to store the resulting addition value in variable a. The statement can be read this way: "a becomes b + c." You may have noticed that variable declarations and statements end with a semicolon (";") symbol to indicate the end of the declaration or the end of a statement. This is mandatory to comply with PL/0 syntax rules.

Sometimes you may be interested in declaring a **constant**. A constant is a value in a memory location that cannot be altered. For example:

    const k = 7;   // constant declaration
    a:= b + k;   // we are adding b + 7

If k is used in the right-hand side of the assignment statement, an error will occur. Therefore, you must not write statements such as

k: = a;   or   k:= a + b;

To write a program in PL/0, there are some syntax rules we have to stick to. A program must begin with the word **main**, followed by constant declarations and variable declarations, then the keyword **begin**, followed by statements, and the keyword **end** right after the last statement. The final touch is the symbol "." (period) following the reserved word **end** to indicate the end of the program. This is an example of a PL/0 program:

```
1 main
2 var a,b,c;
3 begin
4    b:= 2;
```

```
    5   c:= 5;
    6   a:= b + c;
    7 end.
```

Sometimes, there is a list of statements that must be executed several times in different parts of a program, and a clever way to avoid this repetition of statements is to group all those statements together under a single name and use the name instead. This technique is known as **subroutine declaration**. In PL/0 this is carried out by using the keyword **procedure** or **function**, followed by a name (identifier). Subroutines or functions can also be used as an approach to structure a program as a combination of modules. Let us use an example to illustrate this concept. There is a line indicating that the top part contains declarations of variables and procedures and the bottom part contains the main program statements.

PROGRAM 3.1

```
main
var n;                  // global variable declaration

function sub1;          // subroutine  sub1 declaration
var a, b, p;            // subroutine local variable declarations
a:= b + x + p;          // subroutine statements begin here
end;                    // end of sub1

function sub2(y);       // subroutine sub2 declaration (with parameter)
var c;                  // subroutine local variable declaration
c:=2 + y;               // subroutine statements start here
sub1;                   // sub2 calls sub1
end;                    // end of sub2
begin
  n := 5;               // main program statements start here
  sub2(n);              // main calls sub2
end.
```

Program 3.1 shows a program with two functions, named sub1 and sub2. Main calls sub2, and a parameter is passed on from main to sub2; then sub2 calls sub1. In figure 3.7 you can see the stack activity for this program. The left-hand side shows the state of the stack while running main. The one in the middle is a snapshot after calling sub2. The shaded area highlights the sub2 AR. The stack on the left-hand side shows the stack once sub2 has called sub1 and the AR for sub1 was inserted into the stack.

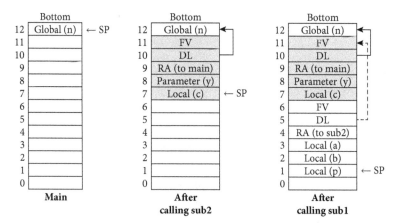

FIGURE 3.7 Stack states when program 3.1 is running.

Sometimes when writing a program, we come to a point that a decision has to be made. In PL/0 as in other programming languages, the programming construct to use is the **if-statement**. There are two variants for the if-statement:

1. **If** *condition* **then** *statement*;
   Example: **If** a > b **then** a := a + 1;

2. **If** *condition* **then** *statement* **else** *statement*;
   Example: **If** a > b **then** a := a + 1 **else** a := 0;

Iterations, also known as loops, are necessary in programming languages to execute a series of statements while a condition holds. Once the condition is not met, the program gets out of the loop. In PL/0 the programming construct to carry out iterations is the **while-statement**. The syntax you must use to write a while-statement is

   while *condition* **do** *statement*;
   Example: **while** a > 5 **do** a := a − 1;

You may have noticed that in both if-statements and while-statements, the syntax rule shows that the word *statement* follows the reserved words **then**, **else**, and **do**. Perhaps this makes you think that only one statement can be placed after these reserved words, but that is not the case. There are two variants of statements you can choose from: single statements and compound statements.

1. In single statements only one statement can be used.
   If a > b **then** a := a + 1;
   while a > 5 **do** a := a − 1;

2. In compound statements several statements can be used, but they must be enclosed between the reserved words **begin** and **end**.

If a > b then begin
    a := a + 1;
    c := d * e;
end;

Recursive Programs

Quicksort is a fast, recursive sorting algorithm invented by C.A.R. Hoare in 1959. The algorithm was published in 1960. In 1980 Hoare received the Turing Award, and in his Turing lecture, "The Emperor's Old Clothes," he makes a statement acknowledging the relevance of recursion in programming languages:

> Due credit must be paid to the genius of the designers of ALGOL 60 who included recursion in their language and enabled me to describe my invention so elegantly to the world.

Recursion is a beautiful and effective principle to handle complex problems. The way it works is by defining the solution of a problem in terms of a simpler version of itself. From a programming standpoint, it can be seen as a powerful method to write concise programs to handle complex problems; it consists of invoking a function that calls on itself. A recursive algorithm has two steps:

1. Explicit condition or base case (to stop the function from calling itself again)
2. The recursive call (where the function calls itself with a simpler version of the problem). We could consider a simpler version of the problem as a smaller data set.

Factorial is a good example to explain recursion. For example, factorial of 5 (5!) is defined as:

$$5! = 5 * 4 * 3 * 2 * 1 = 120$$

The following PL/0 program is a recursive program to compute factorial. We call function fact with parameter n = 5, say fact(5). The function will verify if n = 1 returns the value 1; otherwise, it computes f = 5 * fact (4). As you see, we are calling function factorial again, but this time with parameter n = 4. The function verifies if n equals 1, but as that is not the case, fact(4) is replaced by 4 * fact(3). This means that f = 5 * fact(4) = 5 * 4 * fact(3). You can continue applying the same reasoning time and again until fact(1) is invoked, then the function will stop calling itself and you finally get:

$$Fact(5) = 5 * 4 * 3 * 2 * 1$$

Now the computation can be carried out, and you will obtain the answer 120.

```
program Factorial;
var f, n;

function fact(n): integer;
begin
 if n = 1 then
    return := 1;
 else
    f := n * fact(n-1);
    return f;
end;

begin
 f:= fact(3);
end.
```

Figure 3.8 illustrates the stack states during the calling sequence of factorial(3). Initially, the main function calls factorial(3), and an activation record is created (see shaded area in figure 3.8, left-hand side). Then the factorial function calls itself, executing factorial(2), and a new

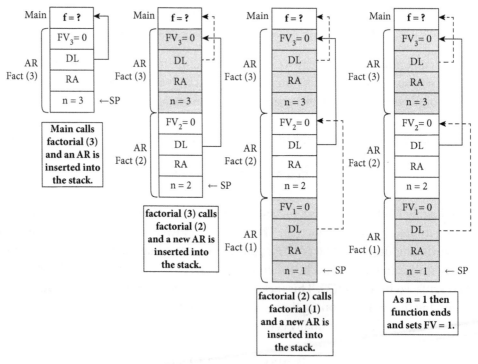

FIGURE 3.8 Stack states while calling factorial recursively.

activation record is created. Then while executing factorial(2), as the explicit condition has not been met, the factorial function calls itself again, but this time with parameter 1 (factorial(1)), and a new activation record is created. As the parameter 1 meets the explicit condition, the function stops calling itself, and the return sequence begins.

Figure 3.9 points into the states of the stack during the returning sequence or computational steps. You will observe in figure 3.9 how the returned value is passed on from one activation record to another. The value n = 1 is copied from the top of the stack into the functional value field (FV_1) and returns to factorial(2). Notice that the AR for factorial(1) is popped out, leaving FV_1 = 1 on top of the stack. Factorial(2) multiplies the values n*FV_1 (2*1) found on top of the stack and stores the resulting value in the FV_2 in the AR of factorial(2). Once factorial(2) returns, its AR is popped out of the stack, leaving the value 2 stored in FV_2. Factorial(3) multiplies FV_2 times its parameter, n = 3, and the resulting value FV2 * n = 6 is stored in FV_3. When factorial(3) ends, it returns the value 6 to f.

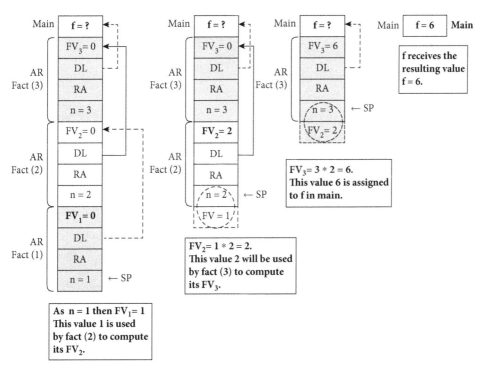

FIGURE 3.9 Stack states while factorial function is returning values.

Lexicographical Levels and Nested Programs

When programmers write programs, they use procedures to make programs look like a set of modules that can be thought of as super-instructions that can be called or used (executed) from practically anywhere within the program according to specific rules that must be followed. For instance, we cannot call a function that has not been declared. Some programming languages, such as PL/0 and JavaScript, allow embedded functions, which means that we can declare functions in the main program, let us call them fun1 and fun2, and inside fun2 we can declare another function, fun3. This creates an embedded static structure for this program, as illustrated in figure 3.10. This treelike structure is organized in levels, and these levels are called **lexicographical levels**. In this example, main is at level 0, functions fun1 and fun2 are at level 1, and fun3 is at level 2. Exploring figure 3.10 a little further, you can observe that in each function there are variables declared, and you will see also some statements. In the lexicographical tree, underneath the function name, you will see the variables declared in each function. Also, you can see a couple of statements in the program, one within fun1 and another inside fun3. In the tree those statements are placed underneath the function name in square brackets. You might notice that in the statement **x := a + b** in fun1, **a** and **b** are accessed locally in fun1, and variable **x** is accessed in main. Similarly, in the statement **e := x + y**, **e** is accessed locally in fun3, **x** is accessed in fun2, and **y** is accessed in main. In the latter case, variables are found in different lexicographical levels, which implies different activation records. To provide access to variables located in different activation records, we must create a new field inside the AR; this field is denoted as the **static link (SL)**.

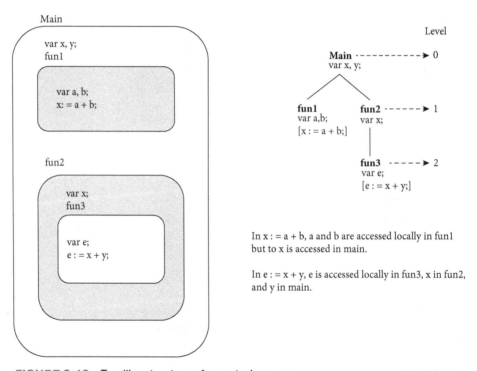

FIGURE 3.10 Treelike structure of a nested program.

In each one of the function activation records, the static link points to the base of the activation record of its ancestor or procedure/function that statically encloses the function. For our example, figure 3.11 shows that the static link of fun3 points to the base of the activation record of fun2, and the static link in the AR of fun2 and fun1 point to the base of the activation record of main. This path is called a **static chain** and can be observed in the stack shown in figure 3.11. Also, you can see in the figure that in the stack and in the static program structure (tree), static links are shown with dashed lines. The stack in figure 3.11 is generated by the following function calls: Main calls Fun2, Fun2 calls Fun3, and Fun3 calls Fun1.

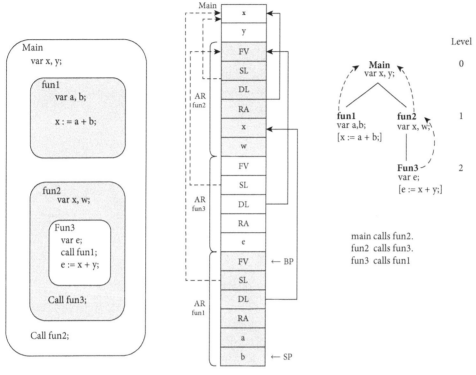

FIGURE 3.11   Static chain in a treelike program structure.

Including the static link in the AR forces us to modify the activation record and the steps taken by instructions CAL and RTN. The new version of the AR layout consists of the following parts: **functional value, static link, dynamic link, return address, parameters**, and **local variables**. Each one of these fields is described as follows:

Activation record

Functional value: Location to store the function returned value.

Static link: Points to the base of the stack frame of the procedure that statically encloses the current function or procedure (the function ancestor).

Dynamic link: Points to the base of the previous stack frame (base of the caller AR).

Return address: Points, in the code segment, to the next instruction to be executed after termination of the current function or procedure.

Parameters: Space reserved to store the actual parameters of the caller function.

Locals: Space reserved to store local variables declared in the called function (callee).

As the activation record was modified with the insertion of the static link, then the steps to be taken by CAL and RTN must be modified accordingly. We show this modification as follows.

06 – **CAL**	**0, L, M**	stack[sp – 1] ← 0;	space to return value
		stack[sp – 2] ← sl	static link (SL)
		stack[sp – 3] ← bp;	dynamic link (DL)
		stack[sp – 4] ← pc;	return address (RA)
		bp ← sp – 1;	
		pc ← **M**;	
00 – **RTN**	**0, 0, 0**	sp ← bp + 1;	
		bp ← stack[sp – 3];	
		pc ← stack[sp – 4];	

SUMMARY

In this chapter, we presented the stack or pushdown storage mechanism as a means of keeping track of subroutine invocations and the steps to be followed to return from a subroutine to the caller. We highlighted the importance of activation records combined with the stack method to implement recursive calls and nested programs. Special attention was given to the static link to illustrate variable visibility from each function. The ISA architecture of VM/0 was enhanced with three new instructions to implement subroutine invocation and subroutine return.

EXERCISES

1. Write a program to evaluate the expression **3 4 * 5 3 * +** using VM/0 assembly language.

2. What is the information stored in the return address and dynamic link when a function is called? And why do we need to save it in the activation record?

3. Describe the steps executed by the instructions CAL 0, 0, M and RTN 0, 0, 0 in VM/0.

4. Why do nested programs need the static link (SL) in their activation record (AR)?

5. When a function is called, do you need the instruction INC to create the activation record?

6. Using pseudocode or the programming language of your preference, write a recursive program to find the greatest common divisor of two numbers (integers). The greatest common divisor of two integers is the largest positive integer that divides both numbers without leaving any remainder.

7. Draw a picture of the stack created by the following program. Initial values are as follows:

   SP = −1, BP = 0, PC = 0. (Assume the stack grows upward.)

0	JMP	0 0 10
1	JMP	0 0 2
2	INC	0 0 6
3	LIT	0 0 13
4	STO	0 0 4
5	LIT	0 0 1
6	STO	0 1 4
7	LIT	0 0 7
8	STO	0 0 5
9	RTN	0 0 0
10	INC	0 0 6
11	LIT	0 0 3
12	STO	0 0 4
13	LIT	0 0 9
14	STO	0 0 5
15	CAL	0 0 2
16	SIO	0 0 2

Bibliographical Notes

As an alternative to the standard infix notation, in 1929 Jan Lukasiewicz[2] developed reverse Polish notation as a new method to evaluate expressions. With this new notation, the expression (3 * 4) + (5 * 6) would be written as 3 4 * 5 3 * +. Reverse Polish notation could be considered the seminal idea that originated the development of recursive programming by Dijkstra[3] and the design of stack-based computers. In 1955 Friedrich L. Bauer and Klaus Samelson introduced the concept of the stack method for expression evaluation.[4,5] Independently, in 1957 the Australian computer pioneer Charles L. Hamblin,[6] based on the works of Lukasiewicz, also proposed the stack mechanism to evaluate expressions. Hamblin's idea inspired the construction of the KDF9 stack computer in the United Kingdom.[7] In 1959 Robert Barton,[8] based also on Lukasiewicz's work, led a group at the Burroughs Corporation in Pasadena, California, in building a stack computer. By 1961 the Burroughs B5500 and its ALGOL-like compiler was operative. Elliott Organick and R. Doran did in-depth studies of the Burroughs stack architecture and give a detailed description of the B5700/B6700 series in their works.[9,10] HP took the road of building stack computers in the 1970s with its HP3000.[11] By the mid-1980s, machines based solely on stack architecture started fading away, and computers kept the stack mechanism mostly for subroutine linkage. However, in the arena of virtual machines, the stack architecture has had a successful comeback since the Java virtual machine (JVM) was implemented. Robert Sebesta presents an excellent chapter on subroutine linkage using a stack mechanism.[1]

Bibliography

1. R. W. Sebesta, *Concepts of Programming Languages*, 11th ed. Upper Saddle River, NJ, Pearson, 2016.
2. J. Lukasiewicz, *Elements of Mathematical Logic*, trans. Olgierd Wojtasiewicz. New York: Macmillan, 1929, p. 124.
3. E. W. Dijkstra, "Recursive Programming," *Numerische Mathematik* 2 (1960), pp. 321–318.
4. F. L. Bauer and K. Samelson, "The Cellar Principle for Formulae Translation," in Proceedings International Conference on Information Processing, Paris, 1959.
5. F. L. Bauer, "The Cellar Principle of State Transition and Storage Allocation," *Annals of the History of Computing* 12, no. 1 (1990), pp. 41–49.
6. C. L. Hamblin, "An Addressless Coding Scheme Based on Mathematical Notations," in Proceedings Weapons Research establishment Conference on Computing, Salisbury, South Australia, June 1957.
7. G. M. Davis, "The English Electric KDF9 Computer System," *Computer Bulletin* (December 1960), pp. 119–120.
8. R. Barton, "A New Approach to the Functional Design of a Digital Computer," in Western Joint Computer Conference, Los Angeles, CA, 1961.
9. E. I. Organick, *Computer System Organization: The B5700/B6700 Series*. New Yrok: Academic Press, 1973.
10. R. Doran, *Computer Architecture: A Structured Approach*. London: Academic Press, 1979.
11. J. Bartlett, "The HP 3000 Computer System," in ACM-IEEE Symposium. on High-Level-Language Computer Architecture, College Park, MD, 1973.

Chapter 4

The Heap

And suddenly the memory returns.
—Marcel Proust
In Search of Lost Time: Swann's Way

CHAPTER OBJECTIVES

- To review the concept of heap storage management.
- To discuss the usage of memory allocators to allow programs to request memory at run time.
- To explore the problems that can arise when memory space is not returned to the heap.
- To understand the way garbage collection works.

INTRODUCTION

When a variable is declared within a program, a memory location is assigned at compile-time, and the memory location is preserved for that variable while the program is running. However, there are programming languages that allow programmers to handle memory dynamically at run time as well. This is carried out by a dynamic memory allocator, which manages a memory area in the process address space called the heap. There are two basic functions to communicate a running program with the heap: an allocation function to request memory space and a free function to return memory space back to the heap.

We initiate this chapter by presenting where the heap resides within the process address space and describing the functions to request memory space from the heap on demand and to return memory space back to the heap. Then we show how a program requests space from the heap and the heap becomes a memory segment with block in use and free blocks. The free blocks can be arranged in a list that can be organized using different strategies. We will describe two of them and explain how memory could be fragmented. Finally, we present a problem that arises when unused blocks are not returned to the heap. Those blocks are called garbage, and therefore, techniques for garbage collection must be used.

VOCABULARY

This is a list of keywords that herald the concepts we will study in this chapter. They are organized in chronological order and will appear in the text in bold. We invite you to take a look at these keywords to find out which ones you are familiar with.

Heap	free( )	Best fit
Memory leak	Storage.alloc(int)	Garbage
PL/1	Memory allocator	Roots
ALLOCATE	Free.storage(ptr)	Root set
FREE	Memory fragmentation	Garbage collection
C	Reserved blocks	Mark-and-sweep
malloc( )	Free blocks	
calloc( )	First fit	

ACTIVATING PRIOR KNOWLEDGE

In this section we will present a series of activities. In some of them you can choose one or more options. Sometimes, if you do not agree with the given answers to choose from, you will be allowed to give your own answer. By the way, this is not a test.

1. If you have to assign some memory space to a program and there are free spaces of different sizes, which one of these options you will choose?

    a. Space almost matches space required ☐
    b. First space found big enough to match the request ☐
    c. Largest space available ☐

2. Assume you have three boxes and a container. The boxes are placed in the container as shown below: First box 1, then box 2, and finally box 3.

Step 1	Step 2	Step 3
5	5	5 Box 3
4	4	4
3	3 Box 2	3 Box 2
2	2	2
1	1	1
0 Box 1	0 Box 1	0 Box 1
Container	Container	Container

    a. Make a list of the free space for each case.
    b. Use three identifiers called P1, P2, and P3, and point them to Box 1, Box 2, and Box 3, respectively.

3. In step 3 in the previous question, there are three free spaces. If a program requests three contiguous memory words, can they be assigned to the program?

    Yes ☐
    No ☐

4. Have you heard the terms *fragmented memory* and *compaction*?

    Yes ☐
    No ☐

5. Skim the chapter and pay attention to the words written in **bold**. Count the number of words you are familiar with.

6. Name two programming languages that support dynamic memory allocation.

    a. _____
    b. _____

7. What is a memory leak?

Programming Constructs for Handling Memory Dynamically

The process address space is a unique memory segment associated with a running program. There is a process address space per program in execution. The **heap** is a memory area within the process address space that can be thought as an array of memory locations (words). Initially, the heap is just a block or segment of free space. Figure 4.1 illustrates the heap within the process address space. To access the heap, there is a pointer called "free" that is pointing to the beginning of the heap segment. The first word in the heap contains the heap length. The main purpose of having a heap is the necessity of using dynamic memory allocation within a running program.

There are two functions to manage the heap at run time: one function is used to request memory dynamically and another to return memory space back to the heap. Programmers are responsible for including instructions in their programs to communicate with the memory allocator at run time in order to request memory space; programmers are also responsible for returning memory space back to the heap. Otherwise, the space not released back will be inaccessible, and it will be considered a **memory leak**. Since the early 1960s, programming languages have provided instructions to handle memory dynamically. A good example is **PL/1** (Programming Language One), a programming language introduced by IBM in 1964 that had two instructions named **ALLOCATE** and **FREE** to request memory and free memory respectively. Nowadays, in the **C** programming language, we can find library functions **malloc( )**, **calloc( )**, and **free( )** for the same purpose of handling memory dynamically. In both cases, the instructions ALLOCATE, malloc( ), and calloc( ) return a memory address pointing to a free space, and instructions FREE and free( ) use the pointer pointing to a memory area to return that space to the heap. In Box 1.1 we will illustrate the use of memory management using allocation and free instructions in PL/1 and in C. For C we will use the function malloc( ).

For simplicity we will assume that the heap is an array of words (memory locations) and there is a memory allocator which is able to assign as many consecutive words as the user requests.

There is as well a pointer to point at the beginning of free words

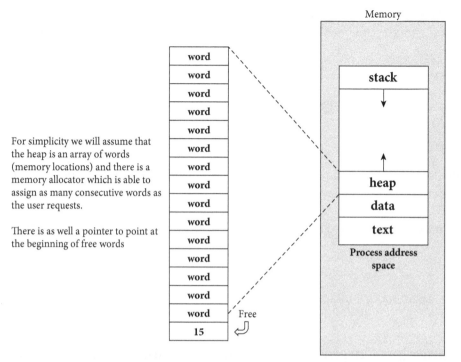

FIGURE 4.1 Heap segment within the process address space.

BOX 1.1 PL/1 EXAMPLE

Description of array ARR declaration but memory is not assigned.

DECLARE ARR (10) FLOAT BASED (PTR_ARR);

Pointer declaration.

DECLARE (PTR_ARR) POINTER;

Reserving storage space for array ARR and PTR_ARR points to the beginning of the array.

ALLOCATE ARR SET (PTR_ARR);

Assigning the value 17 to the third element of the array.

PTR_ARR -> ARR(3) = 17;

// Returns the memory space used by array ARR back to the system.

FREE ARR;

(Continued)

C example:
```
// Pointer declaration.
int *arr;
// Reserves storage space for array pointed to by arr.
arr = malloc(10 * sizeof(int));
// Assigns value 17 to the third element of the array.
// You can replace *(arr + 2) by arr[2] if you wish and do arr[2] = 17.

*(arr + 2) = 17;
// Returns the memory space used by array arr back to the system.
free(arr)
```

As you can see, the outcome of the above statements in PL/1 and C programming languages is practically the same, and the main difference lies in the syntax. The main reason for using dynamic memory allocation in a program is that sometimes the data size is not known in advance. For instance, if a program needs to read n values to populate an array and the number n is unknown at run time, then dynamic memory allocation is convenient. An array can be declared statically at compile-time and will do the job while n is less than or equal to the values to be read in. If the number of values to populate the array is much smaller than n, there will be a waste of memory space. A runtime error might occur when the number of values to populate the array is greater than n.

Requesting Storage Dynamically

User programs explicitly request a number of words from the heap by using an allocate function. The allocate function includes and integer parameter to indicate the number of memory words requested, and it returns a pointer pointing to the assigned memory area. We will name this function ***storage.alloc (int)***. If a user program request n words, the program must execute the function *storage.alloc (n)* and the **memory allocator** will return $n + 1$ words. The first word of the assigned memory block contains its length. Figure 4.2(a) illustrates the heap as one free memory block, then figure 4.2(b) shows the heap state after the execution of the instruction ptr1=storage.alloc(2) where the user program requests two memory words. You might notice the allocator assigns three words. The first one indicates the block size, and the other two are the words to be used by the program. The function returns a memory address (address 1 in this case), and this address is assigned to pointer variable ptr1. You can see as well that the first word of the free block contains its length. In figure 4.2(c) you will see the state of the heap after instruction ptr2 = storage.alloc(3) was executed. The program requests three memory words, and four memory words are given to the program. The first word tells us the block length, ptr2 points to the beginning of the three word blocks the program has access to, and free points to location 7.

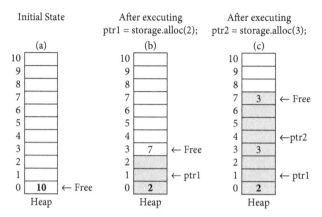

FIGURE 4.2 Heap state after two executions of the allocation function.

In figure 4.3 we present the execution of three more instructions, starting at the heap state in figure 4.2(c). In the first step in figure 4.3(a), the program executes the instruction:

$$ptr3 = storage.alloc(1)$$

At this moment you can observe that there are three pointer variables pointing to three different memory blocks: ptr1, ptr2, and ptr3. There is also a free pointer, pointing to a free memory word. Now we will present the function **free.storage (ptr)**, which is used to free a memory block. In figure 4.3(b) we show the heap state right after the execution of the instruction

$$free.storage\ (ptr2).$$

Surely you realized that there are two free blocks, and we can start talking about creating a list of free blocks shortly, but for the time being we are just presenting the way instructions storage.alloc (int) and free.storage (ptr) work. Finally, figure 4.3(c) shows the heap state after executing the instruction

$$ptr4 = storage.alloc\ (1).$$

When several memory request and free operations have been carried out, memory might be fragmented. By **memory fragmentation** we mean that the free space is not a continuous single block; instead, free spaces are spaced out within the heap. This is a serious matter because sometimes memory requests might not be satisfied even though the free space available

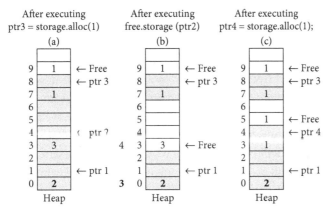

FIGURE 4.3 The heap state after executing a memory allocation, free, and allocation again.

is greater than or equal to the requested memory space. For example, let us assume that a program executes

ptr5=*storage.alloc(2)* and the heap state is the one shown in figure 4.3(c).

You will realize that two free spaces are available but are not continuous. As none of the free spaces is big enough to meet the request, the allocator will not be able to satisfy the program request.

As the memory allocators must find a free space each time a request is made, a linked list of free spaces (free blocks) is necessary to manage the access to all free blocks. Figure 4.4 illustrates the state of the heap, including the free space linked list after executing the set of operations describe below. In this example, we must assume that initially the heap is a single free space block. P, X, W, Y, and K are pointer variables.

```
P := storage.alloc(2);
X := storage.alloc(1);
W:= storage.alloc(1);
Y:= storage.alloc(1);
Free (W);
K:= storage.alloc(2);
W:= storage.alloc(4);
Free (K);
```

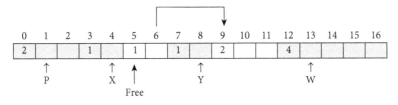

FIGURE 4.4 Linked list of free blocks in the heap.

Now that you have a better idea of the heap as a pool of available memory to be assigned on demand, let us take a closer look at heap free space management. We will base our description on Knuth's *Art of Computer Programming*, volume 1. There are two types of blocks in the heap: reserved blocks and free blocks.

Reserved blocks are the ones that have been assigned to a program dynamically on demand. These blocks have a tag in the first word to identify the block as reserved ("+") and the block size. In figure 4.5 you can see a number at the beginning of the reserved block that indicates its block size or length. Then there will be a number of words, which represent the allocated space to be used by the program. We will add a third component to the reserved word, and this is an additional word with a tag. **Free blocks** are organized similarly, and they represent the memory space that can be requested. We will explain shortly the reason for adding the third component or word to the reserved and free blocks.

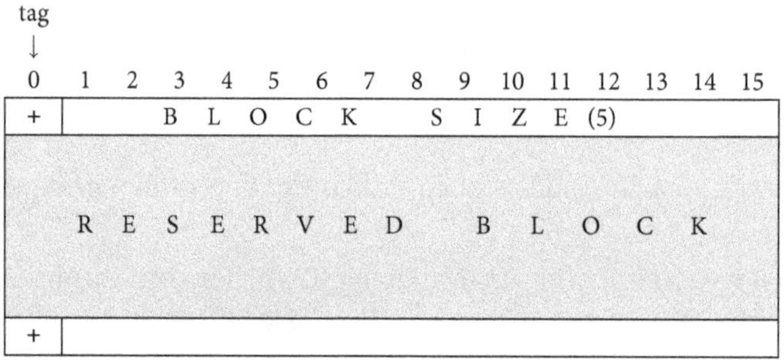

```
tag
 ↓
 0  1  2  3  4  5  6  7  8  9  10 11 12 13 14 15
 +  |     B  L  O  C  K     S  I  Z  E  (5)
    |
    |          R  E  S  E  R  V  E  D     B  L  O  C  K
    |
 +  |
```

FIGURE 4.5 Description of a reserved block.

As mentioned earlier, free block organization is similar to reserved blocks. The first word has a tag minus ("−") to indicate the block is free and then the block size or length. Then there are several words of free space, and the last word has a tag ("−") and a link to connect a free block with the next free block in the free block list. A free block is shown in figure 4.6.

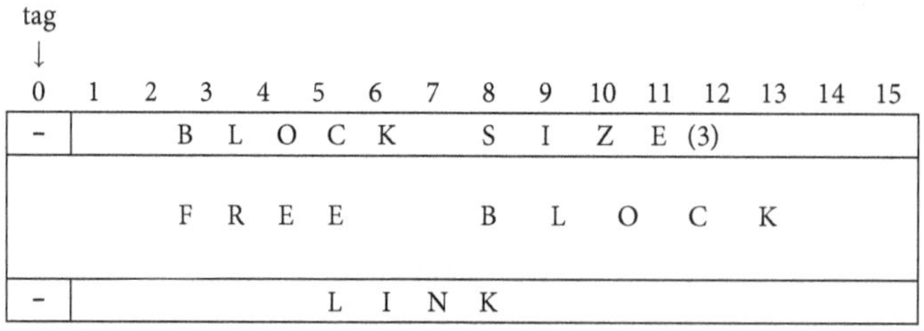

```
tag
 ↓
 0  1  2  3  4  5  6  7  8  9  10 11 12 13 14 15
 −  |     B  L  O  C  K     S  I  Z  E  (3)
    |          F  R  E  E        B  L  O  C  K
 −  |                 L  I  N  K
```

FIGURE 4.6 Description of a free block.

The reason for having a tag at either end of a block is because it will be used to coalesce two adjacent free blocks whose tags are equal. For instance, when a *free.storage (ptr)* is executed and the reserved block becomes a free block, its tags are changed from "+" to "−." Then the new free block tags can be compared with the tags of adjacent blocks, and if there is a match, two free blocks can be coalesced into a single one. In figure 4.7 we show an example where the reserved block size is 5 and the free block size is 3.

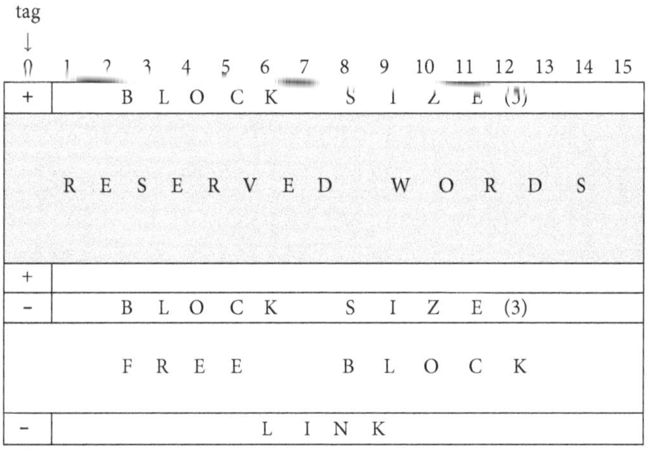

```
tag
 ↓
 0  1  2  3  4  5  6  7  8  9  10 11 12 13 14 15
+|        B  L  O  C  K        S  I  Z  E  (5)   |
 |                                                |
 |           R E S E R V E D    W  O R D S        |
 |                                                |
+|                                                |
-|        B  L  O  C  K        S  I  Z  E  (3)   |
 |           F  R  E  E        B  L  O  C  K     |
-|                     L  I  N  K                 |
```

FIGURE 4.7 Adjacent reserved and free blocks.

Once the free.storage (ptr) instruction has been executed to free the reserve block and the reserved block becomes free, the two adjacent blocks coalesce into a new free block whose size is 10. The reason block size is 10 instead of 8 is because there are four words for housekeeping information and only two are needed. Therefore, the last word of the reserved block and the first one of the free block are added to the free block as available space. Figure 4.8 depicts the state after the free.storage (ptr) instruction was executed and the reserved block became free.

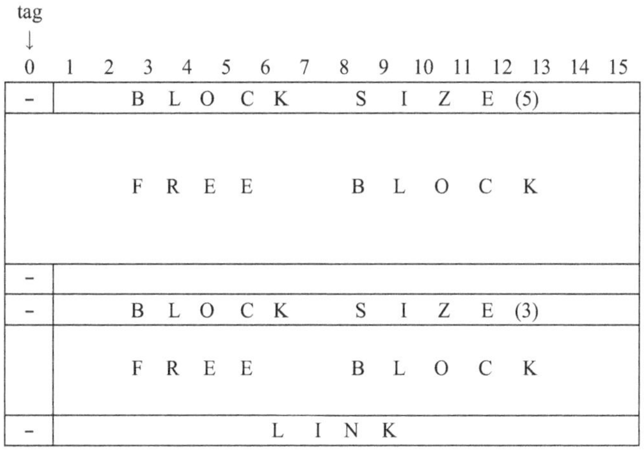

```
tag
 ↓
 0  1  2  3  4  5  6  7  8  9  10 11 12 13 14 15
-|        B  L  O  C  K        S  I  Z  E  (5)   |
 |                                                |
 |           F  R  E  E        B  L  O  C  K     |
 |                                                |
-|                                                |
-|        B  L  O  C  K        S  I  Z  E  (3)   |
 |           F  R  E  E        B  L  O  C  K     |
-|                     L  I  N  K                 |
```

FIGURE 4.8 Free block created by coalescing two free blocks.

Finally, in figure 4.9 you can see how the two free blocks are coalesced into a single free block whose size is:

New free block = first block size + second free block size + 2 = 5 + 3 + 2 = 10

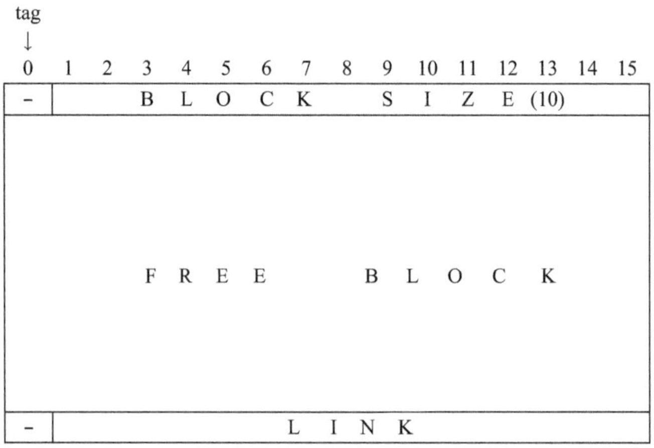

```
tag
 ↓
 0   1   2   3   4   5   6   7   8   9  10  11  12  13  14  15
┌───┬───────────────────────────────────────────────────────────┐
│ - │          B   L   O   C   K       S   I   Z   E  (10)     │
├───┼───────────────────────────────────────────────────────────┤
│   │                                                           │
│   │                                                           │
│   │              F   R   E   E       B   L   O   C   K       │
│   │                                                           │
│   │                                                           │
├───┼───────────────────────────────────────────────────────────┤
│ - │                      L   I   N   K                        │
└───┴───────────────────────────────────────────────────────────┘
```

FIGURE 4.9 Free block created by coalescing two free blocks.

In case there are three adjacent free blocks, we can do it in two steps. First, two free blocks are coalesced into a single free block, and then the new created free block is coalesced with the third one.

Let us assume a program requests n consecutive words from the heap list of free blocks. There are several techniques to manage the free block list, and two of them are **first fit** and **best fit**. In the former case, the allocator assigns the first free block it finds whose size is greater than or equal to n ($\geq n$). On the other hand, best fit searches in the free list for a block either of size n or the smallest free block whose size is greater than n. According to Donald Knuth, the best fit was practically the standard to be followed since it keeps big blocks of free space. However, it increases the number of tiny blocks, and the proliferation of these very small blocks fragments heap memory. Figure 4.10 illustrates the allocation of a block of size two using both techniques. On the left-hand side you can see the heap state before the request is made. The number next to the white blocks indicates the length of the free block. In the center you can see the heap after the request has been satisfied using first fit. Then on the right-hand side you can see the heap state using best fit. The word *new* in the shaded areas indicates the space given to meet the request.

Why We Must Return Allocated Memory

When storage allocation and storage deallocation must be handled explicitly, it is the programmer's responsibility to request heap space and free unneeded heap space to avoid memory leaks. Let us use an example to illustrate this concept. In program 4.1 there is a line indicating

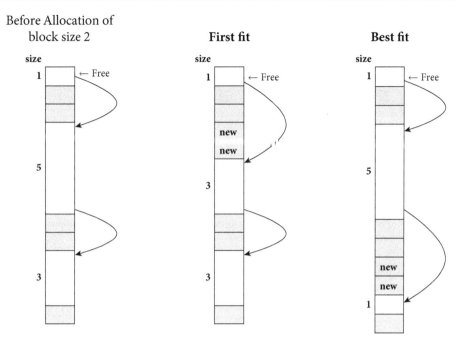

FIGURE 4.10 First fit and best fit allocations for a block of size two.

that the top part contains declarations of variables and functions, and in the bottom part you will see main program statements.

PROGRAM 4.1
```
main
var n;                      //global variable declaration
function sub2(y);           //subroutine sub2 declaration (with parameter)
var ptr;                    //subroutine local variable declaration
ptr:= storage.alloc(5);     //sub2 request memory dynamically
end;                        //end of sub2
begin
  n := 5;                   /*main program statements start here
  sub2(n);                  /*main calls sub2
end.
```

Program 4.1 shows a program with one function named sub2. Main calls sub2, and a parameter is passed on from main to sub2; then sub2 requests memory dynamically using the statement ptr := storage.alloc(6). In figure 4.11 you can visualize the stack activity for this program. The left-hand side shows the state of the stack while running main. The one in the middle is a stack snapshot after calling sub2. You might notice sub2 AR with variable ptr pointing to the heap.

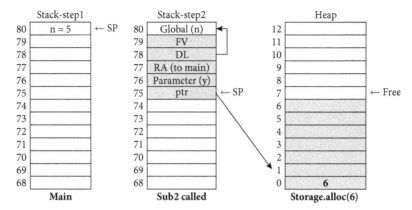

FIGURE 4.11 Stack and heap interaction after executing instruction ptr:= storage.alloc(6).

Figure 4.12 illustrates a memory leak because once sub2 ends, the pointer ptr does not exist, because ptr was a local variable that was deleted once the activation record for sub2 was removed from the stack. There are six unreachable words in the heap from location one to six. If this occurs frequently during program execution, many heap blocks will be unreachable and memory leaks will proliferate. These unreachable and useless heap spaces are considered **garbage**.

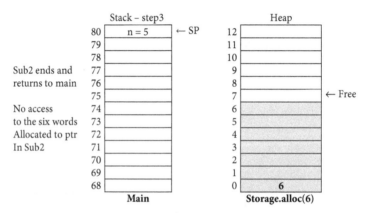

FIGURE 4.12 Stack and heap state after returning from subroutine sub2.

When the programmer does not return unused memory chunks, a potential problem of heap space fragmentation might arise, and it could happen that all free space is greater than a request but the request cannot be granted because the free space is scattered out in the heap.

Garbage Collection

In general, all chunks of heap memory allocated to the program are also known as objects or nodes when linked lists are used. All memory addresses directly accessible by the program are denoted as the **roots**, and the collection of roots is known as the **root set**. Examples of roots are global objects in the data section, local objects in the stack, and heap memory chunks allocated dynamically. We will focus solely on those objects found in the heap. We have seen in previous sections how the heap manager or allocator handles the allocation and deallocation of memory objects on demand. But requesting and returning memory chunks to the heap is the programmer's responsibility. As you know, the heap memory chunks that are not accessible but are considered used space are called garbage, and therefore **garbage collection** must be implemented to return unused heap space to the list of free blocks. There are many techniques to implement garbage collection. One of these techniques is called **mark-and-sweep**, and this is the one that we will describe.

Mark-and-sweep is a two-phase algorithm oriented to distinguish between live objects (reserved words) and unreachable space, or garbage. In the mark phase, the algorithm uses the root set, and starting at each root pointing to the heap, it marks out the block pointed to by the variable. If the marked block points to another live object or reserve block, as in the case of a linked list, then all blocks in the list are marked out. Figure 4.13 shows the heap initial state before the mark phase begins. You can see that the first root points to a single block, and the second root points to a linked list with three blocks.

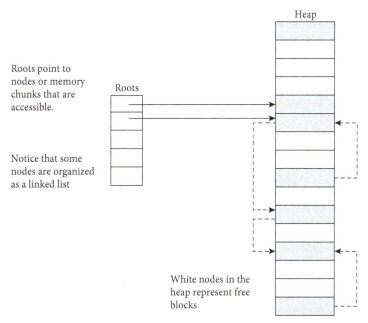

FIGURE 4.13 Initial heap state before using the mark-and-sweep algorithm.

Figure 4.14 shows the heap state after the execution of the mark phase. Four blocks are marked, and you can also see three blocks that are unreachable.

In the sweep phase, we begin with a heap consisting of live objects (marked) and unmarked ones, or garbage. The sweep algorithm exhaustively examines the heap sequentially, word by

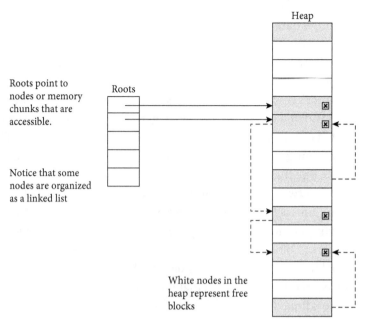

FIGURE 4.14 Heap state after the mark phase.

word, searching for unmarked objects; for each unmarked object found, the space is reclaimed and added to the list of free space. Figure 4.15 shows the heap free space right after the sweep phase.

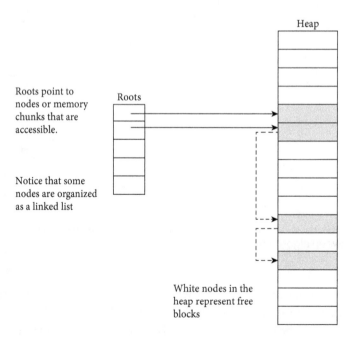

FIGURE 4.15 Heap state after the sweep phase.

SUMMARY

In this chapter, we presented heap storage, a memory segment in the process address space used to provide memory chunks to a program on demand. We highlighted how the storage allocation and deallocation is carried out and described the list of free blocks and two techniques to handle it. Special attention was given to memory leaks, when the program does not return the unused memory back to the heap. Due to memory leaks, we showed that many areas of the heap could be unreachable, and therefore a garbage collection algorithm must be used to collect those unreachable blocks and transform them into free space. A method for garbage collection was explained.

EXERCISES

1. Draw the state of a heap of size 20 after the following set of instructions is executed.
   P := storage.alloc(2);
   X := storage.alloc(1);
   Y:= storage.alloc(1);
   Free (W);
   K:= storage.alloc(2);

2. How many words are taken from the heap when the instruction storage.alloc(6) is executed?

3. If you have to assign some memory space to a program and there are free blocks of spaces of different size, which one of these options will you choose?
   a. Best fit   ☐
   b. First fit   ☐
   c. Worst fit   ☐

4. In a heap with 16 words, execute the following instructions:
   P := storage.alloc(2);
   X := storage.alloc(1);
   W:= storage.alloc(1);
   Y:= storage.alloc(1);
   Free (W);
   K:= storage.alloc(2);
   W:= storage.alloc(1);
   Free (K);
   Free (P):

To compare first fit and best fit, you will execute the following instructions right after the execution of Free (P) above. Use both methods and compare the results:

R := storage.alloc(1);
S := storage.alloc(2);
T := storage.alloc(2);

Is the final result the same using both techniques?

5. Why do we use tags in both ends of reserved and free blocks?
6. Use the heap in figure 4.4 and remove variable P. Mark all spaces pointed to by X, Y, and W. Then examine the heap from location 0 to 16 and insert all unmarked words (garbage) in the free list and show the final state of the heap.
7. Write an algorithm using pseudocode for the description given in question 6.

Bibliographical Notes

An excellent source to study the fundamentals of dynamic memory allocation is the first volume of *The Art of Computer Programming* by Donald Knuth.[1] Adam Webber presents a good introduction to heap management and garbage collection.[2] The term *garbage collector* was proposed by John McCarthy in 1960.[3] Paul Wilson presents an accessible and comprehensive survey on garbage collection techniques.[4] A fresh introduction to heap management and garbage collection using examples in C can be found in Bryant and O'Hallaron.[5]

Bibliography

1. D. E. Knuth, *The Art of Computer Programming: Fundamental Algorithms*, 3rd ed., vol. 1. Upper Saddle River, NJ: Addison-Wesley, 1997.
2. A. B. Webber, *Modern Programming Languages: A Practical Introduction*. Wilsonville, OR: Franklin Beedle & Associates, 2003.
3. J. McCarthy, "Recursive Functions of Symbolic Expressions and Their Computation by Machine, Part I," *Communication of the Association for Computing Machinery* 3, no. 4 (1960), pp. 184–195.
4. P. R. Wilson, "Uniprocessor Garbage Collection Techniques," in International Workshop on Memory Management, St. Malo, France, 1992.
5. D. Bryant and D. R. O'Hallaron, *Computer Systems: A Programmer's Perspective*, 2nd ed. Boston, Prentice Hall, 2003.

Credits

Fig. 4.5: Donald E. Kruth, "Description of a Reserved Block," The Art of Computer Programming: Fundamental Algorithms, 3rd ed., vol. 1. Copyright © 1997 by Addison-Wesley.

Fig. 4.6: Donald E. Kruth, "Description of a Reserved Block," The Art of Computer Programming: Fundamental Algorithms, 3rd ed., vol. 1. Copyright © 1997 by Addison-Wesley.

Fig. 4.7: Donald E. Kruth, "Adjacent Reserved and Free Blocks," The Art of Computer Programming: Fundamental Algorithms, 3rd ed., vol. 1. Copyright © 1997 by Addison-Wesley.

Fig. 4.8: Donald E. Kruth, "Free Block Created by Coalescing Two Free Blocks," The Art of Computer Programming: Fundamental Algorithms, 3rd ed., vol. 1. Copyright © 1997 by Addison-Wesley.

Fig. 4.9: Donald E. Kruth, "Free Block Created by Coalescing Two Free Blocks," The Art of Computer Programming: Fundamental Algorithms, 3rd ed., vol. 1. Copyright © 1997 by Addison-Wesley.

Chapter 5

Lexical Analyzers and Symbol Tables

The limits of my language mean the limits of my world.
—Ludwig Wittgenstein
  Tractatus Logico-Philosophicus, 5.6

CHAPTER OBJECTIVES

- To introduce the concepts of alphabets and vocabulary in the context of programming languages.
- To explore the way a lexical analyzer transforms each lexical unit of a programming language into an internal representation known as a token.
- To understand the way the symbol table saves identifiers and their attributes to assist the compiler in generating code.

INTRODUCTION

A compiler is a translator that transforms a program written in a high-level language to another representation, usually called a target language. Examples of target languages are machine language, assembly language, or other representations known as intermediate code. In the compilation process, we can identify several steps: lexical analysis, syntax analysis, semantic analysis, and code generation. In this chapter, we will discuss lexical analysis and the symbol table, also known as an external name table. The lexical analyzer or scanner is the name given to the program that carries out the lexical analysis, which means it proves the validity of all the symbols used in the program. In this step, the scanner transforms each syntactic unit or symbol of the source program into a token or internal representation to ease the task of the syntax analyzer.

Programming languages provide programmers with a vocabulary and syntax rules to allow them to write programs. A peculiarity of programming languages is that they leave a window open to programmers to permit them to insert external names into programs. Those external names, also known as identifiers, are used to identify constants, variables, and subroutines. By subroutines we mean functions, procedures, and methods. A symbol table is a data structure used to gather external names and their attributes.

VOCABULARY

This is a list of keywords that herald the concepts we will study in this chapter. They are organized in chronological order and will appear in the text in bold. We invite you to take a look at these keywords to find out which ones you are familiar with.

Alphabet	Newline	Start state
Symbols	Lexical analysis	Final state
Characters	Scanner	Attributes
Vocabulary	Lexemes	Insert function
String	Internal representation	Lookup function
Sentence	Token	Mark function
Statement	Regular expression	Sentinel
Grammar	(a)	Variable address
Terminal symbols	ab	Data index (dx)
Numerals	a | b	Global variable
Identifiers	a*	Data area
Symbol table	Empty string (ε)	Local variable
Separators	Transition diagrams	Activation record
White space	States	
Tab	Actions	

ACTIVATING PRIOR KNOWLEDGE

In this section we will present a series of activities. In some of them you can choose one or more options. Sometimes, if you do not agree with the given answers to choose from, you will be allowed to give your own answer. By the way, this is not a test.

1. What is a variable?

    An identifier ☐
    A name ☐
    A memory location ☐
    A reserved word ☐

2. Mark the words denoting an identifier.

    while ☐   a17 ☐   17 ☐   _hello ☐   x ☐

3. Assume you have a vocabulary of two letters {a, t}.

    How many words of length two can you build combining the two symbols? _____
    How many of those words are meaningful to you? _____

4. Using the following example, ";" = 08 and ":=" = 20, we can assign to each word (symbol) below a number; for example:

"end" = 22   "begin" = 21   "." = 19   "," = 17
"if" = 23   "+" = 04   ">" = 13   "then" = 24

Using the numbers associated with each word above, we invite you to translate the following statements (use 02 x each time you find an x and for numbers 03 followed by the number):

Hint: **begin x := 5 + 2 end** can be translated into **21 02 x 20 03 5 04 03 2 08**

a. if x > 7 then x := x + 64;
b. + if 64 x then x := ; > x 7

5. Skim the chapter and pay attention to the words written in **bold**. Count the number of words you are familiar with.

6. Do comments in a program generate executable code?

   Yes   ☐
   Sometimes   ☐
   No   ☐
   I don't know ☐

7. Is a variable name an identifier?

   Yes   ☐
   No   ☐
   Sometimes ☐

On Programs and Compilers

It would be convenient to begin this chapter by reviewing some basic concepts to set up the appropriate environment to discuss lexical analyzers and symbol tables. Let us begin with the algorithm concept. An algorithm describes the steps to be followed to solve a specific problem, and a program is an algorithm expressed in a programming language. We can think of a program as the result of a creative process of our minds; likewise poetry and painting. A programming language is a notation that allows us to write programs with two purposes: to instruct the computer to carry out a specific task and to allow communication among programmers to exchange knowledge. Programs have been used to solve complex problems, as expressed in this quotation from Dijkstra:

> We recognize the battle against chaos, mess, and unmastered complexity as one of computing science's major callings.
> —Edsger W. Dijkstra, *Some Beautiful Arguments Using Mathematical Induction* (1978)

In the domain of systems software, there are programs like operating systems and compilers that can be considered good examples of programs that "battle against chaos, mess, and unmastered complexity." Of the two programs just mentioned, we shall put our attention on compilers. A compiler is a translator that transforms a program written in a high-level language (text) to machine language, assembly language, or a similar representation known as intermediate code. In the compilation process, we can identify three basic steps: lexical analysis, syntax analysis, and code generation. Lexical analysis will be the subject of this chapter.

Before exploring lexical analyzers or scanners in detail, we need to introduce the fundamental elements that characterize a programming language because these elements or syntactic units will be read by the scanner. Therefore, we will present the concepts of alphabet and vocabulary as the basis of designing a programming language.

On Alphabets

Alphabets are finite sets of **symbols** or **characters** that can be combined to create words. We can use a single character from an alphabet to create a word, or we can link together a sequence of characters to create a word, which means that we can have words of different length. As an example, we can use the English alphabet (the Greek letter sigma, Σ, is commonly used to denote alphabets) and define it as:

$$\Sigma = \{a, b, c, d, e, f, g, h, i, j, k, l, m, n, o, p, q, r, s, t, u, v, w, x, y, z\}$$

You can choose one character from Σ and create a word; for example, **a**.

You can choose two characters from Σ and create words as well; for example, **is** and **he**.

You can select three characters from Σ and create a word; for example, **she**.

You can select four characters from Σ and create words; for example, **good** and **nice**.

You can select six characters from Σ and create words; for example, **person**.

Observing the four-letter example closely, you will realize that the character **o** was used twice. With an alphabet, we can build a selected group of words to create a **vocabulary** as means of communication. For example, with the words defined above, we can create a vocabulary, which we will call V:

$$V = \{a, is, he, she, good, nice, person\}$$

Assuming that we share the same vocabulary, you should be able to read and understand the following sentences:

She is a nice person.
He is a good person.

In the context of programming languages, the term **string** denotes a sequence of characters, without forgetting that a single character is also a string. Concerning the word **sentence**, we can use two words, which have an identical meaning: sentence and **statement**. Programming languages are notations that allow us to write programs, and each time you choose a high-level programming language to write a program, the programming language provides you with a vocabulary to choose symbols from and a **grammar** to be followed. In this book, we have been using the language PL/0, and as in any other language, in PL/0 we need to identify the vocabulary, reserved words, and special symbols that we accept as valid. Given the following program written in PL/0, let us find the vocabulary step-by-step. Each time we identify a symbol provided by PL/0, we will add it to the PL/0 vocabulary.

For instance, in the program shown below, we notice that there are many words in boldface. These are called reserved words or keywords. We will add them to the PL/0 vocabulary (PL0V) as shown in step 1.

Step 1:

```
const two = 2;                  PL/0 Vocabulary
var   x, y, z;
procedure mult;                 PL0V = {const  var   procedure  begin
 var a, b;                              while  do    if         odd
 begin                                  then   end   read       call
  a := x;  b := y; z := 0;              write
  while b > 0 do                        }
   begin
    if odd x then z := z + a;
    a := two * a;
    b := b / two;
   end
 end;
begin
 read x;
 read y;
 call mult;
 write z;
end.
```

As we need to identify all the symbols used in the PL/0 programming language, we invite you to observe the example program again, focusing on arithmetic and relational operators such as "+", "*", and ">" and punctuation symbols such as ";", ",", and ")". In step 2, we show the PL/0 vocabulary with relational and arithmetic operators, punctuation symbols, and reserved words.

Step 2:

In this step you will see that there are also some operators { + − * / < = > <= != >= :=} and special symbols { ( ) [ ] , . ; : } in boldface that will be added to the PL/0 vocabulary as well.

```
const two = 2;
var  x, y, z;
procedure mult;
  var a, b;
  begin
    a := x;  b := y; z := 0;
    while b > 0 do
      begin
        if odd x then z := z + a;
        a := two * a;
        b := b / two;
      end
end;
begin
  read x;
  read y;
  call mult;
  write z;
end.
```

PL/0 Vocabulary

PL0V = {const   var   procedure begin
        while   do   if   odd
        then   end   read   call
        write   +   −   *
        /   <   =   >
        <=   !=   >=   :=   (
)   [   ]   ,   .
        :   ;
        }

All the symbols included in the PL/0 vocabulary above are called **terminal symbols**. In addition to the terminal symbols, you can also observe in the program **numerals** 2 and 0. Although in the program there are only two numerals {2, 0}, we can use all numerals from zero to nine, and this will allow programmers to use numerals of different length made from the symbols {0 1 2 3 4 5 6 7 8 9}. Numbers can be used in a PL/0 program and considered as terminal symbols by the scanners. In step 3 we show PL/0 vocabulary plus a set of numerals used to generate numbers.

Step 3:
```
const two = 2;
var  x, y, z;
procedure mult;
  var a, b;
  begin
    a := x;  b := y; z := 0;
    while b > 0 do
      begin
        if odd x then z := z + a;
        a := two * a;
        b := b / two;
      end
```

PL/0 Vocabulary

PL0V = {const   var   procedure begin
        while   do   if   odd
        then   end   read   call
        write   +   −   *
        /   <   =   >
        <=   !=   >=   :=   (
)   [   ]   ,   .
        :   ;
        }

```
end;
begin
  read x;
  read y;
  call mult;
  write z;
end.
```

And any number created from the set of numerals can be treated as a terminal symbol:
{0   1   2   3
 4   5   6
 7   8   9}

Taking a closer look at the program in step 3, you will see that there are some letters and the words "two" and "mult." Those letters and words are **identifiers**. They are external names provided by programmers, and they do not belong to the fixed PL/0 vocabulary. These external names are called identifiers, and they are used to name constants, variables, and functions in a program. Including identifiers in a program is an ingenious way to add flexibility to programming languages. To keep track of identifiers in a program during the compilation process, the compiler uses a data structure known as a **symbol table**. Finally, we have to mention that there are also symbols to identify comments (/* and */) and **separators** such as **white space** (ws), **tab** (\t), and **newline** (\n) that must be recognized by the scanner; but once recognized, they are discarded because they do not generate executable code.

Example: \t a := ▢ 2 * a; \n /* comments */
              ws

Now that we know all the terminals symbols that belong to PL/0 vocabulary and the acceptance of external numbers and identifiers of any size, we can show the set of symbols that define the alphabet for PL/0:

Σ =   {a, b, c, d, e, f, g, h, i, j, k, l, m, n,
       o, p q, r, s, t, u, v, w, x, y, z, 0, 1, 2,
       3, 4, 5, 6, 7, 8, 9, , +, −, *, /, <, =, >, :,
       ., , , , ; }

Do not forget that by using concatenation—joining two or more characters drawn from the PL/0 alphabet—we can build a valid string or word in the PL/0 programming language. For example, "while", "if", or "a:= b + c".

Lexical Analysis

Although some compilers can use a preprocessing stage before **lexical analysis**, the **scanner** can be considered the first stage in a compiler. In this stage, the scanner reads in the program character by character to identify syntactic units known as **lexemes**. A lexeme is a syntactic unit with a meaning. Once a lexeme has been identified, the scanner will assign an **internal representation** or **token** to the lexeme, which explicitly identifies (categorizes) it.

The purpose of the scanner is to break down the source program into its elementary symbols or tokens, and to carry out this transformation, the following steps are taken:

1. Read input one character at a time.
2. Group characters into syntactic units (lexemes).
3. Remove spaces, comments, and control characters.
4. Assign an internal representation (token) to each lexeme.
5. Detect errors and generate error messages.

When designing a scanner, you have to define the token types and give each lexeme (symbol) an internal representation (token value). For example:

Symbol	Token	Symbol	Token	Symbol	Token	Symbol	Token
Null	01	=	09	,	17	**while**	25
Identifier	02	!=	10	;	18	**do**	26
Number	03	<	11	.	19	**call**	27
+	04	<=	12	:=	20	**const**	28
−	05	>	13	**begin**	21	**var**	29
*	06	>=	14	**end**	22	**procedure**	30
/	07	(	15	**if**	23	**write**	31
odd	08	)	16	**then**	24	**read**	32

Once token values have been assigned to special symbols and reserved words, the following translations can be done by the scanner.

Example 1:

Input: **if** x > 7 **then** x := x + 64;
Output: **23 02 x 13 03 7 24 02 x 20 02 x 04 03 64 18**

Example 2:

Input: + if 64 x then x := ; > x 7
Output: **04 23 03 64 02 x 24 02 x 20 18 13 02 x 03 7**

As the scanner does not check on grammar, both inputs are considered correct, and they will be translated to the internal representation with no error messages emitted. The parser in a subsequent step will report that example 2 does not follow the grammar rules and will emit a syntax error message. Note that we are using 02 for identifiers followed by the variable name and 03 for numbers followed by the numeral.

Regular Expressions

The identifiers and numbers inserted by a programmer into a program can be names and numbers of any length, and this brings up a new challenge. In the case of reserved words, a unique word with a predetermined length has to be found in a table but this cannot be done with identifiers and numbers because there are a huge number of them. **Regular expressions** will help us to cope with the problem of recognizing identifiers and numbers. Regular expressions were proposed by Stephen Kleene in 1956.

Definition: A **regular expression** is a notation for representing patterns. They are used to match strings in a language, describing all valid strings (of a language) that can be built from an alphabet.

We will introduce regular expressions informally through some examples. Let us define two alphabets, denoted letter and digit, as shown below:

>letter = {A, B, ..., Z, a, b, ... , z} and digit = {0, 1, 2, 3, ... , 8, 9}
>Letter is the alphabet of uppercase and lowercase letters, and digit is the alphabet of numerals.

Any symbol from either letter or digit is a regular expression of length one. To create strings or words of different length, we will describe some basic operators that will allow us to represent patterns of different length.

If **a** and **b** are regular expressions (symbols of the alphabet), then:

If **a** is a regular expression, then **a** in parentheses (**a**) is also a regular expression.

a . b denotes concatenation of two regular expression to create a string of length two (we will use the notation "ab" instead of a . b).

a | b means choose one among alternatives.
For example: (a | b) (a | b) denotes {aa, ab, ba, bb}.
All strings of length two over the alphabet Σ = **{a, b}**.
"ab" is obtained by selecting **a** from the first regular expression and **b** from the second one.

a* The operator * is called Kleene's star and denotes the language consisting of all finite strings of any length, including the string with no length or **empty string (ε)**:

$$\{ε, a, aa, aaa, aaaa, ...\}$$

Note: ε denotes the empty string or string of length zero.
For example, if Σ = {0, 1} is an alphabet,

$$\Sigma^* = \{\varepsilon, 0, 1, 00, 01, 10, 11, 000, 001, ...\}$$

For example: (**a** | **b**)* denotes the set of all strings consisting of zero or more instances of a or b.

$$\{\varepsilon, a, b, aa, ab, ba, bb, aaa, ...\}$$

Note that a regular expression is a type of grammar that describes a set of strings and can be used to denote a language over an alphabet.

Now with the help of regular expressions and their associated operators, we are well equipped to create regular expressions for representing patterns for matching identifiers and numbers. Be aware that the symbol "→" has to be read as "is defined as."

letter	→ A | B | ... | Z | a | b | c | ... | z
digit	→ 0 | 1 | 2 | 3 | 5 | 6 | 7 | 8 | 9
identifier	→ letter (letter | number)*
numbers	→ digit (digit)*

The definition for identifiers must be read this way:

An identifier	is defined as	begins with a letter	followed by a letter or number zero or more times
identifier	→	letter	(letter | number)*

Using regular expressions, the scanner is capable of identifying strings that match the definitions of identifiers and numbers. For identifiers, we have assigned the internal representation (token) 02 followed by the identifier name, and for integers 03 followed by the number. We invite you to take a careful look at the following example.

Input: **if** day > 5 **then** pay := base + 64;
↓
Scanner
↓
Output: **23 02** day **13 03** 5 **24 02** pay **20 02** base **04 03** 64 **18**

Transition Diagrams

It is possible to represent regular expressions graphically using a **transition diagram**. Each transition diagram has the following components:

States → represented by circles
Actions → represented by arrows between the states (labels on top)
Start state → represented by an arrowhead pointing to a state (beginning of a pattern)
Final state → represented by two concentric circles (end of pattern)

All transition diagrams are deterministic, which means that there is no need to choose between two different actions for a given input. The following transition diagram recognizes the lexemes matching the token identifier.

The transition diagram begins in state one (start). In this state a character is read in, and if the character is a letter there is a match and we move to state two (2); otherwise, it moves toward some other state, which means we are not in the presence of an identifier or reserved word. Once in state two (2), characters are read. As long as there are letters, these match the description of an identifier or reserved word, but if a digit is read in, we know we are still matching the description for identifiers but not for reserved words. The state diagram will keep reading characters in state two while they are letters or digits. As soon as the next character read is not a letter or a digit, we move to the accepting state (3), which means that the lexeme has been found and a token (**id**) is returned. Note that the last character read that brings us to state three (3) does not belong to the recognized identifier.

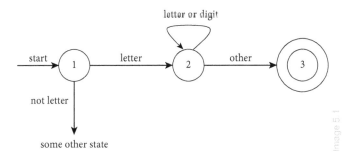

Symbol Table

The symbol table or external name table is a central data structure in the development of compilers. This table stores all identifiers (external names) used in a program. The symbol table can be populated by the scanner (partially) or by the parser. If the scanner populates the symbol table, then for each identifier found, the scanner inserts the name in the symbol table and returns a token and a pointer to the location where the name resides in the symbol table. If the parser populates the symbol table, then it inserts more information, such as the kind of identifier (constant, variable, or procedure), the name of the identifier, the address if it is a variable, the value in case of a constant, and so on. All the pieces of information associated with the identifier that are inserted in a symbol table are known as **attributes**. For instance, if we insert the name of a variable in the symbol table, its address is an attribute. We will assume that the symbol table will be populated in the parser phase of the compiler.

There are different ways to implement a symbol table. It can be organized as a list, a tree structure, or a hash table. The most efficient approach to implementing a symbol table is to use hashing, and we encourage readers, as an exercise, to implement the symbol table we will explain in this chapter, using a hash table. Now we will explain how to populate a symbol table using a linear array to implement an unordered list. This is an easy approach, which will allow you to understand how to manage the symbol table using three basic operations:

Insert(identifier): This operation is used to insert an identifier and its attributes in the symbol table each time a declaration is found.

Lookup(identifier): This is operation used to look for an identifier in the table each time we use it in the program after the declaration. If the name is found, the function returns a pointer (index); otherwise, it returns a zero, which means that the identifier has not been declared.

Mark: This operation is used for tagging identifiers that are not needed any longer. Sometimes this operation is called delete.

Each entry in the linear array is a data structure that will represent an identifier and its attributes. The fields of this data structure, which is based on the one proposed by Wirth for PL/0, are described below:

```
char name[11];    // name up to 11 chars
int kind;         // const = 1, var = 2, procedure = 3.
int val;          // number (ASCII value)
int level;        // L level
int adr;          // M address
int mark;         // 0 = in use for code generation; 1 = unavailable (no active)
```

Note: Position zero in the array is called the sentinel.

Index	0	1	2	3	4	5	6	7	8	9	10	11
Kind												
Name												
Value												
Level (L)												
Address (M)												
Mark												

Depending on the kind of identifier, we store different information in the symbol table:

For constants, you must store kind = 1, name and value.
For variables, you must store kind = 2, name, L and M.
For procedures, you must store kind = 3, name, L and M.
For all of them, "mark" is initialized to zero, which means "active," and when the value becomes one, the entries with value one are considered inaccessible or deleted.

Now we will show you how to populate the symbol table using the small PL/0 program shown below:

1 **const** pi = 3.14;
2 **var** x, y, w;
3 x := y + pi.

When this program passes through the scanner, we obtain the following tokens: lines 1 and 2 translation is represented by the first two rows underneath, and line 3 is associated to the third row:

28 02 pi 09 03 3.14 18
29 02 x 17 02 y 17 02 w 18
02 x 20 02 y 04 02 pi 18

Identifiers are inserted starting at position 1 in the symbol table, and position 0 is used to detect identifiers used within the program but not defined or declared. Position 0 is called the **sentinel**, and each time a search is carried out, the identifier name (say, salary) is copied in the field name in position 0. Using array notation, this is written as table[0].name = salary. There is also a table pointer (tp) initialized to one (tp = 1), and each time a name is inserted in the symbol table, the tp is incremented by one. Let us observe the first line of the program where a constant is defined:

const	pi	=	3.14	;
28	02 pi	09	03 3.14	18

When token 28 is read in, it indicates that the kind is a constant value (kind=1). It is followed by token 02, which indicates an identifier is expected, and back-to-back an identifier named pi will be found. The next token is 09, which means the equal sign, and it is followed by the token 03, which indicates that a value is expected and the value is 3.14. Finally, a semicolon token (18) stops the constant definition. With all that information, the constant pi and its attributes are inserted in position 1 using the function insert(pi), and tp is incremented by one and now points to position 2 in the array. This can be seen in symbol table state 1.

Symbol table state 1

Index	0	1	2	3	4	5	6	7	8	9	10	11
Kind		1										
Name		pi										
Value		3.14										
Level		n/a										
Address		n/a										
Mark		0										

(tp points to index 2)

Let us take a closer look at the variable declarations in line 2.

```
var   x   ,   y   ,   w   ;
29    02 x   17   02 y   17   02 w   18
```

You can observe the reserved word **var** (29), which identifies a variable name (kind=2), then three identifiers preceded by 02, and then the name of the identifiers. There is a comma (token=17) in between identifiers. The declaration ends up with a semicolon (token=18). Recall that each time an identifier is inserted in the symbol table, the tp is incremented by one. Symbol table state 2 shows the state of the table after inserting constant pi and the three variables x, y, and w. From now on, index variable "tp" will be written above the index row instead of using an arrow pointing to the next available entry in the symbol table.

Symbol table state 2

Index	0	1	2	3	4	5	6	7	8	9	10	11
Kind		1	2	2	2							
Name		pi	x	y	w							
Value		n/a	n/a	n/a	n/a							
Level		n/a	0	0	0							
Address		n/a	4	5	6							
Mark		0	0	0	0							

(tp above index 5)

At this point, a question probably arises in your mind: How is the variable address determined?

The **variable address** depends on the number of fields used in the stack as control information to preserve the environment of the caller plus any other information that might be used; for instance, returning a value (FV) and/or a link to reach a variable in another activation record (SL). In figure 5.1 we present three examples:

1. Four stack positions will be used in the activation record as control information (RA, DL, SL, FV). In this case, the variable addresses will begin at location 4 (a displacement of four from the base pointer).
2. Three stack positions will be used in the activation record as control information (RA, DL, SL). In this case, the variable addresses will begin at location 3 (a displacement of three from the base pointer).
3. Two stack positions will be used in the activation record as control information (RA, DL). In this case, the variable addresses will begin at location 2 (a displacement of two from the base pointer).

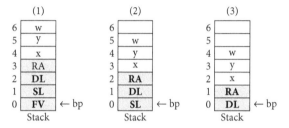

FIGURE 5.1 Different ways to determine the address of a variable in the run-time stack.

It is convenient to initialize a **data index (dx)**, whose initial value is the address where the first declared variable will be stored in the stack. In the symbol table example we are developing in this chapter, the initial value is dx = 4, and it matches the stack (1) in figure 5.1. But if you implement your activation record as in (2), the initial value of dx would be 3, and if case (3) is used, dx = 2. Recall that each time an identifier is inserted in the symbol table, dx is incremented by one.

We will proceed to carry out an exercise of code generation using the information stored in symbol table state 2 in order to explain how function lookup (identifier) works. If the identifier to be found is y, the name "y" is stored in table[0].name. Function search works backward from tp toward zero. There is a match because y is found in position 3, and the address in that entry is five (5), which will be used to generate the instruction LOD R0, 0, **5**.

seek = lookup(y)

		seek			tp						
Index	0	1	2	3	4	5	6	7	8	9	10	11
Kind		1	2	2	2							
Name	y	pi	x	y	w							
Value		3.14	n/a	n/a	n/a							
Level		n/a	0	0	0							
Address		n/a	4	5	6							
Mark		0	0	0	0							

But if the identifier we are looking for is k, then when we execute seek = lookup (k). The index of k is zero, and that means that the variable we are trying to find in the symbol table has not been declared.

seek = lookup (k)

	seek					tp					
Index	0	1	2	3	4	5	6	7	8	9	10	11
Kind		1	2	2	2							
Name	k	pi	x	y	w							
Value		3.14	n/a	n/a	n/a							
Level		n/a	0	0	0							
Address		n/a	4	5	6							
Mark		0	0	0	0							

Line 2 in the program reads: x := y + pi, and the code generated would be:

LDO	R0, 0, 5	// Load y in register R0
LIT	R1, 0, 3.14	// Load 3,14 in register R1
ADD	R0, R0, R1	// add y plus 3.14 and place resulting value in register R0
STO	R0, 0, 4	// store the content of R0 in x

You can verify that the addresses of variables y and x in the instruction LDO and STO match the addresses in the symbol table for those identifiers. Let us take our previous example an extended with a procedure declaration. Inside the procedure, two local variables x and p are declared as shown below

```
const pi = 3.14;
var x, y, w;
procedure sum;
   var x, p;
```

In symbol table state 3, after inserting procedure identifier "sum," you might notice that procedure address is equal to "?" because at that moment code has not been generated and the address of the first instruction of the procedure is unknown.

Symbol table state 3

							tp					
Index	0	1	2	3	4	5	6	7	8	9	10	11
Kind		1	2	2	2	3						
Name	sum	pi	x	y	w	sum						
Value		3.14	n/a	n/a	n/a	n/a						
Level		n/a	0	0	0	0						
Address		n/a	4	5	6	?						
Mark		0	0	0	0	0						

State 4 shows the symbol table once the two local variables in procedure sum are added to the table. Notice that the lexicographical level is 1 because procedure sum is embedded within the main program. Each time a procedure is nested with another procedure, the lexicographical level of all variables declared in the nested procedure is incremented by one in the symbol table.

Something else you should pay attention to is that there are two variables with the same name (x). That will not create any conflict, because they represent two distinct memory locations; **global variable** x points to location 4 in the **data area (main)** in the process address space, and **local variable** x declared in the procedure sum points to location 4 in the function **activation record** in the stack. When an instruction within the procedure sum refers to x, it will access the local variable x declared in procedure sum (the one at index = 6). Any reference to variable x outside procedure sum will access the global variable x (the one at index = 2).

Symbol table state 4

									tp			
Index	0	1	2	3	4	5	6	7	8	9	10	11
Kind		1	2	2	2	3	2	2				
Name	p	pi	x	y	w	sum	x	p				
Value		3.14	n/a	n/a	n/a	n/a	n/a	n/a				
Level		n/a	0	0	0	0	1	1				
Address		n/a	4	5	6	?	4	5				
Mark		0	0	0	0	0	0	0				

In the next case, we will add another procedure declaration to the example under study and include a statement in each procedure.

```
const pi = 3.14;
var x, y, w;
procedure sum;
   var x, p;
   begin
     x := p + w;   ← access global variable w and local variables x and p.
   end;
procedure add;
   var a, b;
   begin
     a := b + x;   ← access global variable x and local variables a and b.
   end;
```

In state 5 we can see the symbol table after the insertion of procedure identifier add and variables a and b into the table. Observing the symbol table carefully, you will notice that the scanner went out of procedure sum and is now working on procedure add. Once the scanner adds variables x and p to the symbol table and code is generated (in the code generation step) for all statements within procedure sum, all variables within the procedure are marked as inactive (mark = 1), as illustrated in symbol table state 5. We must recall that searching in the symbol table is carried out backward from the position tp is pointing to toward index location zero. Be aware that when the code generator handles the statement a := b + **x** in procedure add, it will find the first x at index 6, but as x is marked (mark =1), then it will continue searching until it finds another **x**, which is at index 2. As this one is not marked, the code generator will use this entry in the symbol table to generate code for the statement a := b + **x**.

Symbol table state 5

Index	0	1	2	3	4	5	6	7	8	9	10	11
Kind		1	2	2	2	3	2	2	3	2	2	
Name	b	pi	x	y	w	sum	x	p	add	a	b	
Value		3.14	n/a	n/a	n/a	n/a	n/a	n/a	n/a	n/a	n/a	
Level		n/a	0	0	0	0	1	1	0	1	1	
Address		n/a	4	5	6	?	4	5	?	4	5	
Mark		0	0	0	0	0	1	1	0	0	0	

tp is at column 11.

All the information stored in the symbol table will be used to generate object code, assembly language, or another type of representation known as intermediate code. If assembly language is generated, another program called the assembler will translate assembly language into object code (binary).

SUMMARY

We began this chapter by presenting programs as an alternative to solve complex problems using computers. To instruct the computer to carry out a specific task, it is necessary to use a programming language, but as programming languages allow us to write programs using plain text and the computer only "understands" binary, a translation from text to binary is required. We can use two translators to carry out this task: a compiler and an assembler. A compiler is a program that translates programs written in a high-level language into assembly language or object code, and the assembler translates assembly language into object code. We discussed one step of the compilation process, the scanner or lexical analyzer. Before examining the scanner, we presented the concepts of alphabet and vocabulary as the basis for creating a programming language and used the PL/0 language as an example. Then we described how the scanner transforms program text into tokens. In this regard, we presented two cases: one where the scanner deals with a finite number of symbols such as reserved words and special characters. In the second case, identifiers and numbers are considered, and we face the problem of an uncountable set of them. Therefore, we presented regular expressions to recognize patterns and handle this second case. Transition diagrams were shown as a way to visualize regular expressions. Finally, we explained how the symbol table is used to manage identifiers and their attributes.

EXERCISES

1. What is a compiler?
2. What is an assembler?
3. Name the three basic steps in the compilation process. For each step, include the name of the input and output files.
4. What are the five steps carried out by the lexical analyzer to transform text into tokens?
5. What is an alphabet?
6. Write down a list containing all PL/0 reserved words.
7. Is a reserved word a terminal symbol?

8. Using the symbol/token table found in page 88, translate the following program text into tokens:

   ```
   read w;
   begin
     x:= 4;
     if w > x then
            w:= w + 1
     else
            w:= x;
   end
   write w;
   ```

9. Let us define the alphabet $\Sigma = \{0,1\}$. Give all strings of length four according to the following regular expressions:

   a. 0 (0 | 1) 1 (0 | 1)
   b. (0 | 1) (0 | 1) (0 | 1) (0 | 1)

10. Give the transition diagram for the regular expression in question 9.

11. What is a symbol table?

12. How is the address attribute assigned to each variable?

13. Give the symbol table for the following program:

    ```
    const k = 5;
    var x, y;
    procedure sum;
      var p, x;
      begin
         Statements...
      end;
    procedure add;
      var a, b;
      begin
         Statements...
      end;
    end.
    ```

14. Give the symbol table for the following program:

```
main
  const k = 5;
  var x, y;
  procedure sum;
    var p, x;
    procedure add;
      var x, b;
      begin
        Statements…
      end;
    begin
      Statements…
    end;
  begin
    Statements…
  end.
```

Bibliographical Notes

The descriptions of the scanner and symbol table in this chapter are based on the PL/0 compiler described by Wirth in his book *Algorithms + Data Structures = Programs*.[1] Karen Lemone[2] presents an accessible introduction to scanners and symbol tables with some examples. Per Brinch Hansen[3] gives details of scanners and symbol table implementation issues; in this source you can find a good explanation for implementing symbol tables using hashing techniques. Of course, the main sources to delve deeper into scanners, symbol tables, and any subject related to compilers are *Compilers: Principles, Techniques, and Tools* by Aho, Lam, Sethi, and Ullman[4] and *Engineering a Compiler* by Cooper and Torczon.[5] Regular expressions were proposed by Stephen Kleene[6] in 1956.

Bibliography

1. N. Wirth, *Algorithm + Data Structures = Programs*. Upper Saddle River, NJ: Prentice Hall, 1976.
2. K. Lemone, *Fundamentals of Compilers: An Introduction to Computer Language Translation*. Boca Raton, FL: CRC, 1992.
3. P. Brinch Hansen, *On Pascal Compilers*. Englewood Cliffs, NJ: Prentice Hall, 1985.
4. A. Aho, M. Lam, R. Sethi, and J. Ullman, *Compilers: Principles, Techniques, and Tools*, 2nd ed. Boston, MA, Addison-Wesley, 2007.
5. L. Torczon and K. Cooper, *Engineering a Compiler*, 2nd ed. San Francisco, CA, Morgan Kaufmann, 2012.
6. S. Kleene, "Representation of Events in Nerve and Finite Automata," in *Automata Studies*, ed. C. Shannon and J. McCarthy. Princeton, NJ: Princeton University Press, 1956, pp. 3–42.

Chapter 6

Syntax Analysis and Code Generation

A parsing algorithm is derived for each nonterminal symbol, and it is formulated as a procedure carrying the name of the symbol. The occurrence of the symbol in the syntax is translated into a call of the corresponding procedure.
—Niklaus Wirth
Compiler Construction

CHAPTER OBJECTIVES

- To introduce the concept of grammar and a metalanguage to describe the grammar of programming languages.
- To explore the way a syntax analyzer parses the program according to a given grammar.
- To understand the way a syntax analyzer interacts with a code generator and generates an intermediate representation, which can be executed on a virtual machine.

INTRODUCTION

This chapter presents syntax analysis and code generation, which are two key components of a compiler. The parser or syntax analyzer reads in a source program represented as a stream of tokens generated by the scanner and determines whether its syntactic structure is well formed. If so, the parser might generate a parse tree or interact with other compiler components; for example, with the code generator to emit executable code or an intermediate representation. Otherwise, a syntax error is reported. The syntax of a programming language is a set of rules that define the structure of the language, and the usage of these rules allows us to write well-formed programs. The chapter will also present a notation called Backus-Naur form, or BNF, which is a metalanguage commonly used to describe the grammar rules of programming languages.

We will assume that the parser/code generator will generate an intermediate representation at the level of assembly language of a virtual machine. This will be considered a parser and code generation step in the compilation process. We will give examples of code generation for several programming constructs

VOCABULARY

This is a list of keywords that herald the concepts we will study in this chapter. They are organized in chronological order and will appear in the text in bold. We invite you to take a look at these keywords to find out which ones you are familiar with.

Grammar	Verb phrase (VP)	Derivation
Productions	Derivation	Left recursion
Syntactic equations	Parse tree	Left factoring
Metalanguage	Context-free grammar (CFG)	Top-down parsing
Backus-Naur form (BNF)	Nonterminal symbol (N)	Bottom-up parsing
Parser	Terminal symbol (T)	Parse tree
Metasymbol	Production rules (P)	Extended Backus-Naur form (EBNF)
Phrase structure grammar	Start symbol (S)	
Noun phrase (NP)	Leftmost derivation	Code generation

ACTIVATING PRIOR KNOWLEDGE

In this section we will present a series of activities. In some of them you can choose one or more options. Sometimes, if you do not agree with the given answers to choose from, you will be allowed to give your own answer. By the way, this is not a test.

1. Which one of these statements is correct?

    Peter eat an apple. ☐
    Peter eats an apple. ☐
    Peter an apple eats. ☐
    An apple eats Peter. ☐

2. In this game there are several rules. Each rule has two parts: the name of the rule and its definition. Each rule name can be replaced by its definition. For instance, imagine that we have these rules:

Name		Definition	
K	→	W K | t	// you can choose either WK or t
W	→	t p K	// you have only one option

    Assume we would like to know the number of ways to go from K to t, starting at K.

    The symbol → can be read as "can be replaced by."

    Only uppercase letters can be replaced by their definition.

    Lowercase letters and other symbols are stopping elements, and no matter what you find after them, you must stop. There are two ways to go from K to t, as shown below.

    K → t   Apply rule 1.
    K → WK → t p K K   Apply rule 1 and replace K by WK, then apply rule 2.

We have found two ways to go from K to t.

Now it is your turn. For the following rules:

E ::= T E'

E' ::= + T E' | ε

T ::= F T'

T' ::= * F T' | ε

F ::= (E) | t | n

  a. Find a path from E to "**(**".

  b. Find a path from E to **t**.

  c. Find a path from T to **n**.

3. When the compiler generates intermediate code, it generates:

   a. Assembly language ☐
   b. Machine language ☐
   c. Object code ☐

4. Does machine language = assembly language?

   Yes ☐   No ☐

Syntax Analysis

Generally speaking, we can define a **grammar** as a collection of rules to guide us on how to put words together into a correct sentence in a language, and this also applies to programming languages. These syntactic rules are also known as **productions** or **syntactic equations**, and they are written using a **metalanguage**. A metalanguage is a language or notation used to describe another language. The common notation to describe the grammar of a programming language is known as **Backus-Naur form** (**BNF**). John Backus and Peter Naur are credited with the creation of this streamlined notation. In a compiler, the task of verifying whether a program is well written is carried out by the syntax analyzer or **parser**. The **metasymbols** used in BNF are:

1. Connectives
   "::="   which can be read as "is defined as"
   "|"   which can be read as "or"
2. Variables
   <...>   These angled brackets are used to surround syntactic rules names.
           For example: <expression> or <statement> or <letter>

Each syntactic rule in a language can be expressed in BNF, using metasymbols. Let us observe the following example of a language grammar with three syntactic rules:

1. <sentence> ::= <subject> <predicate>
2. <subject> ::= **Peter** | **Ada**
3. <predicate> ::= **writes** | **talks**

In this example there are three syntactic rules, and you have to read them this way:

1. <sentence> is defined as a <subject> follow by a <predicate>
2. A <subject> is defined as the name **Peter** or **Ada**.
3. A <predicate> is defined as the verb **writes** or **talks**

With these rules, we define four possible valid sentences:

Peter writes   **Peter talks**   **Ada writes**   **Ada talks**

In the early 1950s Noam Chomsky developed **phrase structure grammars** as a means to describe the structural description of languages. In a phrase structure grammar, the words are grouped into phrases. Let us assume that the phrases are classified into **noun phrases (NPs)** and **verb phrases (VPs)**. For example, the following phrase

"the boy read the book"

can be described, using a modified version of the original Chomsky notation, by the following grammar:

1. SENTENCE → NP~VP   // The symbol → is equivalent to ::= in BNF
2. NP → *the~boy* | *the~book*   // ~ can be read as "follows by" and "|" can be read as "or"
3. VP → VERB~NP   // Uppercases are called nonterminals.
4. VERB → *read* | *took*   // Lowercases are called terminals.

Using this grammar, we can verify whether the sentence "The boy read the book" follows the grammar rules:

SENTENCE	using rule 1, SETENCE can be replaced by NP~VP
NP~VP	using rule 2, NP~VP can be replaced by the~boy~VP
the~boy~VP	using rule 3, the~boy~VP can be replaced by the~boy~VERB~NP
the~boy~VERB~NP	using rule 4, the~boy~VERB~NP can be replaced by the~boy~read~NP

the~boy~read~NP   using rule 2, the~boy~read~NP can be replaced by the~boy~read~the~book

the~boy~read~the~book   We have verified that the sentence follows the grammar rules!

Nonterminals are syntax rule names, and they can be replaced by their definition. Each time we replace a nonterminal by its right-hand side, we call it a **derivation**. Terminals are names that are atomic and cannot be expanded further. A graphical representation of the hierarchical structure of the derivation is called a **parse tree**. Figure 6.1 illustrates the parse tree for the derivation just explained. The strings obtained after each derivation are called sentential forms.

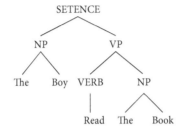

FIGURE 6.1 Parse tree for the sentence "The boy read the book."

There is a type of phrase structure grammar called **context-free grammar (CFG)**, which is called context free because the grammar rules can be applied regardless of the linguistic concept. A context-free grammar consists of a set of recursive rewriting rules to describe the syntax of a context-free language. BNF is a notation used to describe the syntax of context-free languages, and programming languages are context-free languages. A context-free grammar consists of four components: **nonterminal symbols (N)**, **terminal symbols (T)**, **production rules (P)**, and the **start symbol (S)**. Formally, it is defined by the tuple CFG = (N, T, P, S). Let us identify these components using an example:

1. A finite set of terminal symbols (T), which require no further definition because they are atomic entities. In figure 6.2 they are enclosed in a dashed circle.

FIGURE 6.2 Terminal symbols.

2. A finite set of nonterminal symbols (N), which represent names of syntactic classes or categories and are defined in terms of either terminal or nonterminal symbols, or as a sequence of terminals and nonterminals. They can be substituted by their definition. In figure 6.3, they are enclosed in dashed lines. You might notice that the syntactic class <sentence> is defined in terms of other nonterminal symbols and the syntactic classes <subject> and <predicate> are defined in terms of terminal symbols. Later in this chapter, we will show you syntactic categories defined as a sequence of terminals and nonterminals (including themself). Notice that for a nonterminal or syntactic class, angled brackets are used.

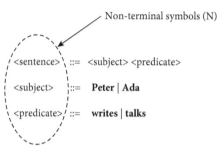

FIGURE 6.3 Nonterminal symbols.

3. A finite set of syntactic equations or productions, which are the grammar rules (P). There is a unique rule for each nonterminal symbol in the grammar. In figure 6.4, they are enclosed in dashed lines, and you can see that in each rule there is a left-hand side, which represents a syntactic category or nonterminal, and a right-hand side, which is a finite string of terminal and/or nonterminal symbols.

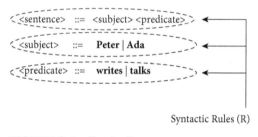

FIGURE 6.4 Productions.

4. The start symbol, which is one of the nonterminal symbols. In general, we can assume that the start symbol is the syntactic class defined in the first production. In figure 6.5 you will see the start symbol enclosed in dashed lines.

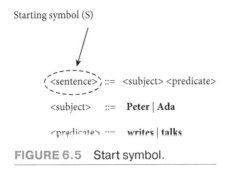

FIGURE 6.5 Start symbol.

Let us move on to an example related to programming languages. The following grammar defines the syntactic classes <expression> and <identifier>:

R1 <expression>   ::= <identifier> * <expression>
R2 | <identifier> + <expression>
R3 | <identifier>
R4 | (<expression>)
R5 <identifier>   ::= v | w | x | y

An expression is generated by the grammar using derivations. We will focus on a type of derivation known as **leftmost derivation**. By a leftmost derivation we mean that the expression will be parsed from left to right, and anytime we find a nonterminal or syntactic class, we can substitute it for one of its definitions (sometimes there is only one option). In the grammar for expressions described above, rules Ri (with i = 1 to 5) stand for the grammar rules. The application of a syntax rule is called a **derivation**. For instance, an <expression> can be replaced by <identifier> by rule R3; this is a derivation. Then, the <identifier> can be replaced by a terminal symbol, say x, chosen from (v, w, x, y) according to rule R5; this is another derivation. We can write these two consecutive derivations as follows:

    <expression> => <identifier> => x   // read symbol "=>" as "derives into"

Now, let us verify whether the expression (x * y) is well written according to the grammar defined above:

R4 <expression>   => (<expression>)
R1   => (<identifier> * <expression>)
R5   => (x * <expression>)
R3   => (x * <identifier>)
R5   => (x * y)

We have just verified that the expression (x * y) follows the grammars rules and can be derived from the start symbol <expression>.

As a second example, we will move on to the syntactic class statement that is frequently used when we write programs, and we will present the assignment statement. Rules Ri (i =1 to 6) below show the grammar for the assignment statement. You can see three syntactic classes or nonterminals, which are <statement>, <expression>, and <identifier>. All other symbols are terminal symbols.

R1	<statement>	::= <identifier> := <expression>
R2	<identifier>	::= v | w | x | y
R3	<expression>	::= <identifier> * <expression>
R4		| <identifier> + <expression>
R5		| <identifier>
R6		| (<expression>)

Let us find out whether we are able to derive x := w * y + v using the assignment statement grammar described above. We will begin with the starting symbol (<statement>).

R1 <statement>	=> <identifier> := <expression>
R2	=> x := <expression>
R4	=> x := <identifier> * <expression>
R2	=> x := w * <expression>
R3	=> x := w * <identifier> + <expression>
R2	=> x := w * y + <expression>
R6	=> x := w * y + <identifier>
R2	=> x := w * y + v

These derivations show that the statement x := w * y + v follows the grammar rules and therefore is syntactically correct. A graphical view of this derivation or parse tree is illustrated in figure 6.6.

One of the problems of the grammar described above is that the arithmetic operations "*" and "+" are defined at the same level in the grammar, and the precedence of the operator "*" over "+" is not granted. To solve this issue, we will rewrite the grammar to give higher precedence to "*" over "+". Two new syntactic classes are created and added to the grammar: <term> and <factor>. We will also simplify the notation by shortening the names of the syntactic classes <factor>, <expression>, <identifier>, <statement>, and <term> by replacing them with F, E, ID, S, and T respectively. The new grammar for the statement is:

R1	S	::= ID := E
R2	ID	::= v | w | x | y
R3	E	::= E + T
R4		| T
R5	T	::= T * F
R6		| F
R7	F	::= (E)
R8		| ID

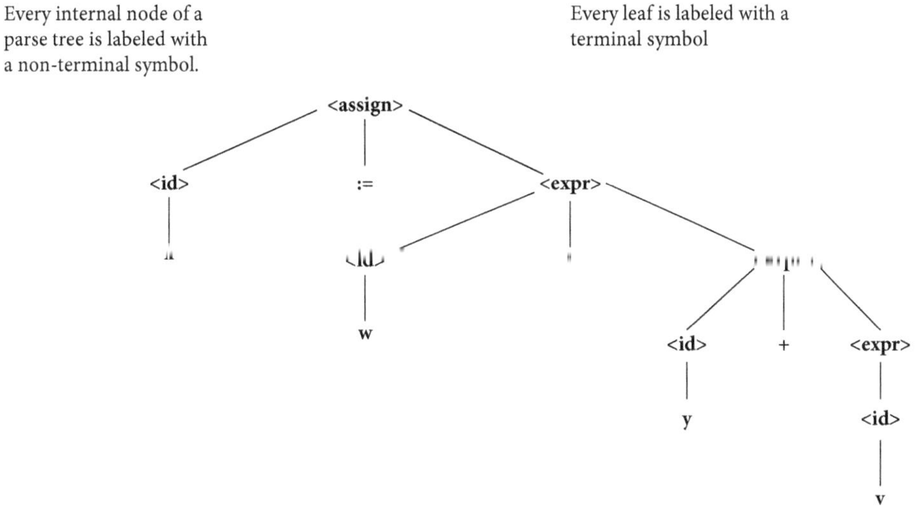

Every internal node of a parse tree is labeled with a non-terminal symbol.

Every leaf is labeled with a terminal symbol

FIGURE 6.6 Assignment statement derivation.

We will use this grammar to parse x := v + y * w. As you can see, we are evaluating the same expression we used in the previous example, and the only difference is that we rearranged the operators and variables, placing the plus and times symbols in different grammar rules. The new grammar enforces precedence of the operations. As usual, we will begin our left derivations with the syntactic class associated with the starting symbol, which is statement (S).

R1 <S>   ==> ID := E
R2   ==> x := E
R3   ==> x := E + T
R4   ==> x := T + T
R6   ==> x := F + T
R8   ==> x := ID + T
R2   ==> x := v + T
R5   ==> x := v + T * F
R6   ==> x := v + F * F
R8   ==> x := v + ID * F
R2   ==> x := v + y * F
R8   ==> x := v + y * ID
R8   ==> x := v + y * w

Figure 6.7 depicts the parse tree for the derivation associated with the assignment statement x := v + y * w.

There is something else we must pay attention to in the assignment statement grammar. If we take a closer look at this grammar, we will notice that the definition of expression E syntactic rule begins with itself, which makes this rule left recursive; and as we are parsing from left to right, this will present a problem for top-down parsing.

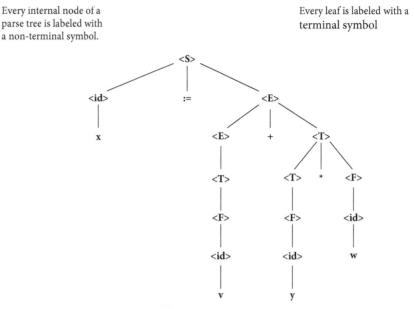

FIGURE 6.7 Second assignment statement derivation.

S ::= id := E
id ::= v | w | x | y
E ::= E + T | T
T ::= T * F | F
F ::= (E) | id

Allow us to give you an idea of what the problem is. In a top-down parser, we have to implement a function or procedure for each syntactic class; then if we implement a procedure for an expression, whose first statement is a call to the procedure expression again, the parser might get into an infinite loop. This is known as the **left recursion** problem, and we can solve this problem by rewriting the grammar to eliminate left recursion.

Let α represent a string of terminals and nonterminals and X represents a syntactic class (nonterminal). In the following grammar you will see that left recursion exists:

X ::= X α | β → replacing X by X α → replacing X again by X αα → replacing X again by βαα

The strings derivable from X are a β followed by 0 or more occurrences of α.

For example, βαααααα

We can rewrite this grammar to avoid left recursion and obtain an equivalent grammar that produces the same strings derivable from X. To do this, we will need to add another syntactic class, say X' to rewrite the new version of the grammar. In addition, we must use the empty string ε to stop the derivations.

X ::= β X'   This grammar is equivalent to X ::= X α | β and generates the same type of strings.
X' ::= αX' | ε

Let us apply this technique to the expression rule E ::= E + T | T
$$\qquad\qquad\qquad\qquad\qquad\qquad\qquad\qquad\quad |\ \ \ |\ \ \ |$$
$$\qquad\qquad\qquad\qquad\qquad\qquad\qquad\qquad\quad X\ \ \alpha\ \ \beta$$

by applying the same technique and replacing X by E, α by +T, and β by T, we can rewrite the expression grammar as:

E ::= T E'
E' ::= + T E' | ε

something similar must be done with the definition of the term (T), which is also left recursive, to transform the syntactic rule T ::= T * F | F into:

T ::= F T'
T' ::= * F T' | ε

now that we have gotten rid of the left recursion in this statement grammar, we can present it as:
S   ::= ID := E
id   ::= v | w | x | y
E   ::= T E'
E'   ::= + T E' | ε
T   ::= F T'
T'   ::= * F T' | ε
F   ::= (E) | ID

At this moment we can write a parser for this grammar using the top-down approach. For each syntactic rule (right-hand side of the equations), we need to write a function or procedure. Before we move on to top-down parsing, we have to review another problem known as **left**

factoring. Sometimes in a production, we need to select between alternatives. If we choose the wrong one, then we need to backtrack and explore another alternative. Getting rid of left factoring means delaying the decision until we can make the right choice. For example, in the following grammar,

$$X ::= \alpha\beta_1 \mid \alpha\beta_2 \mid \alpha\beta_3$$

assuming α and β are strings made of terminals and nonterminals. Then if we choose $\alpha\beta_1$ and after parsing α we arrive at β_1 and there is not a match, then backtracking is required, and another choice, say $\alpha\beta_2$, has to be made but similar result can be obtained, and then we have to try with $\alpha\beta_3$. This problem can be solved by rewriting the grammar as follows:

$$X ::= \alpha\, X'$$
$$X' ::= \beta_1 \mid \beta_2 \mid \beta_3$$

The rewritten grammar allows us to parse the complete string α, and then call X'. Within X' we choose one β_i, and if there is not a match, then we can try another path, and so on. However, you can see that we do not have to undo everything and restart parsing from the beginning of α time and again. A typical example where left factoring is necessary is the <if-then-else statement>:

<if-then-else statement> ::= **if** expression **then** statement **else** statement
| **if** expression **then** statement

Taking a closer look at the **if-then-else**, you can verify that " **if** expression **then** statement" is identical in both definitions, and only when the **else** is found can a decision be made. This can be rewritten as:

<if-then-else statement> ::= if expression then statement X'
< X'> ::= else statement | ε

Top-Down Parsing

Although there are different ways to parse, the two more popular are **top-down parsing** and **bottom-up parsing**. We will focus on top-down parsing in this book. The idea behind top-down parsing consists of constructing a **parse tree** for an input string of tokens provided by the scanner. The way to build the parser for a given grammar is to implement a procedure or function for each syntactic class in the grammar (nonterminals). Once the parser is implemented, it will get a token from the scanner and call the function that represents the starting symbol in the grammar (for example, the assignment statement denoted in the grammar by S). Let us explore an example using the assignment statement grammar described in the previous section. The grammar is expressed this time in the **extended Backus-Naur form (EBNF)** proposed by Niklaus Wirth.

program ::= var-declaration statement "." .
var-declaration ::= "var" ident {"," ident}";"
statement ::= ident ":=" expression
expression ::= term expression-prime
expression-prime ::="+" term expression-prime | ε
term ::= factor term-prime
term-prime ::= "*" factor term-prime | ε
factor ::= "(" expression ")" | ident
ident ::= "v" | "w" | "x" | "y"
digit ::= "0" | "1" | "2" | "3" | "4" | "5" | "6" | "7" | "8" | "9".

Based on Wirth's definition for EBNF, we have the following notation rules:

[ ] means an optional item.
{ } means repeat 0 or more times.
Terminal symbols are enclosed in quotation marks.
A period is used to indicate the end of the definition of a syntactic class.

In this grammar you can see that a program is defined as variable declarations, follow by a statement, followed by "." which represents the end of program.

program ::= var-declaration statement "." .

The handling of var declaration and the population of the symbol table were explained in the previous chapter, and therefore we will focus on parsing the assignment statement to create the parse tree by calling the function "statement." Let us work with the following program:

var x, y;
x := y + x. // Represented by the following token list **02 x 20 02 y 04 02 x 19** as shown below.

Input: x := y + x.
↓
Scanner
↓
Output: 02 **x** 20 02 **y** 04 02 **x** 19

In this example we would call function statement using as input the first token 02, which represents an identifier symbol, and the identifier name x just follows the 02 token. Procedure statement could be implemented as follows:

```
procedure statement;
  begin
    if token != "identifier-symbol" then ERROR.    // "identifier-symbol" = 02
    else
     begin
       get (next token)                            // gets name x from the token string
       id := token;                                // id stores x
       i := find-in-symbol-table (id);             // i = 0 is the sentinel location;
                                                   //    i != 0 variable found in ST
       if i = 0 then ERROR;                        // variable not declared
       get (next token);
       if token != "becomes-symbol" then ERROR;    // "becomes-symbol" = 20
       get(next token);
       call expression;
       if token != "." ERROR;
     end;
  end;
```

The procedure statement just described outlines the generation of the following parse tree at the moment the procedure expression is about to be invoked.

As procedure statement calls procedure expression, and expression calls term, and term calls factor, these function calls generate the complete parse tree for the assignment statement. Following, you will find a description of procedures expression, expression-prime, term, term-prime, and factor.

```
procedure expression;                    procedure term;
  begin                                    begin
    call term;                               call factor;
    call expression-prime;                   call term-prime;
  end;                                     end;

procedure expression-prime;              procedure term-prime;
  begin                                    begin
    if token != "+" then ERROR;              if token != "*" then ERROR;
    begin                                    begin
     addop := "+";                            multop := "*";
     get (next token);                        get (next token);
     call term;                               call factor;
     call expression-prime;                   call term-prime;
    end;                                     end;
  end;                                     end;
```

```
procedure factor;
  begin
    if token = "identifier-symbol" then
      begin
        get (next token)              // get identifier name from the
                                      //   token list
        id := token;
        i := find-in-symbol-table (id);  // using sentinel technique,
                                      // i = 0 is the sentinel location.
        if i = 0 then ERROR;          // variable not declared
        id := symbol-table[i].name;   // id found
        print ("id found")
        get (next token)
      end;
    else
    if token = "(" then               // there is a match, "(" found.
      begin
        get (next token)
        call expression;
        if token = ")" then print     // there is a match, ")" found.
        else ERROR;                   // error message: ")" left paren-
                                      //   thesis expected
        get (next token)
      end
    else ERROR;
  end;  // end procedure factor
```

Now that we have described the parsing procedures to implement a parser for the assignment grammar, the next step will be to show how to integrate code generation along with the parsing process. This will be the subject of the next section.

Intermediate Code Generation

Although some compilers might separate parsing and **code generation**, these two stages can be combined into a single module. An excellent example of this approach is the PL/0 compiler developed by Wirth in his textbook *Data Structures + Algorithms = Programs*. To illustrate this approach, we will take the same small program we used in the previous section to explain the top-down parser/code generator. Let us see the example again:

        var x, y; ← Let us work with the declaration first.
        x := y + x.

Recall that the scanner reads in variable declarations and generates tokens to feed in the parser.

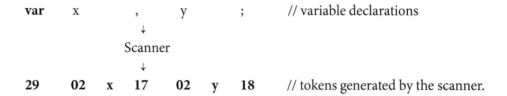

You can see the reserved word **var** (29), which identifies the variable kind. This is followed by the variable token, the value two (02). There are two identifiers preceded by 02 and then the identifier names. There is a comma (17) in between identifiers. The declaration ends up with a semicolon (18) to indicate end of variable declarations. Recall that each time an identifier is inserted into the symbol table, the symbol table pointer (tp) is incremented by one, and it always points to the next free location on the symbol table. The symbol table underneath shows the state of the symbol table once the parser has inserted the variables x and y in the symbol table.

Symbol table after inserting x and y

Index	0	1	2	3	4	5
Kind	–	2	2			
Name		x	y			
Value	–	0	0			
Level	–	0	0			
Address	–	4	5			
Mark	–	0	0			

If you do not recall why the addresses of x and y are 4 and 5 respectively, please take a look at figure 5.1 in chapter 5, where an explanation is given on variable address generation.

We will proceed with the parsing and code generation for the assignment statement using the same example:

var x, y;
x := y + x. ←

The tokens generated by the scanner for this assignment statement are:

02   x   20   02   y   04   02   x   19

Token 20 represents ":=", 04 represents "+", and 19 is ".".

At this stage in the parsing process, the parser reads in token 02 and calls procedure statement (assignment statement). The version of the procedure statement that you will see underneath includes code generation.

```
procedure statement;
  begin
    if token != "identifier-symbol" then ERROR.
    else
      begin
        get (next token)                      // gets name x from the token string.
        id := token;                          // id stores x name
        i := find-in-symbol-table (id);       // i != 0 means x found in symbol table.
        if i = 0 then ERROR;                  // variable not declared
        if symbol_table[i].kind != 2 then ERROR; // It is not a variable identifier
        get (next token);
        if token != "becomes-symbol" then ERROR;
        get(next token);
        call expression;
        if i != 0 then emit (STO, RF[rp], 0, symbol_table{i}.address)
                  rp := rp - 1;
        if token != "." ERROR;                // "." Means EOF.
    end;
end;
```

Note: RF means register file, and rp means register index. If rp = 3, register 3 is selected from the register file; then if we assume that the lexicographical level is zero and variable x address is taken from the symbol table, the instruction generated by the emit instruction would be "STO 3, 0, 4".

Procedure statement will verify whether token = 02 (identifier symbol) then get the next token and verifies whether the variable name is in the symbol table. If it is, the index pointing to the variable entry is kept in variable i. Then the parser get the next token (20) and verifies that it is the expected symbol ":=". Then, if there is a match, it gets a new token and calls procedure expression.

```
procedure expression;                   procedure term;
  begin                                   begin
    call term;                              call factor;
    call expression-prime                   call term-prime
  end;                                    end;
```

By observing procedure expression, you will see that the first instruction calls procedure term. Once in term, you will realize that term calls procedure factor. Let us see what factor does to generate code. Factor compares the token to the identifier symbol (02), and if there is a match, it gets a new token, which is the variable name, and verifies the presence of the name in the symbol table. If it is found, then a free register must be selected from the register file (RF). The RF is handled as stack and managed with a register pointer (rp) whose initial value is rp = −1. To assign a free register, the following operations are necessary: rp = rp + 1, and then use RF[rp].

```
procedure factor;
  begin
    if token = "identifier-symbol" then
      begin
        get (next token)                      // get identifier name from the token
                                              list
        id := token;
        i := find-in-symbol-table (id);       // i != 0 name found in symbol table.
        if i = 0 then ERROR;                  // variable not declared
        rp := rp + 1;                         // to select free register
        emit (LOD, RF[rp], 0, symbol_table[i].address)
        get (next token)
      end;
    else
    if token = "(" then                       // there is a match, "(" found.
      begin
        get (next token)
        call expression;
        if token = ")" then print ("there is a match");  // there is a match,
                                                          ")" found.
        else ERROR;                           // ")" left parenthesis expected
        get (next token)
      end
    else ERROR;
end;  // end procedure factor
      // error message: "(" right parenthesis expected
```

After generating the code LOD 0 0 5 for variable x, procedure factor gets a new token and returns. Then it calls term-prime, but as the token is not equal to "*", term-prime returns, and procedure term ends its execution and then returns to procedure expression. The next instruction in procedure expression is call expression-prime.

```
procedure expression;           procedure term;
  begin                           begin
    call term;                      call factor;
    call expression'                call term'
  end;                            end;
```

Once procedure expression-prime starts execution, this is what it does:

1. Verifies the token = "+".
2. If there is a match, saves the operator in variable addop.
3. Gets next token (in our example 02, which means identifier symbol)
4. Calls term.

```
procedure expression-prime;                procedure term-prime;
  begin                                      begin
    if token != "+" then ERROR;                if token != "*" then ERROR;
    begin                                      begin
      addop := "+";                              multop := "*";
      get (next token);                          get (next token);
      call term;                                 call factor;
      rp = rp + 1;                               rp = rp + 1;
      if addop == "+" then                       if addop == "times(*)" then
        emit (ADD RF[rp], RF[rp], RF[rp+1])        emit (MUL RF[rp], RF[rp],
                                                         RF[rp+1])
      else                                       else
        emit (SUB RF[rp], RF[rp], RF{rp+1});       emit (DIV RF[rp], RF[rp],
                                                         RF[rp+1]);
      call expression-prime;                     call term-prime;
    end;                                       end;
  end;                                       end;
```

Term will call factor, and once in factor, we will follow the steps of factor (as we did before) and realize that the instruction LOD 1 0 4 will be generated. Then, again, there is a return from factor, and as the new token is different from "*", term-prime returns, term returns, expression-prime is called, and as the token is equal to "+", expression-prime generates the operation ADD 0 0 1 and calls itself recursively. Then, as the new token is different from "+", expression-prime returns to expression, and expression returns to procedure statement to the instruction right after call expression. In that instruction, the operation STO 0 0 4 is generated. In summary, the parser/code generator produces the following code:

LOD 0 0 5   // Load y in register R0

```
LOD 1 0 4      // Load x in register R1
ADD 0 0 1      // Get the contents of R0 and R1, add them up, and store the result in R0
STO 0 0 4      // Store R0 in x
```

This code generated for the expression x:= y + x. can be executed in the machine explained in chapter 2.

It is worthwhile to mention that when code is being generated, there is a variable called code index (cx) that points to the memory location where the next line of code must be placed. Each time a line of code is placed in the text (code) segment, cx is incremented by one. The initial value for cx is zero.

Let us explore another example of parsing and code generation, the if-then statement. The grammar rule for the if-then statement is:

<statement> ::= **if** <condition> **then** <statement>

The code snippet to parse the statement **if** <condition> **then** a:= b + 5 and generate code is:

```
if (token = ifsym)                  // does token match the if-simbol?
  begin
   get (next token);                // get a new token
   condition( );                    // call condition and return a true or
                                    false value
   if (token != thensym) then       // does token match the then-simbol?
    error();                        // then expected
   else
    get (next token);               //get a new token
   ctemp := cx;
   emit(JPC, 0, 0, 0);
   statement ( );                   // emit code for a :+ b + 5;
   code[ctemp].m = cx;
  end
```

The way we will parse the statement **if** <condition> **then** a:= b + 5 will be illustrated in the next four figures. Initially, the parser/code generator verifies whether the token read is equal to the "if" symbol. If it does not, some other actions could be taken because the token could be associated with another statement. But let us assume that there is a match, then the program gets a new token and then call condition. We assume that the function condition will be executed and will return a true or false value in register zero. Then the parser/code generator verifies whether the next token represents the reserved word "then." If it does, no error will be emitted, and the program gets a new token. In the next instruction, the code index (cx) is copied in the variable ctemp, as illustrated in figure 6.8.

The next step in the program is the generation of a dummy jump on condition (JPC) instruction, as shown in figure 6.9. This instruction will be modified later on by the parser/code generator to set up the address where the jump will be made if the condition is false.

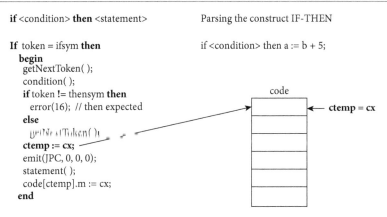

FIGURE 6.8 Code index is copied in a temporary variable.

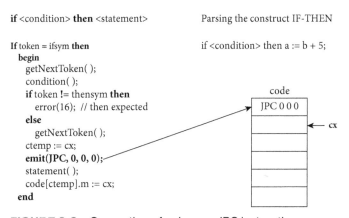

FIGURE 6.9 Generation of a dummy JPC instruction.

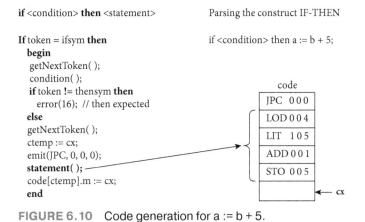

FIGURE 6.10 Code generation for a := b + 5.

Then the function statement is called to parse and generate code for the assignment statement a:= b + 5. As we have studied the parsing and code generation of the assignment statement, we can verify that the code generated for the assignment statement will be the one shown in figure 6.10.

At this moment the code index (cx) is pointing to the next position, just after the last code generated by the assignment statement function, as presented in figure 6.11. Also, you can see in the figure that the JPC dummy instruction, generated earlier in the code generation process, was modified to point to cx. With the modification of the dummy statement, once the condition is evaluated, if the condition is false, the program counter will be overwritten, and the next instruction to be executed will be the one pointed to by cx.

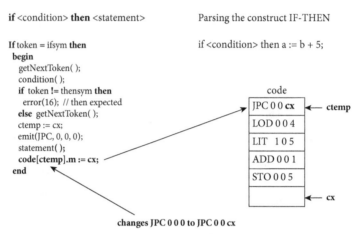

FIGURE 6.11 Modification of the JPC dummy statement.

Now that we know how to parse and generate code for the if-statement, we can include the if-statement in the original grammar proposed at the beginning of this section, and it will look like this:

program ::= var-declaration statement ".".
var-declaration ::= "var" ident {"," ident}";"
statement ::= ident ":=" expression
        | **if** <condition> **then** <statement>
expression ::= term expression-prime
expression-prime ::="+" term expression-prime | ε
term ::= factor term-prime
term-prime ::= "*" factor term-prime | ε
factor ::= "(" expression ")" | ident
ident ::= "v" | "w" | "x" | "y"
digit ::= "0" | "1" | "2" | "3" | "4" | "5" | "6" | "7" | "8" | "9".

Based on Wirth's definition for EBNF, we have the following notation rules:

[ ] means an optional item.
{ } means repeat 0 or more times.
Terminal symbols are enclosed in quotation marks.
A period is used to indicate the end of the definition of a syntactic class.

Let us assume that you are interested in adding the while-do statement to the grammar. Formally speaking, you are interested in extending the grammar with:

while <condition> **do** <statement>

With the experience you have gained so far in inserting the if-then statement into the grammar, it will be easier for you to extend your parser/code generator for the while-do by observing the following code snippet:

```
if (token = whilesym) then
  begin
    ctemp1 := cx;
    getNextToken( );
    condition( );
    ctemp2 := cx;
    gen(JPC 0, 0, 0)         // Insert dummy instruction with no address
    if(token != dosym) then
      error( ); // do expected
    else
      getNextToken( );
    statement ( )
    gen(JMP 0, 0, cx1);
    code[ctemp2].m = cx;     // Fix address in the dummy instructions
  end
```

We have guided you through the necessary background to write a parser/code generator for a simple grammar. We encourage you to continue developing parser/code generation algorithms for the grammar presented in this chapter. This way you will end up with your first compiler.

SUMMARY

This chapter is the natural sequel of chapter 5, and both chapters combined give you a basic knowledge of compilers as a foundation for reading textbooks or taking a compiler course to delve into the vast and beautiful domain of compiler construction. We introduced the concept of context-free grammar (CFG) and the way to describe CFG using the BNF metalanguage and its extension known as EBNF. Then we moved on to top-down parsing and showed two techniques known as left factoring and left recursion, which are useful for shaping grammars for top-down parsing. These two techniques avoid the problems of backtracking and getting into infinites loops when writing a parser. We explained top-down parsing using a small assignment statement grammar and described the necessary procedures to implement it and create parse trees, emphasizing that each syntactic class is implemented as a recursive procedure. As an example, we used an assignment statement of the type "x := y + x". Furthermore, we modified all parsing procedures to interweave parsing and code generation in each one of the procedures. To illustrate the way those parser/code generation procedures work, we took the same example used in parsing to describe code generation for the assignment statement. The code generated was assembly language instructions for the architecture explained in chapters 2 and 3. We presented as well the algorithms for parsing and code generation for the if-then and while-do statements.

EXERCISES

1. What is parsing?
2. What is BNF, and what do we use it for?
3. What is the difference between terminal and nonterminal symbols?
4. Name two approaches to building parsers.
5. Are syntactic classes and productions equivalent concepts?
6. What is EBNF?
7. Name the program that generates the tokens to be consumed by the parser.
8. Consider the following grammar:
   K → K ; W
   K → W
   W → W # M
   W → M
   M → (K)
   M → a

Rewrite the grammar to avoid left recursion (capitals are nonterminals, and all other symbols are terminals).

9. Consider the left recursive grammar:
   $S \to S\beta_1 \mid S\beta_2 \mid S\beta_3 \mid \alpha_1 \mid \alpha_2$
   Rewrite the grammar in order to eliminate left recursion.

10. When generating code, where can the parser get variable addresses?

11. Write a program to implement a virtual machine that interprets the instruction set architecture described in chapters 2 and 3 (programming project).

12. Write a program to implement a parser/code generator for the following grammar.

    The code has to be generated for the VM of question 11 (programming project).

```
program ::= block ".".
block ::= const-declaration var-declaration statement.
constdeclaration ::= ["const" ident "=" number {"," ident "=" number} ";"].
var-declaration ::= ["var" ident {"," ident} ";"].
statement ::= [ident ":=" expression
            | "begin" statement {";" statement} "end"
            | "if" condition "then" statement
            | "while" condition "do" statement
            | "read" ident
            | "write" ident
            | e].
condition ::= | expression rel-op expression.
rel-op ::= "="|"<>"|"<"|"<="|">"|">=".
expression ::= [ "+"|"-"] term {("+"|"-") term}.
term ::= factor {("*"|"/") factor}.
factor ::= ident | number | "(" expression ")".
number ::= digit {digit}.
ident ::= letter {letter | digit}.
digit ;;= "0" | "1" | "2" | "3" | "4" | "5" | "6" | "7" | "8" | "9".
letter ::= "a" | "b" | ... | "y" | "z" | "A" | "B" | ... |"Y" | "Z".
```

Based on Wirth's definition for EBNF, we have the following rules to read the grammar described above:

[ ] means an optional item.
{ } means repeat 0 or more times.
Terminal symbols are enclosed in quotation marks.
A period is used to indicate the end of the definition of a syntactic class.

Bibliographical Notes

Noam Chomsky is considered the creator of context-free languages.[1] John Backus and Peter Naur proposed BNF as a metalanguage to describe the syntax of context-free languages.[2,3] The description of the parser/code generator in this chapter is based in the PL/0 compiler described by Niklaus Wirth in his book *Algorithms + Data Structures = Programs*.[4] The books by Karen Lemone[5] and Kenneth Louden[6] present an accessible introduction to parsing. Per Brinch Hansen[7] gives detailed implementation of a parser and code generator for a virtual machine. The main source to delve deeper into the parser, code generation, and all nuts and bolts on compiler construction is the book *Compilers: Principles, Techniques, and Tools* by Aho, Lam, Sethi, and Ullman.[8]

Bibliography

1. N. Chomsky and M. P. Schützenberger, "The Algebraic Theory of Context Free Languages," in *Computer Programming and Formal Languages*. Vol. 35, Edited by P. Braffort, D. Hirschberg, North-Holland, 1963, pp. 118–161.
2. J. Backus, "The Syntax and Semantics of the Proposed International Algebraic Language of the Zurich ACM-GAMM Conference," IFIP congress, 1959, pp. 125–131.
3. J. Backus, F. Bauer, J. Green, C. Katz, J. McCarthy, A. Perlis, H. Rutishauser, et. al., "Algol 60 revised report," Edited by P. Naur. *Communication of Association for Computing Machinery*, 6, no. 1 (1963), pp. 1–17.
4. N. Wirth, *Algorithm + Data Structures = Programs*. Upper Saddle River, NJ: Prentice Hall, 1976.
5. K. Lemone, *Fundamentals of Compilers: An Introduction to Computer Language Translation*. Boca Raton, FL: CRC, 1992.
6. K. Louden, *Compiler Construction: Principles and Practice*. Boston, MA, PWS, 1997.
7. P. Brinch Hansen, *On Pascal Compilers*. Englewood Cliffs, NJ: Prentice Hall, 1985.
8. A. Aho, M. Lam, R. Sethi, and J. Ullman, *Compilers: Principles, Techniques, and Tools*, 2nd ed. Boston, MA, Addison-Wesley, 2007.

Chapter 7

Assemblers, Linkers, and Loaders

One of the principal goals of my books is to show how high-level constructions are actually implemented in machines, not simply to show how they are applied.
—Donald Knuth
The Art of Computer Programming, vol. 1

CHAPTER OBJECTIVES

- To explore assemblers as translators from assembly language to object code.
- To describe the static linker as a program that combines more than one object code into a single executable linkable file.
- To discuss the different type of loaders; specifically, absolute loader, boot loader, and relocating loaders.

INTRODUCTION

Assembly language is considered a low-level programming language, and it defines the instruction set architecture (ISA) of a specific processor. Therefore, we could say that the processor is basically an interpreter of assembly language instructions. Assemblers are programs that translate assembly language into an executable version of the program, which we refer to as object code or executable linkable file. Linkers are programs, which can take two or more object code files to create a single executable file. Loaders are programs whose main task is to store an executable file in the computer memory for execution.

We begin this chapter with a description of the process of translating assembly language to object code or executable file. Then we introduce the static linking step as a way to combine several object codes into an executable linkable file. Loaders are presented as system programs that store user programs in memory for execution. Finally, three types of loaders will be described: the absolute loader, which loads a program in a fix memory location; the boot loader, which loads the operating system; and the relocating loader, which loads a program in any memory location.

VOCABULARY

This is a list of keywords that herald the concepts we will study in this chapter. They are organized in chronological order and will appear in the text in bold. We invite you to take a look at these keywords to find out which ones you are familiar with.

Assembler	Header	Executable and Linkable Format (ELF)
Object code	Text section	Static linking
Assembler directives	Data section	Linker
Labels	Relocation section	Absolute loader
.begin	Symbol table section	Bootstrap loader
.data	Debugging section	Relocation loader
.end	Loader	Relocation bits
Object file format	a.out	

ACTIVATING PRIOR KNOWLEDGE

In this section we will present a series of activities. In some of them you can choose one or more options. Sometimes, if you do not agree with the given answers to choose from, you will be allowed to give your own answer. By the way, this is not a test.

1. What is the language a computer executes?

    Object code ☐
    Binary ☐
    Assembly language ☐

2. What is the name of the program that translates assembly language into an object code file?

    Compiler ☐   Interpreter ☐   JVM ☐   Assembler ☐

3. Assume that ADD can be encoded as 0001 and we can use three registers identified as A, B, and C. If A is coded as 0011, B as 0010, and C as 0001, write down using binary digits the instruction ADD C B A.

4. How many instructions can be encoded using 4 bits, excluding 0000?

    15 ☐
    12 ☐
    16 ☐
    If the answer is not given above, please give yours. _____

5. An assembler is a program that translates
   a. From Python to binary ☐
   b. From assembly language to binary ☐
   c. From object code to assembly language ☐
   d. From assembly language to object code ☐

6. To execute a program, the OS must load the program from a disk. Where does the operating system load programs in a computer system?

   In the CPU ☐
   In memory ☐
   50 percent in memory and 50 percent in the CPU ☐

7. Skim the chapter and pay attention to the words written in **bold**. Count the number of words you are familiar with.

8. Are programs always loaded in the same memory location?

   Yes ☐   No ☐   Very often ☐   I don't know ☐

9. The operating system uses the loader to load user programs from a disk. How are the loader and operating systems loaded into memory?

Translating Assembly Language to Object Code

Assembly languages could be considered the first major step toward the development of high-level notations to program computers. Kathleen Britten is credited as the implementer of the first assembly language. **Assemblers** are programs that translate assembly language into an executable version of the program, and they were developed in the late 1940s. We will describe a very simple assembly language to explain the translation process carried out by the assembler. Nevertheless, we must recall that to program a computer in assembly language, the programmer needs a basic knowledge of computer organization. In this regard, we will describe the different components of a hypothetical one address tiny computer.

- The computer has a processor with three registers: the accumulator (A) for data values; the program counter (PC), which points to the next instruction to be executed; and the instruction register (IR) to place the instructions in.
- All input/output devices are connected to the accumulator.
- The computer has a main memory (RAM). We can assume any size, and we refer at it as MEM.
- The instruction format consists of two fields:

    Opcode → Tells the computer the action to be carried out. (opocde = operation code)
    Operand → This field identifies a <memory address> or a <device number>.

There are nine instructions in the tiny computer assembly language, and we describe them as follows.

opcode (binary)	mnemonic	meaning
0001	LOAD <x>	A ← MEM[x]
0010	ADD <x>	A ← A + MEM[x]
0011	STORE <x>	MEM[x] ← A
0100	SUB <x>	A ← A − MEM[x]
0101	IN <Device_#>	A ← read from Device
0110	OUT <Device_#>	A → output to Device
0111	HALT	Stop
1000	JMP <x>	PC ← x
1001	SKIPZ	If A = 0 Skip next instruction

Example:

Instruction: LOAD <17>

Meaning: A ← MEM[17]

Description: Load in accumulator the contents of memory location 17.

As you can see, all instructions work with the accumulator register except JMP and HALT. Therefore, there is no need to explicitly include the accumulator register in the instructions, and that is why we write "LOAD <17>" instead of "LOAD A, <17>". At the bit level, the instruction format of this one-address architecture consists of 16 bits: 4 bits to represent instruction opcodes (op) and 12 bits for addresses or device numbers.

op	address		
0001	0000	0001	0001

For instance, the instruction LOAD <17> would be coded as "0001 0000 0001 0001" and the instruction to input a value is IN <5>, where 5 identifies the keyboard. The encoding of IN <5> would be "0101 0000 0000 0101". Figure 7.1 shows a view of the computer organization of the tiny computer. In this arrangement, the instruction LOAD <1> is stored in memory location 13, and the contents of memory location 1 is the value 33.

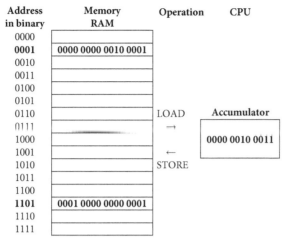

FIGURE 7.1 Instruction LOAD <1> is executed, and the value stored in location <1> is copied into the accumulator.

Now we will proceed to give you a closer description of all the instruction set architecture of the tiny computer.

01 - LOAD <X>
Loads the contents of memory location X into A (A stands for accumulator).

02 - ADD <X>
The data value stored at address X is added to the A register, and the result is stored back in A.

03 - STORE <X>
Store the contents of the A register into memory location X.

04 - SUB <X>
Subtracts the value located at address X from the value stored in A and stores the result back in A.

05 - IN <Device #>
A value from the input device is transferred into A.

06 - OUT <Device #>
Print out the contents of A in the output device.

Device #	Device
5	Keyboard
7	Printer
9	Screen

For instance, you can write **IN <5> "23"** where "23" stands for the value you are typing in. It is worthwhile to let you know that device numbers were randomly chosen.

07 - HALT
The machine stops execution of the program (control returns to the OS).

08 - JMP <X>
Causes an unconditional branch to address X. PC ← X (the next instruction to be executed is the one at address X).

09 - SKIPZ
If the contents of A = 0, the next instruction is skipped.

Another interpretation for SKIPZ is: If A = 0 then PC = PC + 1. The reason is that in the fetch cycle the PC is incremented by one to point to the next instruction. Then SKIPZ increments the PC by one again if the condition is met, and this means that one instruction is skipped.

Figure 7.2 illustrates a more detailed view of the tiny computer executing the fetch cycle. Initially, the PC is pointing to the instruction placed in memory location 20. When the fetch cycle begins, the instruction is placed in the instruction register (IR), and the program counter is incremented by one to point to the next instruction to be executed (the one located at memory address 21) in the next fetch cycle. When the instruction in the IR is executed, the computer prompts the user to input a value and waits for the user's action. The user types in the value 18 and hits the Return key. At that moment the value 18 would be placed in the accumulator register (A). This is indicated by the dashed line in figure 7.2.

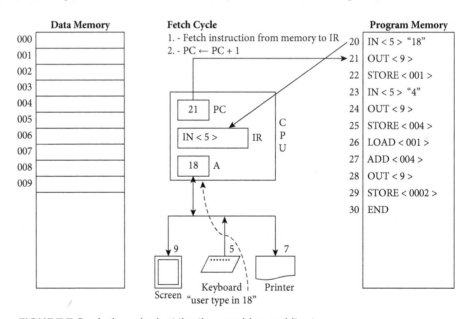

FIGURE 7.2 A closer look at the tiny machine architecture.

As an introduction to the translation process carried out by an assembler, we will use a small program to give you an idea of the two-step process. In figure 7.3 you will see a small program on the top left-hand side, and in the top right-hand side you can see a table with all instructions of the tiny computer and their binary representation. From now on, we will refer to this table as the opcode table. Figure 7.3 shows an assembler reading in a program and transforming each instruction into a binary representation. To convert each instruction opcode into binary, the opcode table is used. For instance, if the instruction "ADD <001>" is read in, the assembler will search in the opcode table the operator ADD, and once found, it will be replaced by the binary value associated with operation ADD. Then for the address, which is expressed as a decimal number, a simple conversion from decimal to binary is carried out. Thus, "ADD <001>" is transformed into "0010 0000 0000 0001". Following the same steps, each instruction is converted into binary. The binary version of the program is called **object code**. Note that if an instruction does not use an address or device number, padding zeros are used in the address field.

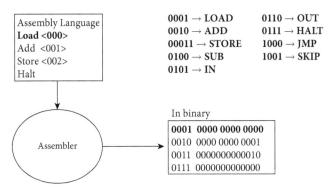

FIGURE 7.3 Translation from assembly language to object code.

To enhance the tiny assembly language, we will add others component needed by the assembler to carry out the translation process. These new components are call **assembler directives** and **labels**. The directives or pseudo-operations are incorporated in the assembler to invoke a specific service from the assembler. These pseudo-operations do not generate code, and the three directives we will be using are ".begin", ".data", and ".end". A description of the service requested by each directive is explain briefly as follows.

.begin	→	tells the assembler where the program instructions begin
.data	→	tells the assembler to reserve a memory location
.end	→	tells the assembler where the program ends

Labels, on the other hand, are symbolic names used to identify memory locations. The next example depicts the usage of assembler directives.

.begin

"Assembly language instructions" (text area)

halt *(return to OS)*
.data *(to reserve a memory location. Tells the assembler where data begin)*

"Data area"

.end *(tells the assembler where the program ends)*

Note: the directive ".end" can be used to indicate where the program starts by using a label next to it. (For example: ".end <insert label here>").

Label	Opcode	Address	
start	.begin		
	in	x005	
	store	a	
	in	X005	
	store	b	Text section (code)
	load	a	
	sub	TWO	
	add	b	
	out	x009	
	halt		
a	.data	0	
b	.data	0	
two	.data	2	Data section
	.end	start	

FIGURE 7.4 Assembly language example program with directives.

Figure 7.4 shows the usage of directives and labels. Directives will help the assembler identify different parts of the program in the translation process. Labels will allow the assembler to create the symbol table. The program in figure 7.4 reads in two values and stores them in variables a and b respectively. Then it computes "a - 2 + b," displays the result, and stops. It is worthwhile mentioning that the letter "x" in front of a number identifies the number as hexadecimal. You might notice that in this assembly language, each ".data" directive is used to reserve memory space for a variable or constant, and the initial value is given for each variable. As you might have noticed, the instruction set of the tiny machine does not provide an instruction to multiply, but that can be solved by writing a program to carry out that task. In figure 7.5 you will see an assembly language program that multiply two numbers. In this example, you will appreciate a couple of interesting details: the usage of comments and the starting memory location expressed in hexadecimal. This address will tell the loader where in memory the program has to be loaded.

	Label	Opcode	Address
01		; This is	
02		; a comment	
03	start	.begin	x200
04	here	LOAD	sum
05		ADD	a
06		STORE	sum
07		LOAD	b
08		SUB	one
09		STORE	b
0A		SKIPZ	
0B		JMP	here
0C		LOAD	sum
0D		OUT	x009
0E		HALT	
0F	sum	.data	x000
10	a	.data	x005
11	b	.data	x003
12	one	.data	x001
13		.end	start

This program is computing a x b.

FIGURE 7.5 Assembly language program to multiply two numbers.

We will use the latter example to explain the two steps used by the assembler to translate the program into object code. In the first pass the assembler scans the program line by line, identifies labels, and creates a symbol table; this is carried out by inserting the label names and their associated addresses in the symbol table, as depicted in figure 7.6.

	Label	Opcode	Address	
01		; This is		
02		; a comment		
03	start	.begin	x200	
04	here	LOAD	sum	x200
05		ADD	a	x201
06		STORE	sum	x202
07		LOAD	b	x203
08		SUB	one	x204
09		STORE	b	x205
0A		SKIPZ		x206
0B		JMP	here	x207
0C		LOAD	sum	x208
0D		OUT	x009	x209
0E		HALT		x20A
0F	sum	.data	x000	x20B
10	a	.data	x005	x20C
11	b	.data	x003	x20D
12	one	.data	x001	x20E
13		.end	start	x20F

Symbol Table

here	x200
sum	x20B
a	x20C
b	x20D
one	x20E

symbol   address

In pass one the assembler examines the program line by line in order to built up the symbol table.

There is an entry in the symbol table for each label found in the program.

FIGURE 7.6 Creation of the symbol table in the assembler first pass.

Then, using the symbol table created in the first pass and the opcode table, the assembler, initiates the second pass to translate the assembly program to object code. This translation is done by replacing each opcode with its binary representation and using the symbol table addresses to calculate the instruction addresses as PC-relative addresses. Symbol table and opcode table data structures are shown below.

opcode table		Symbol table	
opcode	mnemonic	symbol	address
0001	LOAD	here	x200
0010	ADD	sum	x20B
0011	STORE	a	x20C
0100	SUB	b	x20D
0101	IN	one	x20E
0110	OUT		
0111	HALT		
1000	JUMP		
1001	SKIPZ		

For instance, the offset between the instruction "LOAD sum" and the "declaration of sum" is 10, because when LOAD sum is fetched for execution, the PC is pointing to the next instruction, "ADD a". That means that the address to be plugged into the instruction is "pc + offset = 10". Observing figure 7.7, you will realize that the instruction in line 04,

LOAD sum is translated as "0001 0000 0000 **1010**"

Label		Opcode	Address				Object code
01		; This is					
02		; a comment					
03	start	.begin	x200			x200	0001000000001010 (10 is the offset)
04	here	LOAD	sum	PC →		x201	0010000000001010
05		ADD	a			x202	0011000000001000 (8 is the offset)
06		STORE	sum		o	x203	0001000000001001
07		LOAD	b		f	x204	0100000000001001
08		SUB	one		f	x205	0011000000000111
09		STORE	b		s	x206	
0A		SKIPZ			e	x207	
0B		JMP	here		t	x208	All addresses are
0C		LOAD	sum			x209	pc-relative. (PC + offset)
0D		OUT				x20A	
0E		HALT				x20B	Recall: PC is always pointing to
0F	sum	.data	x000			x20C	the next instruction to be fetched.
10	a	.data	x005			x20D	
11	b	.data	x003			x20E	
12	one	.data	x001			x20F	
13		.end	start				

FIGURE 7.7 Partial generation of the object code file in the assembler second pass.

The address is 0000 0000 1010 (decimal 10) because that is the distance from the address PC is at to the place variable sum is declared in. Similarly, you can take a closer look at the instruction in line 06, which is "STORE sum" and is translated into "0010 0000 0000 **1000**". In this case variable sum is at a distance of 8 from the PC.

Another interesting instruction to look at in figure 7.8 is the one at line 0B (JMP here). As the instruction indicates a jump backward, the address in the instructions has to be a negative number, and we will express it in one's complement. Therefore, the instructions will be translated as:

$$\text{JMP here} \rightarrow 1000\ 1111\ 1111\ 1000\ //\ (-7)$$

Label		Opcode	Address			Object code	
01		; This is					
02		; a comment					
03	start	.begin	x200				
04	here	LOAD	sum		x200	0001000000**1010**	(9 is the offset)
05		ADD	a	PC →	x201	0010000000001010	
06		STORE	sum	o	x202	001100000000**1000**	(7 is the offset)
07		LOAD	b	f	x203	0001000000001001	
08		SUB	one	f	x204	0100000000001001	
09		STORE	b		x205	0011000000000111	
0A		SKIPZ		s	x206	1001000000000000	
0B		JMP	here	e	x207	1000**1111 1111 1000** (-7)	
0C		LOAD	sum	t	x208	0001000000000010	
0D		OUT	x009		x209	0110000000000000	
0E		HALT			x20A	0111000000000000	
0F	sum	.data	x000		x20B	0000000000000000	
10	a	.data	x005		x20C	0000000000000101	
11	b	.data	x003		x20D	0000000000000011	
12	one	.data	x001		x20E	0000000000000001	
13		.end	start				

One's complement

FIGURE 7.8 Object code file generated in the assembler second pass.

In figure 7.8 you will see that the whole assembly program has been translated into binary, and in general we refer to this as object code. However, the object code is not only the data section and the text section as shown in figure 7.8; it has several sections. For instance, an **object file format** or executable file format could have the following sections.

Header: In the header we will find information about all sections within the file; for example, program name or id. In addition, the header has the starting address and length for each section within the file.

Text section: Executable instructions.

Data section: Data.

Relocation section: Addresses to be fixed by the loader and/or linker.

Symbol table section: Global symbols in the program (labels in the program).

Debugging section: Source file and line number information, and the description of data structures.

In figure 7.9 we show an object file with fewer sections to illustrate the concepts of starting section and section length. In the figure, the section starting addresses point to the beginning of each section within the file; and concerning section length, as an example, we show the length of the relocation section only.

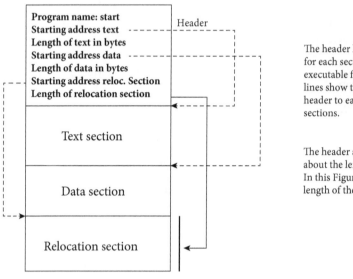

FIGURE 7.9 Executable linkable format.

The object code or executable file resides in the hard drive and is place there by the assembler. To execute the object file, another program called the **loader** is required. Loaders load programs from the hard drive into memory for execution.

The executable format we have explained in this chapter will allow you to grasp the concept of object code or executable file in a straightforward manner. Our format resembles the **a.out** format of early versions of the UNIX system. Figure 7.10 shows the UNIX a.out format. Executable formats in general are more elaborate, and we invite readers to explore the **Executable and Linkable Format** (**ELF**), which is object code format used on modern Linux systems.

A Note on Static Linking

Sometimes we need to combine the object code produced by our program with libraries that implement common functions or with other object programs we have previously written and

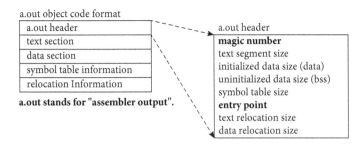

magic number: indicates type of executable file.
bss: is an acronym for block storage start.
entry point: starting address of the program

FIGURE 7.10 Assembler out format of original UNIX systems.

compiled. Libraries are precompile functions that can be shared by all programs. This process of combining two or more object codes into a single executable file is called **static linking** and is carried out by a program called the **linker**. The input of the linker is object code, and library functions in object file format, and the output is a single executable file. It is worth mentioning that object code can be executed directly without passing through the static linker. However, using library functions allows us to avoid rewriting functions that are already implemented and can be used by the programs we write. Another view of the linking process is the creation of an executable file from several modules of a large program that have been compiled separately and need to be merged into a single executable file for execution. This is called separate compilation, and it has the advantage of each single component of the large program being able to be modified and compiled independently of the other files without the necessity of compiling the whole program again. Figure 7.11 illustrates the linking process.

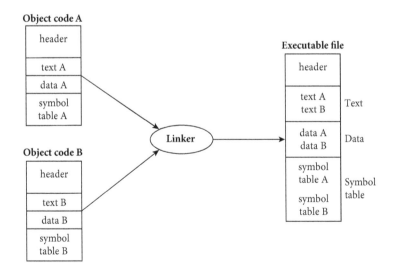

FIGURE 7.11 Linker merging two object codes into an executable file.

Loaders

Loader programs along with interrupt handlers could be considered the first step toward the development of an operating system. The concept of a loader program was a significant step because loaders were programs capable of loading programs into memory for execution. Without loaders, the programs had to be loaded manually one instruction after the other, in binary, using a set of switches in a dashboard. There are different types of loaders, and we will present three of them in this chapter:

Absolute loaders: load a program into a specific memory location.

Bootstrap loaders: stand-alone programs not residing in memory (RAM), which are used to boot the computer system and load the operating system.

Relocating loaders: load a program in any memory location where there is room available.

Absolute Loader

Assemblers and loaders could be considered the first two pieces of systems software developed to help humans write programs in a symbolic language and load the executable program in the computer memory for execution. These loaders were called absolute loaders, and they were able to load an object code in a specific memory location. In those early days when the first loaders were created, the programmer was responsible for including the absolute address in the directive ".begin" or ".orig". The program in the translation process was contained in a single object file, and the file was loaded in memory as a monolithic entity. The steps taken by the absolute loader are as follows.

1. The header record is checked to verify that the correct program has been presented for loading.
2. The absolute loader will load the program at a memory location, say x200, as indicated in the header in figure 7.12.
3. Each text record is read and placed at the indicated address in memory.
4. Each data record is read and moved to the indicated memory address. All data is placed right after text.
5. When the "end" record (EOF) is encountered, the loader passes on control to the user program by jumping to the specified address (x200 in our example) to begin execution.

Figure 7.12 illustrates the steps taken by the absolute loader for loading a user program in a specific memory location. The area used for the program is called the runtime environment or process address space. The loader gets from the header the program starting address and starts placing the text from that memory location onward. Once all instructions have been loaded, the loader begins to store the data section into the memory data area.

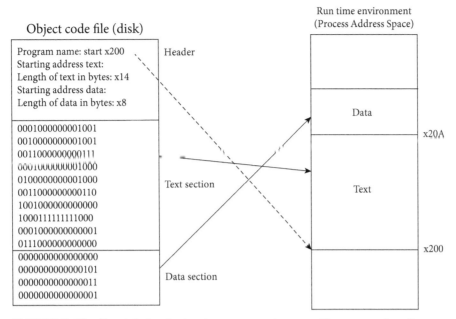

FIGURE 7.12 Absolute loader loads a program in a specific memory location.

Bootstrap Loader

At this point, a question is perhaps wandering around in your mind:

If the loader has to be in memory to run and load the user program, how is the loader program loaded into memory?

To answer this question, we must present the concept of the initial program loader (IPL). Early programmable computers had toggle switches in the front panel that allowed the operator to place a small program into memory before starting the CPU. This program was called the initial program loader. In modern computer systems, the initial program loader is called the bootstrap loader. The bootstrap process begins with the CPU executing a stand-alone program contained in ROM or erasable programmable read-only memory (EPROM) at a predefined address, whose elementary functionality is to search for a device eligible to participate in booting and to load into memory another program from a specific address in the device. The bootstrap loader does not have the full functionality of an operating system, but it is capable of loading into memory a more elaborate loader that we will call "loader2". Figure 7.13 depicts these actions.

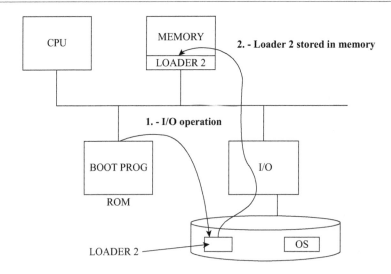

FIGURE 7.13 Bootstrap loader loads loader2 in memory.

Loader2 is a program that, once in memory, takes control of the computer system and is capable of loading another program. An example of a loader2 to load a program starting at location zero is given below.

	Loader2	
0		
	OS will be loaded here	
99998		
99999	LC = 0	LC = Location counter
100000	**read**	Read a record from program in disk.
100001	**if** (EOF) **then** PC = 0	If EOF pass control of CPU to the OS.
100010	**Else** {STORE at LC	Store the read record at location LC.
100011	LC = LC + 1	Increment LC by one.
100100	JMP 100000}	Jump back to location 100000.

Now that loader2 is in control of the computer system, it will be able to load another program into memory and transfer control of the computer system to the new loaded program; let us assume that the program to be loaded is the operating system. Once the operating system has been loaded, the loader transfers control of the computer system to the operating system by setting the PC = 0. From that moment onward, the operating system, using a loader, will be able to load user programs for execution. Figure 7.14 shows the second step of the bootstrap process.

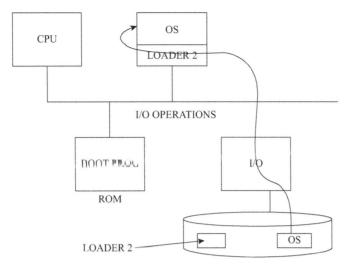

FIGURE 7.14 Loader2 loads OS and transfers control to the OS.

Relocating Loaders

Absolute loaders load a program at a specific memory location, but it is often desirable to have two or more programs residing in memory sharing the different resources of a computer system. Let us assume a situation where two programs have to be loaded at the same memory location; the relocating loader would load one of the two programs in a different location and would modify instruction addresses to resolve the references within the program. Relocating loaders are able to load a program into memory wherever there is a free space big enough to meet the memory requirements. The example we will use to illustrate the way a relocating loader works is a variant of an example proposed by Peter Calingaert.

It would be impractical to assign starting addresses to each program to plan program execution, and therefore we can assume that assemblers generate code that starts at address zero for all programs; but they can also emit with each line of text (code) **relocation bits** indicating what fields in the object code must be modified when the program is loaded in an address different from zero. For example, if the program will be loaded at address 50, relocation bits equal to 1 indicate what part of the instruction must be modified, which means that the value 50 must be added to that part of the instruction. In the example below, the relocation bits associated with the instruction "13 **33 35**" are "0**11**". The interpretation here is 13 stays as is because its associated relocation bit has value zero. The address 33 has its associated relocation bit with value one; this means that the relocation address is 83 (33 + 50). Similarly, 35 is transformed into 85 as its relocation address.

Loc#	Len	Rbits	Text	RLoc#	Rtext
00	3	011	13 33 35	50	13 83 85

In this example,

Loc# → Stands for memory address of the instruction.

Len → Stands for instruction length in bytes.

Rbits → Relocation bits 0 means as is and 1 means must be modified.

Text → Object code before relocation.

Rloc# → Memory address where the program will be loaded.

Rtext → Object code after relocation.

An example of relocation is shown in figure 7.15; the example is a variant of the one presented in Calingaert's textbook on assemblers, compilers, and program translation. In the example, you will see on the left-hand side a program written in assembly language; in the middle, the translation of the program before relocation; and on the right-hand side, the program after relocation. Taking a closer look, you will see that all memory addresses to be modified in the before-relocation version of the program have their relocation bits equal to one. The instruction format has two fields, and therefore we will use two relocation bits: one bit associated with the opcode and the other for the address. The program will be loaded starting at memory address 50.

	Source program			Before relocation			After relocation	
Label	opcode	address	Loc #	Len	reloc	text	Loc #	text
00	in	x005	00	2	00	5 005	50	5 005
01	store	a	01	2	01	3 010	50	3 050
02	in	x005	02	2	00	5 005	52	5 005
03	store	b	03	2	01	3 011	53	3 051
04 here	load	sum	04	2	01	1 00F	54	1 05F
05	add	a	05	2	01	2 010	55	2 050
06	store	sum	06	2	01	3 00F	56	3 05F
07	load	b	07	2	01	1 011	57	1 051
08	sub	one	08	2	01	4 012	58	4 052
09	store	b	09	2	01	3 011	59	3 051
0A	skipz		0A	2	00	9 000	5A	9 000
0B	jmp	here	0B	2	01	8 004	5B	8 054
0C	load	sum	0C	2	01	1 00F	5C	1 05F
0D	out	x009	0D	2	01	6 009	5D	6 009
0E	halt		0E	2	00	7 000	5E	7 000
0F sum	.data	x000	0F	2	00	0 000	5F	0 000
10 a	.data	x000	10	2	00	0 000	60	0 000
11 b	.data	x000	11	2	00	0 000	61	0 000
12 one	.data	x001	12	2	00	0 001	62	0 001

Relocation constant to be added is 50

FIGURE 7.15 Relocation loader example.

Taking a closer look at figure 7.15, you can see that the relocation bits and instructions are interleaved. This would make the loading of the program more cumbersome because the loader has to discern between bits that represent instructions and the one representing the relocation bits. This problem can be resolved by collecting all relocation bits into a relocation segment in the object file; this way, the loader can read in an instruction from the text segment and the relocation bits associated with the instruction from the relocation segment. Recall that the header in the object format has the starting address and length of the text and relocation segments. Figure 7.16 shows a view of the object code file, highlighting the first four instructions and associated bits of the example illustrated in figure 7.15.

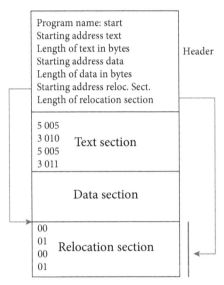

FIGURE 7.16 Relocation segment in the object code format.

SUMMARY

In this chapter we reviewed the concepts of assemblers and loaders. We introduced a tiny assembly language instruction set architecture (ISA) for a hypothetical one address machine (tiny machine). Then we explained the actions taken by each instruction when they are executed. The ISA allows us to write simple programs for the tiny computer. Then we presented a two-pass assembler and explained the process of translating assembly instructions into object code. We presented the concept of linking and gave an example to illustrate the linking step. Then we introduced the concept of loaders, and three type of loaders programs were described: the absolute loader, which is able to load a program in a specific memory location; the bootstrap loader, which does not reside in memory but is a stand-alone program that is able to load another program into memory and to pass on control of the CPU to the new loaded program; and relocation loaders, which are programs capable of loading a program in any available memory location if the space is large enough for the program to fit in.

EXERCISES

1. Write down a program to multiply three numbers using the ISA of the tiny machine.
2. Transform the following program written in binary into tiny machine assembly language.

    0001 0000 0001 0001
    0010 0000 0010 0000
    0011 0000 0001 0010

3. Convert the following program expressed in hexadecimal into assembly language of the tiny machine.

    10 12
    20 0F
    30 18

4. What is the difference between an assembler and a loader?
5. Name four fields found in the header of the object file format explained in this chapter.
6. What is the difference between a relocating loader and relocating bits?
7. Does assemble-and-go mean to translate to object code and load the program for execution?
8. What is a linker?

Bibliographical Notes

For many years, small assembly languages have been designed for educational purposes to initiate students into the area without getting into the complexities of more elaborate assembly languages, such as the one available for actual processors. We believe that once students understand the basis of assembly language, they are better prepared for an in-depth study of assembly language, assemblers, linkers, and loaders. There are two must-read textbooks related to designing a computer and using programming notations to program them.[1,2] A good description of assemblers and loaders can be found in Barrow.[3] In *Assemblers, Compilers, and Program Translation*,[4] Peter Calingaert presents a detailed description of assemblers, linkers, and loaders. An in-depth description of linkers can be found in O'Hallaron and Bryant,[1] and a good illustration of relocating loaders can be found in Beck.[5] An excellent source that explains assemblers and loaders in detail is presented by David Salomon.[6] Patterson and Hennessy[2] provide a detailed introduction to assemblers, linkers, loaders, and object file format. Booth and Britten[7] and Burks, Goldstine, and Von Neuman[8] provide seminal works in the area of digital design of computers and implementation of computer notations to program them.

Bibliography

1. R. E. Bryant and D. R. O'Hallaron, *Computer Systems: A Programmer's Perspective*, 3rd ed. Boston, MA: Prentice Hall, 2016.
2. D. A. Petterson and J. L. Hennessy, *Computer Organization and Design: The Hardware/Software Interface ARM Edition*. Cambridge, MA: Morgan Kaufmann, 2017.
3. D. W. Barrow, *Assemblers and Loaders*, 3rd ed. New York: North-Holland, 1978.
4. P. Calingaert, *Assemblers, Compilers, and Program Translation*. Potomac, MD: Computer Science Press, 1979
5. L. Beck, *System Software: An Introduction to System Programming*, 3rd ed. Addison Wesley, Reading, MA, 1996.
6. D. Solomon, *Assemblers and Loaders*. Chichester, West Sussex: Ellis Horwood, 1993.
7. A. Booth and K. Britten, *General Consideration in the Design of an all Purpose Electronic Digital Computer*. Princeton, NJ: Princeton University Press, 1947.
8. A. W. Burks, H. H. Goldstine, and J. Von Neuman, *Preliminary Discussion of the Logical Design of an Electronic Computer Instrument*. Princeton, NJ: Princeton University Press, 1946.

Credits

Fig. 7.6: P. Calingaert, "Assembler Pass One," Assemblers, Compilers, and Program Translation. Copyright © 1979 by Springer Verlag Heidelberg.

Fig. 7.7: P. Calingaert, "Assembler Pass Two," Assemblers, Compilers, and Program Translation. Copyright © 1979 by Springer Verlag Heidelberg.

Fig. 7.8: P. Calingaert, "Assembler Object Code," Assemblers, Compilers, and Program Translation. Copyright © 1979 by Springer Verlag Heidelberg.

Fig. 7.15: P. Calingaert, "Relocating Loader," Assemblers, Compilers, and Program Translation. Copyright © 1979 by Springer Verlag Heidelberg.

Chapter 8

Understanding the Interrupt Mechanism

Because your question searches for deep meaning, I shall explain in simple words.
—Dante Alighieri
  Inferno, canto II, trans. Mark Musa

INTRODUCTION

An operating system (OS) is a complex program or set of programs, and in general it is defined as an event-driven program. The three main functions of an operating system are to manage system resources efficiently, create a friendly interface between users and the computer system, and provide an environment for user programs to run. The interrupt mechanism is an essential component of a CPU because it allows the interaction between the operating system and user programs. Furthermore, the interrupt mechanism tells the OS when to take control of the computer system to assist a user program or to take the appropriate actions to protect user and system programs from malicious or undebugged user programs.

VOCABULARY

This is a list of keywords that herald the concepts we will study in this chapter. They are organized in chronological order and will appear in

CHAPTER OBJECTIVES

- To understand the implementation of an interrupt mechanism.
- To discuss the usage of the interrupt mechanism and other registers for knowing the status of the running program.
- To understand the difference between software interrupts and hardware interrupts.
- To explore the implementation of system calls and their usage to allow user programs to request service from the operating system.

the text in bold. We invite you to take a look at these keywords to find out which ones you are familiar with.

Interrupt mechanism	Mode	Timer register
Interrupts	User mode	Process control block (PCB)
Trap	System mode	System call
Overflow	Two-mode mechanism	Supervisor call (SVC)
Flag	Privileged instruction (PI) flag	System call vector table (SCVT)
OV flag	Mode bit	SVC flag
Interrupt handler (IH)	Program status word (PSW)	Runtime library
Operating system	OLD-PC	Interrupt vector
New program counter (NEWPC)	OLD-R0	Kernel
Hardware/software interface	I/O flag	Software interrupts
Fence register	I/O interrupt	Hardware interrupts
Memory protection (MP) flag	Timer	
Privileged instruction	Timer interrupt (TI) flag	

ACTIVATING PRIOR KNOWLEDGE

In this section we will present a series of activities. In some of them you can choose one or more options. Sometimes, if you do not agree with the given answers to choose from, you will be allowed to give your own answer. By the way, this is not a test.

1. Is an interrupt equivalent to an unexpected event?

2. Skim the chapter and pay attention to the words written in **bold**. Count the number of words you are familiar with.

3. Why does the operating system provide a stack for each running program?

4. How does the operating system know that user programs need assistance?

    A flag in the CPU ☐
    An unexpected event indicator ☐
    An interrupt ☐

    If the answer is not given above, please give yours. _____

5. How does the user request service from the operating system?

    With an SVC ☐
    With a system call ☐
    Using Extracode ☐

    If the answer is not given above, please give yours. _____

6. Why does a timer allow the operating system retake control of the CPU?

To detect an infinite loop in a program	☐
To prevent a user program monopolizing the CPU	☐
The two statements above are true .	☐

7. Do you recall the meaning of the following concepts from previous chapters?

Program counter (PC)	☐
Stack pointer (SP)	☐
Base pointer (BP)	☐

8. Think about the concept of hardware/software interface. What does it mean to you?

9. When the operating system is running, does it have its own stack?

10. Look up the meaning of the word *kernel* in a dictionary.

From Fetch-Execute to Fetch-Execute-Interrupt

We will simplify the architecture presented in chapter 2 by using a subset of its ISA to focus exclusively in the **interrupt mechanism**. The simplified version of VM/0 will have only one register, and the instruction format will have only three fields: opcode, a register address (R0), and a memory address (ADDRESS). The reduced ISA consists of four instructions:

01 - LOAD R0, <ADDRESS>
Load contents at memory location ADDRESS into register R0.

02 - ADD R0, <ADDRESS>
Add contents of memory location ADDRESS to register R0, and store the result in R0.

03 - STORE R0, <ADDRESS>
Store the register R0 contents in memory location ADDRESS.

04 - END
Program stops running.

Note that the field we refer to as <ADDRESS> was called **M** in chapter 2.

With the four instructions just mentioned, you can write programs, and they can be executed in this new version of VM/0. For example, in program 8.0 below, the first instruction loads the contents of memory location <200> into R0. Then the instruction ADD takes the contents of R0 and memory location <210> and add them up, and the resulting value is stored in R0. The third instruction, STORE, takes the contents of R0 and stores it in memory location <205>. Finally, when the last instruction is executed, the program stops running.

Program 8.0:

LOAD   R0, <200>
ADD   R0, <210>
STORE R0, <205>
END

As in any other CPU, there exists a two-step instruction cycle. These two steps are known as the fetch-execute loop or instruction cycle. Basically, in fetch, the CPU uses the address stored in the program counter (PC) to access a memory location in the text segment for retrieving an instruction. Figure 8.1 depicts the actions taken in the fetch step. These steps are described below:

1. The address stored in the program counter (PC) is copied into the memory address register (MAR).
2. The PC is incremented by one.
3. The instruction stored in the address pointed to by MAR is copied into the memory data register (MDR).
4. The instruction stored in MDR is copied into the instruction register (IR).
5. The opcode (IR.OP) is sent to the control unit (CU).

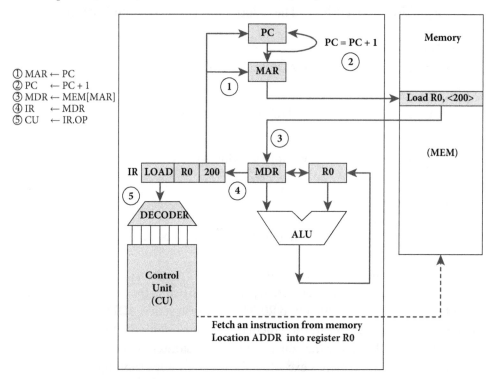

FIGURE 8.1 Tiny VM/0 CPU executing fetch.

Once the fetched instruction reaches the IR, the opcode is given to the control unit to initiate the execution step. The execution of the load instruction is shown in figure 8.2. The instruction stored in the IR indicates that the contents of memory location <200>, which is 2020, has to be loaded (copied) into the MDR register and then copied from the MDR into register zero (R0).

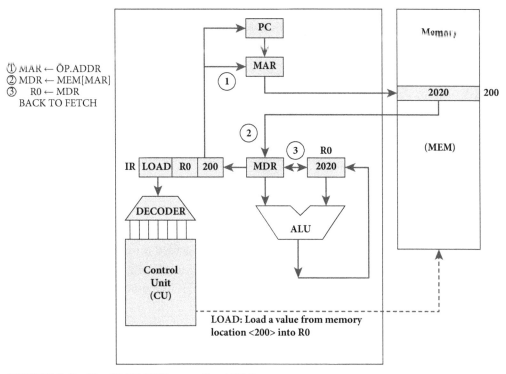

FIGURE 8.2   Tiny VM/0 CPU executing LOAD.

Each time an instruction is executed, the CPU goes back to the fetch step. The actions taken by each of the instructions of the ISA considered in this chapter are described as follows.

Instruction Cycle

Fetch Step

```
MAR  ← PC
PC   ← PC+1
MDR  ← MEM[MAR]
IR   ← MDR
CU   ← IR.OP
```

Execute Step (Choose one instruction sequence depending on the value of IR.OP.)

01 LOAD

MAR ← IR.Address	Copy the IR address value field into MAR.
MDR ← MEM[MAR]	Load the content of a memory location into MDR.
R0 ← MDR	Copy the content of MDR into R0 register.

Back to Fetch

02 ADD

MAR ← IR.Address	Copy the IR address value field into MAR.
MDR ← MEM[MAR]	Load the content of a memory location to MDR.
R0 ← R0 + MDR	Add up contents of MDR and R0 and store result in R0.

Back to Fetch

03 STORE

MAR ← IR.Address	Copy the IR address value field into MAR.
MDR ← R0	Copy the content of R0 into MDR.
MEM[MAR] ← MDR	Copy the contents of MDR in memory.

Back to Fetch

04 END

STOP ← 0	The program runs to completion properly and the CPU stops.

Following the fetch-execute instruction cycle, it is easy to verify that program 8.0 would be executed according to the following sequence of steps.

Executing program 8.0 from the standpoint of the instruction cycle.

```
FETCH
EXECUTE  →  LOAD R0, <200>
FETCH
EXECUTE  →  ADD R0, <210>
FETCH
EXECUTE  →  STORE R0, <205>
FETCH
EXECUTE  →  END (program stops)
```

The CPU of the tiny VM/0 is able to execute programs but cannot detect program errors, such as an overflow. This occurs, for example, when the resulting value obtained after executing an ADD instruction is greater than the maximum value register R0 can store. If this situation is not detected, the program will continue running and giving wrong results. In a critical application this might lead to a catastrophe. To handle this type of unexpected event, more hardware should be incorporated into the CPU to create an **interrupt mechanism**. This mechanism leads us to extend the instruction cycle with an additional step to check on unexpected events called **interrupts**. The new instruction cycle would be fetch-execute-interrupt. Let us illustrate the way program 8.0 would be executed using this new instruction cycle.

Program 8.0:

FETCH
EXECUTE → LOAD R0, <200>
INTERRUPT (is there any interrupt?)
FETCH
EXECUTE → ADD R0, <210>
INTERRUPT (is there any interrupt?)
FETCH
EXECUTE → STORE R0, <205>
INTERRUPT (is there any interrupt?)
FETCH
EXECUTE → END (program stops)
INTERRUPT (is there any interrupt?)

The first interrupt type to be studied is known as **trap**. We will describe the mechanism to implement three traps and their names are: overflow, memory protection and privileged instruction.

Traps

We will refer to all interrupts associated with program errors or instructions involving malicious program actions as traps. To understand better the hardware necessary to implement traps, let us first present the steps to be taken by the tiny VM/0 CPU to execute the fetch-execute cycle for the ISA presented above. To run a program, the STOP value is set to one, and the PC points to the address where the first program instruction resides in memory. Then the CPU initiates the instruction cycle repeatedly until STOP gets the value zero.

This description of the ISA does not check on interrupts, and therefore there is no way to determine, say, an overflow after several executions of instruction ADD. One way we can detect an **overflow** is by adding a flip/flop or **flag** to the arithmetic logic unit (ALU) to check for overflow. Initially, the flag is set to zero, and if an overflow occurs its value becomes one. We will call this flag the **OV flag** (overflow flag). Figure 8.3 shows the OV flag attached to the tiny VM/0 ALU.

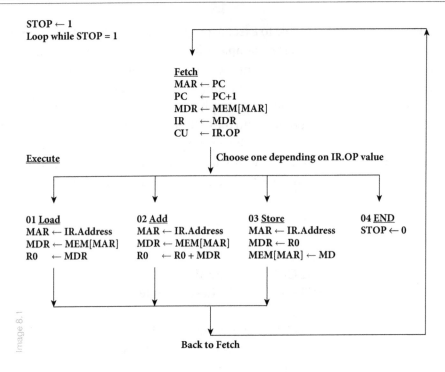

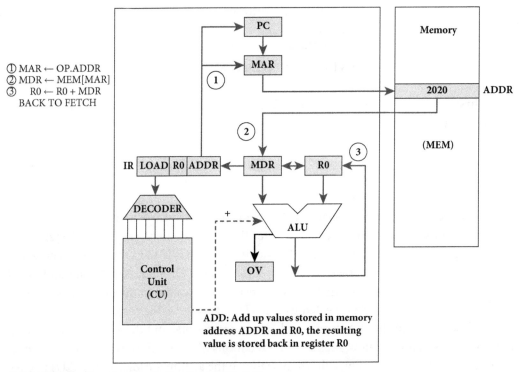

FIGURE 8.3 Overflow flag in the tiny VM/0 ALU.

Attaching this OV flag to the ALU leads us to redesign the ISA interpretation in the CPU. First, we must add a new step to the ISA instruction cycle to check on interrupts. The new step will be "05 INTERRUPT". Then the step "back to fetch" at the end of each instruction will be replaced by "go to interrupt". Once in the interrupt step, the CPU verifies whether OV = 0 or OV = 1. If OV = 1, the computer stops and a red light in the front panel turns on to indicates that there is an overflow; otherwise, the action taken is "back to fetch". The new description of the actions taken by the VM/0 CPU to execute the ISA is shown below:

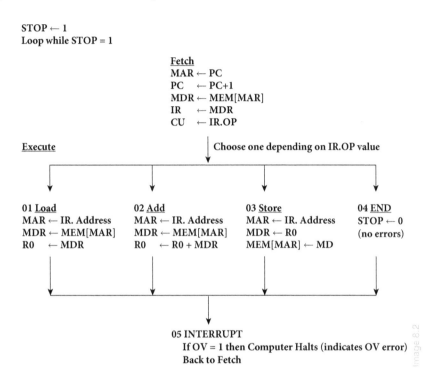

At this moment we have a computer that stops to indicate the program has run to completion properly, or it suddenly halts, indicating with a red light that an overflow has occurred. We can do better than stopping the computer each time a program runs to completion or an overflow is detected. A more clever approach is to have another program in memory to handle interrupts. This program is known as the **interrupt handler (IH).** This way, as soon the overflow flag is asserted, CPU control is transferred to the IH to handle the interrupt. In this case the IH will abort the running program and be able to take other actions. For instance, it could call another function to proceed with loading a new program. The interrupt handler is the first extension (software) layer developed to extend hardware functionality, and it is the first step toward implementing an **operating system**. To implement this enhanced mechanism, a new register will be added to the CPU. We will refer to this register as the **new program counter (NEWPC),** and its contents, a memory address, point to the first instruction of the interrupt handler. This new register obliges us to modify the interrupt step in the CPU as follows: When

OV = 1, instead of stopping the CPU, the content of the NEWPC is copied into the PC, and then the CPU goes back to fetch. In the next instruction cycle, fetch will retrieve the first instruction of the interrupt handler. What the interrupt mechanism has accomplished is to switch from a user program to a system program (the interrupt handler). This new enhancement in the interrupt mechanism is known as the **hardware/software interface**. The mechanism, in the presence of an unexpected event, permits the CPU to transfer control of the computer system to the interrupt handler. This new arrangement is illustrated in figure 8.4. The CPU interrupt step will look as described below:

05 INTERRUPT
    If OV = 1 Then PC ← NEWPC
    Back to Fetch

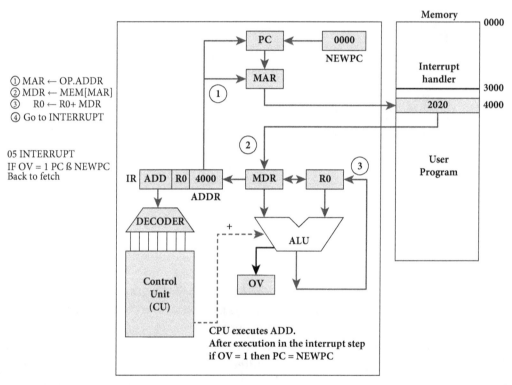

FIGURE 8.4 NEWPC register to transfer control to interrupt handler.

As you can see in figure 8.4, the interrupt handler and a user program are stored in memory at the same time, and there is a boundary or fence between them at memory location 3000. Sharing memory space raises a new problem. The user program could eventually execute an instruction that might modify the interrupt handler routine. For example, if the user program executes the instruction **STORE R0, <2000>**, the instruction would modify the handler routine. This must not be allowed, because this way any user program will be able to alter (hack) the interrupt handler and take control of the computer system. To cope with this issue, more hardware has to be added to the CPU to make the interrupt mechanism stronger. The hardware needed is as follows:

- **Fence register:** A new register loaded with the address that sets a boundary between the interrupt handler routine and the user program (3000 in our example).
- **Device for address comparisons:** To compare the fence register contents with any addresses that the user program attempts to access (the address field in IR).
- **A flip/flop:** A **memory protection (MP) flag**, which is set to 1 if a memory violation occurs (trying to access a memory location between addresses zero and 3000).

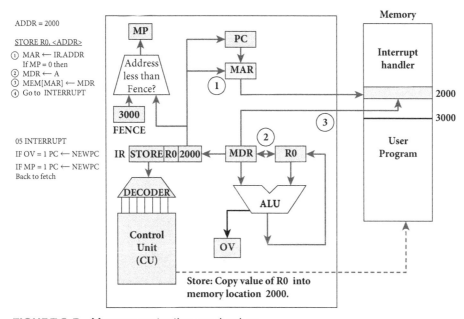

FIGURE 8.5   Memory protection mechanism.

The new hardware added checks whether IR.ADDR > fence register value, and if the condition holds, the CPU keeps MP = 0 and the instruction is executed. Otherwise, the MP flag gets the value one, and the CPU does not execute the instruction but initiates the INTERRUPT step. This new mechanism, as illustrated in figure 8.5, implements a trap to protect the interrupt handler from undebugged and malicious programs. Now the interrupt step is able to handle two traps, as shown in the following description.

```
05 INTERRUPT
    If OV = 1 Then PC ← NEWPC
    If MP = 1 Then PC ← NEWPC
    Back to Fetch
```

When one of these two events is detected by the CPU, the interrupt handler initiates execution to take control of the computer system, and the user's running program is aborted. The implementation of this new interrupt requires some changes in the actions taken by the instructions LOAD, ADD, and STORE. Below you will find the new description of the execution sequence for the four instructions of the simplified version of the VM/0 computer.

01 LOAD
    MAR ← IR.Address
    If MP = 0 Then
        MDR ← MEM[MAR]
        R0 ← MDR
    go to INTERRUPT

02 ADD
    MAR ← IR.Address
    if MP=0 Then
        MDR ← MEM[MAR]
        R0 ← R0 + MDR
    go to INTERRUPT

03 STORE
    MAR ← IR.Address
    if MP = 0 Then
        MDR ← R0
        MEM[MAR] ← MDR
    go to INTERRUPT

05 INTERRUPT
    if OV = 1 Then PC ← NEWPC (OV)
    if MP = 1 Then PC ← NEWPC (MP)
    Back to Fetch

04 END
    STOP ← 0 (no errors)

The ISA must provide new instructions to interact with the new hardware added. For example, a "**LOAD-FENCE-REGISTER, <address>**" instruction is used to set up the fence register. With this new instruction to load the fence register, a new problem arises because a user program could set up the fence register to any value, say zero (address zero), and then the user program would be able to modify the interrupt handler and eventually take control of the whole system. As you can see, the fence register is not protected. To solve this new problem, the instruction set must be split into **privileged instructions**, which are prohibited to user programs, and standard instructions, which can be executed by any program running in the computer. To distinguish between times when privileged instructions are or are not allowed to be executed, the computer operates in two **modes:**

        User mode: 0
        System mode: 1

In user mode, only a subset of the instruction set (standard instructions) can be used by the running program, but a program running in system mode has access to all instructions (standard and privileged instructions). To implement a **two-mode mechanism**, some hardware has to be added to the CPU:

- A flip/flop: This **privileged instruction (PI) flag** is set to 1 if a user program tries to execute a privileged instruction.
- Another flip/flop denoted as the **mode bit:** This allow the CPU to know whether the running program is a user program or a system program.
- A device to compare values: Create a mechanism in the CPU to avoid the execution of privileged instructions by user programs. The device will output a 1 if the condition is met.
- Divide the ISA in two groups: The instruction set has to be organized in such a way that all privileged instructions have operation codes greater than a given number. For example, if the ISA has 120 instructions, privileged instructions will have operation codes greater than 59.

Example:

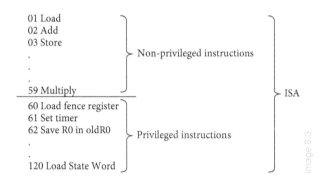

image 8.3

To understand the way a two-mode mechanism works, we will provide two examples: assume first that mode = 0 and the user program tries to execute an instruction whose opcode is 75. Observing the left-hand side in figure 8.6, you will see that the mode value passes through an inverter (NOT gate), and its value is changed to a 1 that is wired to the AND gate on one of its inputs. The other input of the AND gate receives its value from the device that compares the opcode (75) with 59, which is the value that sets up the boundary between standard and privileged instructions. As 75 is greater than 59, the outcome of comparing these two values will be a 1 that is sent to the other input of the AND gate. As the two inputs are one, the output of the AND gate, a 1, is stored in the PI flag. When PI =1, it triggers the privileged instruction interrupt because a user program intends to execute a privileged instruction. On the right-hand side in figure 8.6, there is another example: we set the mode bit to 1 and assume the program is executing the same instruction with opcode = 75. In this case, when the mode value (a 1) passes through the NOT gate, it is transformed into a zero. That zero value enters the AND gate, and the resulting value of the AND gate will be zero because AND gates only emit a value of 1 when all inputs are 1. This way the PI flag remains zero.

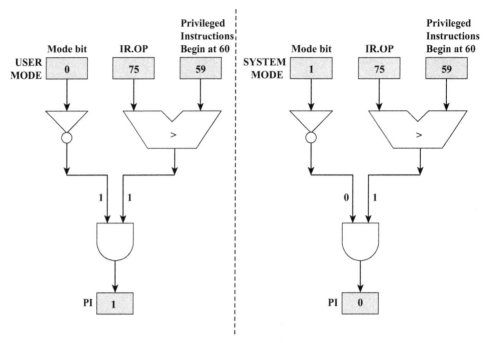

FIGURE 8.6 Two-mode mechanism implementation.

It is worth mentioning that the interrupt handler, as a system program, has the right to execute privileged instruction, and therefore when CPU switches from a user program to the interrupt handler, the mode bit must be set to 1. The interrupt step in the instruction cycle is now able to handle three traps, as shown in the following description.

```
05 INTERRUPT
    If OV = 1 Then PC ← NEWPC; Mode ← 1;
    If MP = 1 Then PC ← NEWPC; Mode ← 1;
    If PI = 1 Then PC ← NEWPC; Mode ← 1;
    Back to Fetch.
```

As we have added more hardware to the CPU, we will start showing the CPU from another perspective to focus more on registers and flags than on the way they connect. We will gather all interrupt flags, the PC, and the mode bit to create the **program status word** (**PSW**). The program status word gives the state of the running program at any time after the execution of an instruction. The PSW can be conceptualized as a logical register because all its hardware components are separated physically.

The Program Status Word

The PSW is a concept that we have borrowed from the IBM/360, a computer from the 1960 and 1970s. The reason we have chosen this interrupt mechanism is because it is a very simple example of the handling of some interrupts in a clear and concise manner. However, we must clarify that our PSW is simpler than the one presented in the IBM/360. You must think of the PSW as a large register that comprises the program counter, interrupt flags, and the mode bit, as illustrated below. It is worth mentioning that some interrupt flags in the illustration of the PSW have not been considered yet, but we will proceed to fill in this gap shortly.

	Interrupt Flags						
Program counter (PC)	OV	MP	PI	I/O	SVC	TI	Mode

Program status word

As you can see in figure 8.7, in addition to the PSW, there are two others registers called **OLD-PC** and **OLD-R0**. As you already know, the NEWPC points to the first instruction of the interrupt handler. All flags are set to zero, and the mode bit is equal to zero because a user program is running and is fetching an instruction at location 4000. After fetching the instruction, you can see that the instruction register (IR) holds the instruction "STORE R0, <2000>".

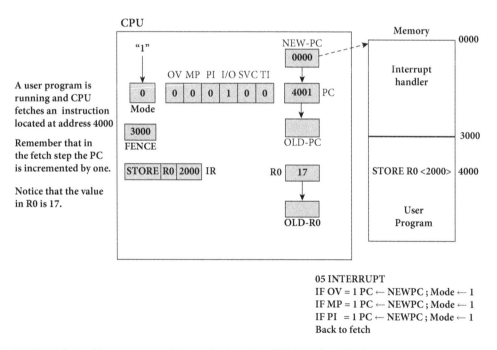

FIGURE 8.7 User program fetches instruction STORE R0, <2000>.

The address 2000 lies in the interrupt handler address space, and therefore the MP bit is set to 1 (MP = 1) because there is a memory violation. Once this trap is detected, the PC is saved in OLD-PC, and R0 is saved in OLD-R0. The main reason for saving these two values is because the contents of the NEWPC will overwrite the PC and R0 will be used by the interrupt handler. Do not forget that the mode bit will be set to 1 because the interrupt handler must run in system mode. Once all these updates are done, the interrupt handler gets control of the CPU, as shown in figure 8.8 PSW. Then the interrupt handler tests interrupt flags in the PSW and realizes that MP =1 and proceeds to abort the running program due to a memory violation.

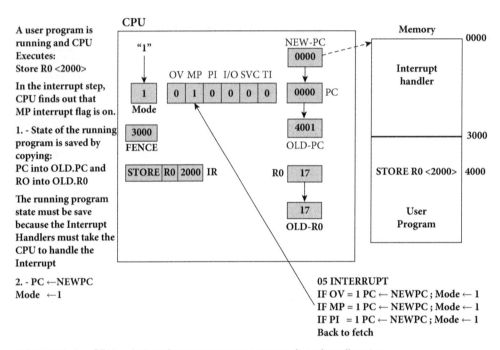

FIGURE 8.8 CPU switches from user to system mode to handle a trap.

I/O Interrupt

This type of interrupt occurs when an I/O device sends a signal to inform the CPU that an I/O operation has been completed. An **I/O flag** is used in the PSW to assert this type of interrupt. This is shown in figure 8.9.

When an **I/O interrupt** occurs, the program state of the running program is saved; thus, it can be restarted from the same point where it left off once the I/O interrupt has been handled. This must be done because the I/O interrupt is associated with another program and not to the running program. Therefore, the running program has to be suspended temporarily. As you can see in figure 8.10, the PC (running program) is saved in the OLD-PC, the content of register R0 is save in a register called OLD-R0 (to save the data the current program was using), and the NEWPC is copied into the PC to pass control to the interrupt handler.

A user program is running and while CPU is executing Fetch-Execute an I/O interrupt occurs.

Remember that in the fetch step the PC is incremented by one.

Notice that the value loaded in R0 is 17.

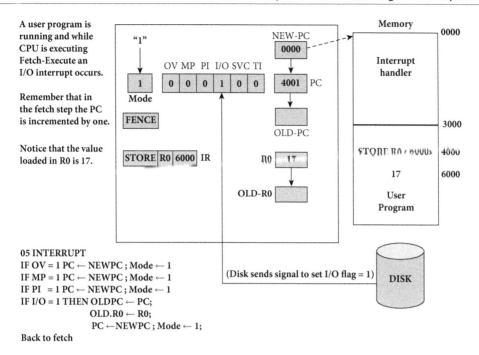

05 INTERRUPT
IF OV = 1 PC ← NEWPC ; Mode ← 1
IF MP = 1 PC ← NEWPC ; Mode ← 1
IF PI = 1 PC ← NEWPC ; Mode ← 1
IF I/O = 1 THEN OLDPC ← PC;
                OLD.R0 ← R0;
                PC ←NEWPC ; Mode ← 1;
Back to fetch

FIGURE 8.9 State of the system when I/O operation occurs.

A user program is running and while CPU is executing Fetch-Execute an I/O interrupt occurs.

In the interrupt step, CPU finds out that I/O interrupt flag is on.

1.-State of the running program is saved by copying:
PC into OLD.PC and
R0 into OLD.R0

2.-The running program state must be saved because the Interrupt Handlers must take the CPU to handle the Interrupt

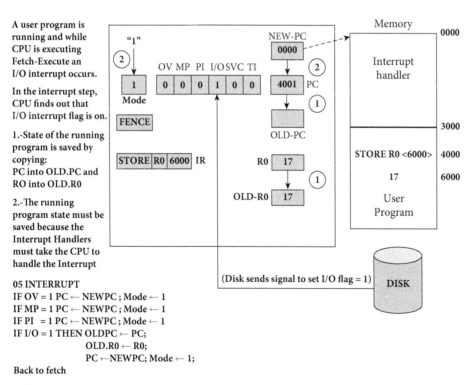

05 INTERRUPT
IF OV = 1 PC ← NEWPC ; Mode ← 1
IF MP = 1 PC ← NEWPC ; Mode ← 1
IF PI = 1 PC ← NEWPC ; Mode ← 1
IF I/O = 1 THEN OLDPC ← PC;
                OLD.R0 ← R0;
                PC ←NEWPC; Mode ← 1;
Back to fetch

FIGURE 8.10 Interrupt handler takes control of the CPU to handle an I/O interrupt.

The interrupt handler takes control of the CPU to handle the I/O interrupt, and once handled, the interrupt handler passes control back to the suspended program. You can see that in the new description of the interrupt step, the I/O interrupt is included.

>05 INTERRUPT
>If OV = 1 Then PC ← NEWPC; Mode ← 1;
>If MP = 1 Then PC ← NEWPC; Mode ← 1;
>If PI = 1 Then PC ← NEWPC; Mode ← 1;
>
>If IO = 1 Then OLD-PC ← PC;
>   OLD-R0 ← R0;
>   PC ← NEWPC;
>   Mode ← 1;
>Back to Fetch.

Once the interrupt handler finishes handling the interrupt, it must emit a couple of instructions to resume the suspended program. This is done using the following privileged instructions:

>Copy OLD-R0 into R0
>Copy OLD-PC into PC

Once these two instructions have been executed, in the next fetch cycle the suspended program will resume execution at the point where it left off.

Timer Interrupt

Sometimes when several programs coexist in memory, processor sharing is required to allow each program to use the CPU for a certain amount of time. Once the time allotted to a running program is used up, the CPU is assigned to another program for a limited time period. Controlling the time each process is allowed to use the CPU can be carried out with a timer interrupt register, by triggering an interrupt when the running program uses up the CPU time assigned by the operating system. This interrupt will be detected by the CPU, which in its turn will activate the interrupt handler to manage the interrupt. To implement the timer interrupt mechanism, we need to add to our CPU another register called **timer** and another flag. This new flag is called the **timer interrupt (TI) flag**. The mechanism works this way:

The **timer register** is set to a specific value.

The timer register is decremented by one at each clock-tick received by the CPU.

When the timer reaches the value zero, a timer interrupt is triggered by setting the **TI flag** to 1.

The interrupt step of the instruction cycle can now detect a timer interrupt when TI = 1 and transfer CPU control to the interrupt handler. In turn, the interrupt handler will save the contents of the PC and R0 to a data structure associated with the running process. That data structure is called the **process control block (PCB)**. There is one PCB associated with each program in memory waiting to get executed in the CPU. We will give a detailed explanation of the PCB in chapter 9. Once the status of the running process has been saved, the supervisor could assign the CPU to another program. By including the timer interrupt, the interrupt step of the instruction cycle will look like this.

```
05 INTERRUPT
    If OV = 1 Then PC ← NEWPC; Mode ← 1;
    If MP = 1 Then PC ← NEWPC; Mode ← 1;
    If PI = 1 Then PC ← NEWPC; Mode ← 1;

    If IO = 1 Then  OLD-PC ← PC;
                    OLD-R0 ← R0;
                    PC ← NEWPC;
                    Mode ← 1;

    If TI = 1 Then  PCB.PC ← PC;
                    PCB.R0 ← R0;
                    PC ← NEWPC;
                    Mode ← 1;

    Back to Fetch.
```

This concept of timer or interval timer allows the interrupt handler to gain CPU control back at fixed intervals. It is worth mentioning that infinite loops cannot be detected by the system just by using the timer interrupt. A program engaged in an infinite loop is ended when the OS realizes that the program has used up all the time allotted for running.

System Calls

As we will be adding more services to the interrupt handler, from now on we will refer to the interrupt handler as the "supervisor," and eventually we will call it the operating system. Sometimes a user program requires some services from the supervisor; for instance, when a user program needs to open a file or to read in from a file. The user program is unable to accomplish these actions by itself because they require the use of privileged instructions. For this reason, the user program must communicate somehow with the supervisor to request the supervisor to carry out those services on its behalf. The mechanism used to request services from the supervisor is known as a **system call** or **supervisor call (SVC)**. A system call is an instruction that triggers a software interrupt, and the format of the system call instructions in a tiny VM/0 is:

SVC B, <index>

Note that instead of register R0 we use a register B, which is a new register added to the CPU. The field "address" in the instruction format is called index in the system call instruction because it will not be treated as a memory address but as an array index. This index will give us the entry point into an array called the **system call vector table (SCVT)**. Each **SCVT element** contents of a different memory address that points to the beginning of a different system program. Each of those programs will execute different services, for example initiate an I/O operation. For example, if a user program executes a system call, say SVC B, <4>, to read data from a file, the system call instruction will load the value "index" into the new CPU register B, and then it will behave as though it were a subroutine call to a read I/O function. The index, entry point 4 in the system call vector table, will be used by the supervisor to find the address of the program code to handle the read operation. The SVC instruction will set to 1 a new flip/flop that we have to add to the PSW, the **SVC flag**. Thus, in the interrupt cycle the system switches from user to supervisor mode. It is worth noting that we are treating system calls in a different way than we have handled the other types of interrupts. All I/O functions can be considered as an I/O runtime library. **Runtime libraries** are precompiled procedures that can be called at runtime. As described earlier, to implement an SVC, a new register call B is added to the CPU to store IR.address, which is the index to search the SCVT for the function to be carried out. The translation of the read instruction to SVC B, <index> instruction might be similar to this:

Source program   **Object program**

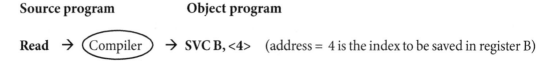

Read → Compiler → SVC B, <4>   (address = 4 is the index to be saved in register B)

We have assigned the value 80 as the opcode of an SVC. The execution steps for SVC R0, <address> are:

80 SVC

    B ← IR.ADDR   (the index value is loaded temporarily in register B)
    SVCFLAG = 1   (set SVC flag to 1)
    Go to Interrupt

The pseudocode for the interaction between user and supervisor programs will look like this:

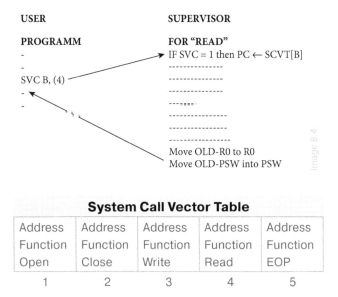

After adding the SVC flag to the PSW, the interrupt step of the instruction cycle can be described as follows.

```
05 INTERRUPT
    If OV = 1 Then PC ← NEWPC; Mode ← 1;
    If MP = 1 Then PC ← NEWPC; Mode ← 1;
    If PI = 1 Then PC ← NEWPC; Mode ← 1;

    If IO = 1 Then  OLD-PC ← PC;
                    OLD-R0 ← R0;
                    PC ← NEWPC;
                    Mode ← 1;

    If TI = 1 Then PCB.PC ← PC;
                   PCB.R0 ← R0;
                   PC ← NEWPC;
                   Mode ← 1;

    If SVC = 1 Then OLD-PC ← PC;
                    OLD-R0 ← R0;
                    PC ← NEWPC;
                    Mode ← 1;
    Back to Fetch.
```

Switching from user mode to system mode to handle interrupts must be done as quickly as possible. As we have seen, the VM/0 CPU transfers control to the supervisor (interrupt handler), and the interrupt handler analyzes the flags and then, depending on which flag has been set to 1, the appropriate actions are taken. A more expedited form of switching directly to the procedure or routine that handles a specific interrupt can be implemented by using the concept of **interrupt vector**. The idea consists of partitioning the interrupt handler in several programs, one for each type of interrupt. Those programs will reside in memory in fixed locations, and the starting addresses of each program are gathered into an array called the interrupt vector. The array resides in main memory as well. Let us suppose that an array of length 6 is stored in memory and each element of the array is associated with each interrupt flag; say the first element of the array is associated with the flag OV, the second with MP, and so on. The content of each element of the array is the beginning address of the program that handles that type of interrupt. Let us name the array the interrupt handler vector (IHV). With this new arrangement, the interrupt cycle will transfer control of the CPU directly to the routine that handles the interrupt that occurred. Thus, for handling interrupts using the concept of interrupt vector, the interrupt step of the VM/0 machine should be modified as follows.

05 Interrupt step

IF OV = 1 THEN	PC ← IHV[0]; MODE ← 1	Load address of OV handler.
IF MP = 1 THEN	PC ← IHV[1]: MODE ← 1	Load address of MP handler.
IF PI = 1 THEN	PC ← IHV[2]; MODE ← 1	Load address of PI handler.
IF TI = 1 THEN	PCB.PC ← PC;	Save PC of the current program in its PCB.
	PCB.R0 ← R0;	Save R0 of the current program in its PCB.
	PC ← IHV[3];	Load address of the timer interrupt handler.
	MODE ← 1	Set mode to system mode.
IF I/O = 1 THEN	OLD-PC ← PC;	Save PC of the current program.
	OLD-R0 ← R0;	Save R0 of the current program.
	PC ← IHV[4];	Load address of the I/O interrupt handler.
	MODE ← 1	Set mode to system mode.
IF SVC = 1 THEN	OLD-PC ← PC;	Save PC of the current program.
	OLD-R0 ← R0;	Save R0 of the current program.
	PC ← IHV[5];	Load address of the SVC interrupt handler.
	MODE ← 1	Set mode to system mode.
BACK TO FETCH		Control unit initiates fetch step again.

Interrupt Handler Vector

IHV	Address Overflow Handler	Address MP Handler	Address PI Handler	Address Timer Handler	Address I/O Handler	Address SVC Handler
	0	1	2	3	4	5

With this new arrangement, we have simplified the interrupt mechanism for identifying the function to be run as soon as possible. Therefore, by copying PC into OLD-PC, R0 into OLD-R0, the state of the running program is saved, and the address of the required handler from the interrupt handler vector is copied into the PC, and setting mode to 1 will allow the supervisor to take control of the system. As the supervisor can manipulate flags depending on the interrupt type, it could reset the flag associated with the interrupt that is being handled.

This modification seems to work quite well when the system is handling just one interrupt, but there are cases where two or three interrupts might occur simultaneously; for example, an SVC and I/O interrupt or timer, SVC and I/O interrupt. As you can see, two or three flags might be on, and the system must handle all interrupts one at a time. Another case is that while an SVC is being carried out, the function executes another system call. This is known as nested interrupts. To sort out this new challenge, we will bring back the stack mechanism we studied in chapter 3. As you know, there is a stack associated with each running program, including a stack for the supervisor (operating system), usually known as the **kernel** stack. In general, a stack is used to control the calling and returning from subroutines by inserting an activation record when the function is called and popping out the activation record when the function ends. By way of analogy, we can think of the handling of interrupts as function calls. To get an idea of the way the system will handle interrupts, we will go back to the I/O interrupt case, but this time we will be dealing with two stacks per process: the process stack and another one to handle interrupts at the system level that we will name the kernel stack. We will be considering the base pointer (BP) and the stack pointer (SP) as additional registers of our simplified VM/0 version. This means that from now on, the state of the running program is given by the PC, BP, SP, mode bit, all flags, R0, and register B.

Let us assume that a user program, say P3, is running and an I/O-interrupt signals the CPU by setting the I/O flag to 1. You already know that the system must suspend the running program (P3) temporarily to handle the I/O interrupt, and this means saving the P3 state before handling the interrupt. This is carried out in three steps:

1. Save the state of the running program (P3) in the process kernel stack. This means gathering the PC, BP, SP, mode bit, all flags, R0, and register B from the CPU and pushing them down into the kernel stack.
2. Handle the I/O interrupt using the CPU.
3. Resume execution of the running program (P3) by popping out the state saved in the kernel stack and copying back the PC, BP, SP, mode bit, all flags, R0, and register B in the corresponding CPU registers.

In the case of nested interrupts, this can be thought as two function calls in a row, and the process kernel stack will create an activation record for each function, thereby ensuring a safely returning sequence.

To conclude this chapter, we will gather all described interrupts to create a taxonomy. We will divide all interrupts into two groups, denoted as software interrupts and hardware interrupt. In the **software interrupt** category, we include system calls (SVC) and traps. These interrupts are synchronous and occur when a program is executing an instruction in the CPU. **Hardware interrupts** are asynchronous and could be triggered at any moment during the instruction cycle. In this category we include the timer and I/O interrupt.

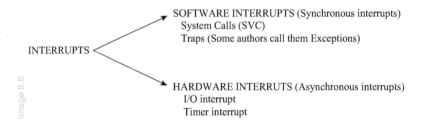

Image 8.5

SUMMARY

In this chapter we described the interrupt mechanism of a hypothetical CPU (tiny VM/0). As in any other computer, the interrupt mechanism allows the CPU to alert the operating system of any unexpected event that might occur while a program is running and transfer control to the operating system. We started out by presenting a classical interrupt mechanism that transfers control to a small program called the interrupt handler, and little by little, we enhanced the interrupt handler with more functionality and renamed it the supervisor, which was the name given in the early days to the operating system. To give enough details about the handling of interrupts, we presented different types of interrupts and showed how they are handled by the interrupt mechanism.

EXERCISES

1. Name an asynchronous interrupt.
2. Is the CPU able to detect an infinite loop within a running program?
3. What is the purpose of the PSW?
4. What is known as the hardware/software interface?
5. What is an interrupt?
6. Can the CPU detect two or more interrupt flags in one instruction cycle?

7. Write down the necessary steps to handle an I/O interrupt.
8. Is the I/O interrupt associated to the running program?
9. What does it mean that an interrupt is asynchronous?
10. We explained three traps in this chapter. Name them.
11. Give the steps of the fetch cycle.
12. What is an operating system?
13. Why do we need an interval timer in a computer system?
14. Give the name of two privileged instructions.
15. Why do system programs need to run in system mode?
16. Name the fields of the PSW.
17. If a program is temporarily interrupted, what information must be saved?
18. What is the advantage of using an interrupt vector?

Bibliographical Notes

The interrupt mechanism and its associated interrupt handler known as the hardware/software interface play a fundamental role in all operating systems. Lister[1] and Tanenbaum[2] offer good descriptions of an interrupt mechanism. The UNIVAC I is credited as the first computer that implemented the concept of overflow trap.[3] The UNIVAC 1103A is credited as the first computer system that implemented an interrupt system.[4] The ATLAS supervisor developed in the late 1950s and early 1960s was the first operating system that implemented extracode routines (system calls).[5] Dijkstra[6] and Brooks[7] share credit for the implementation of the vectored interrupt system. Madnick and Donovan[8] give a detailed description of the PSW in the IBM/360. Silberschatz, Galvin, and Gagne[9] provide a good introduction to system calls.

Bibliography

1. A. M. Lister, *Fundamentals of Operating Systems*, 2nd ed. New York: Macmillan, 1979.
2. A. S. Tanenbaum, *Modern Operating Systems*, 2nd ed. Englewood Cliffs, NJ: Prentice Hall, 2001.
3. Remington Rand, *Programming for the UNIVAC Fac-Tronic System*. Philadelphia, PA: Remington Rand, 1953.
4. J. Mersel, "Program Interrupt on the Univac Scientific Computer," in Western Joint Computer Conference, San Francisco, CA, 1956.
5. T. Kilburn, R. B. Payne, and D. J. Howarth, "The Atlas Supervisor," in the American Federation of Information Processing Societies, Eastern Joint Computer Conference, Washington, DC, 1961.
6. E. W. Dijkstra, *Communication with an Automatic Computer*. Amsterdam: Mathematisch Centrum, 1959.
7. F. P. Brooks, "A Program-Controlled Program Interruption System," in IRE-ACM-AIEE '57 (Eastern Joint Computer Conference), Washington, DC, 1957.
8. S. E. Madnick and J. J. Donovan, *Operating Systems*. New York: McGraw-Hill, 1974.
9. A. Silberschatz, P. B. Galvin, and G. Gagne, *Operating System Concepts*. Hoboken, NJ: Wiley, 2013.

Chapter 9

Processes and Threads

The reference of "evening star" would be the same as that of the "morning star," but not the sense.
—Gottlob Frege
On Sense and Reference

INTRODUCTION

The word *process* refers to a program in execution. A process is implemented using a data structure called the process control block or process descriptor, and associated with the process descriptor is a memory area called the process address space. The information in the process control block is known as the context and is used to keep track of program execution. In a multiprogramming environment, several processes are able to reside in memory simultaneously, thereby allowing processor sharing in order to enhance CPU utilization. Since the early 1960s, the words *process*, *task*, and *thread* have been in essence the same concept. The designers of the MULTICS and THE operating systems used the word *process*, while the term *task* was used by the designer of the IBM/360 operating system to refer to the same entity. *Thread* was a term suggested by Victor Vyssotsky to refer to a program in execution.

We begin this chapter by looking at the concept of process from different perspectives. Then we explain process implementation and the states a process can be in while a program is running. While discussing process creation, we will show the difference between a program and a process. Finally, thread implementation for single-threaded programs will be described, and then multithreading will be explained.

CHAPTER OBJECTIVES

- To introduce the process concept and states it can be in.
- To understand interrupts as events that move a process from one state to another.
- To understand the difference among programs, processes, and threads.
- To explore the implementation issues of processes and threads.

VOCABULARY

This is a list of keywords that herald the concepts we will study in this chapter. They are organized in chronological order and will appear in the text in bold. We invite you to take a look at these keywords to find out which ones you are familiar with.

Process	Text	I/O interrupt
Program in execution	Process state	Page fault
Time sharing	Ready	Wait for page
Compatible time-sharing system (CTSS)	Running	Page loaded
	Waiting on I/O	Explicit I/O
MULTICS	Suspended	Implicit I/O
THE	End	Page
Multiprogramming	Abend (abnormal end)	Executable program file
Dispatch	Dispatch	Thread
Concurrent execution	SIO	Unit of execution of a process
Process control block (PCB)	Timer	Thread control block (TCB)
Process address space	EOP	Lightweight process
Stack	Trap	Multithreading
Heap	Stop	Multitasking
Data	Resume	Multicore

ACTIVATING PRIOR KNOWLEDGE

In this section we will present a series of activities. In some of them you can choose one or more options. Sometimes, if you do not agree with the given answers to choose from, you will be allowed to give your own answer. By the way, this is not a test.

1. What is a program?

    Code ☐
    An algorithm expressed in a programming language ☐
    A series of instructions ☐
    If the answer is not given above, please give yours. _____

2. Mark the words denoting the same concept.

    Task ☐   Thread ☐   Process ☐   Job ☐

3. Mark the segments that belong to the process address space.

    Data ☐   CPU ☐   Text ☐   Stack ☐

4. In the context of OS, is it true that Program = Process?

   Yes ☐
   No ☐
   Sometimes ☐
   If the answer is not given above, please give yours. _____

5. Skim the chapter and pay attention to the words written in **bold**. Count the number of words you are familiar with.

6. To execute a program, the OS must load the program from a disk. Where does the operating system load programs?

   In the CPU ☐
   In memory ☐
   50 percent in memory and 50 percent in the CPU ☐

7. Take a look at the concepts below and mark the ones you know.

   Process control block (PCB) ☐
   Thread control block (TCB) ☐
   Context switch ☐
   Process address space ☐

Process Concept

Gottlob Frege in his remarkable work *On Sense and Reference* describe an interesting example to illustrate that the names "evening star" and "morning star" refer to the same planet (Venus). A similar situation occurs in the context of operating systems, with the different names given to a program in execution. The concept of process is central to the study of operating systems, and you will find, in the literature, that the words *process*, *task*, and *thread* are used to denote the same concept. Intuitively, you can think of a process as an activity or series of activities that are carried out to achieve an objective. In the context of operating systems, a **process** is defined as a **program in execution**. The origin of the word *process* in the context of operating systems was used for the first time circa 1962, when a team of scientists at MIT led by Fernando Corbató used the word *process* when they were designing and implementing a **time-sharing** system on an IBM 7090. This system was later known as the **compatible time-sharing system (CTSS)**. The concept of process as we know it today was used, originally and independently, by the designers of the **MULTICS** operating system at MIT and the designers of the **THE** operating system at the Technische Hogeschool Eindhoven (Eindhoven University of Technology) in Netherlands. We think it would be convenient at this moment to quote some definitions of *process* to reinforce the grasping of the process concept:

We use the word process to denote the execution of a program.
—V. A. Vissotsky, F. J. Corbato, and R. M. Graham, *The Structure of the Multics Supervisor* (1965)

A process is a locus of control within an instruction sequence. That is, a process is that abstract entity which moves through the instructions of a procedure as the procedure is executed by a processor.
—Jack Dennis and Earl C. Van Horne, *Programming Semantics for Multiprogrammed Computations* (1966)

The execution of a program is a sequential process.
—Edsger W. Dijkstra, *Cooperating Sequential Processes* (1966)

A process is controlled by a program and needs a processor to carry out this program.
—Arie Nicolaas Habermann, *Introduction to Operating System Design* (1976)

When there is a single program in memory (a process) executing instructions in the CPU, it leads to the degradation of CPU utilization. A good example can be found in this scenario: think of a running program that initiates an I/O operation. The CPU remains idle until the I/O operation is completed, and this implies CPU time is wasted. A solution to this problem is provided by **multiprogramming**. Although the term *multiprogramming* might suggest multiple programmers writing programs simultaneously, what it actually means is the presence of multiple programs residing in memory at the same time, waiting for CPU time. Having several programs in memory simultaneously allows the operating system to **dispatch** a program (assign the CPU to the program) each time the CPU is idle. Going back to the example described above, in the context of a multiprogramming system, if the running program executes an I/O operation, the program will wait until the I/O operation completes, and the operating system will dispatch another program. This way we will have a couple of programs engaged in two different activities simultaneously: one running instructions in the CPU and another carrying out an I/O operation. Multiprogramming allows the "apparent" **concurrent execution** of two or more programs by a single CPU (processor sharing), and simultaneously, multiprogramming allows "true" concurrency (parallelism) by allowing two or more processes to carry out different activities on different devices at the same time.

A process is created each time a program is loaded for execution. To create a process, the operating system uses a data structure called the **process control block (PCB)**; along with the PCB, the operating system also assigns to each process a memory area known as the **process address space**. Therefore, we could say that a process is represented in a computer system by its PCB and its process address space. When the program ends, the operating system regains the memory area used by that process.

Process Control Block

Process activity or evolution of a running program is controlled by the operating system using a data structure called the process control block (PCB) or process descriptor. This data structure stores information about the process, and we will name a few of the data fields of the PCB: the program counter, stack pointer, state, contents of some CPU registers, mode bit, files opened, priority, and so on. This arrangement is illustrated in figure 9.1. We will refer to all that information in the PCB as the context, and to assign the processor to a program (dispatching), part of the context must be copied in the CPU.

PCB	Description
id	process number
bp	base pointer
sp	stack pointer
pc	program counter
registers	contents of some processor registers
state	
mode	tells if this is a user or a system process
priority	for scheduling purposes
open files	Tells about the files the process is using
. . .	additional information about the process

FIGURE 9.1 Process control block.

Process Address Space

The process address space is a memory area that the operating system assigns to a process, and it is organized into four segments or sections:

- **Stack** segment
- **Heap** segment
- **Data** segment
- **Text** segment

The text segment is used to store the executable program, and it is located at the beginning of the process address space starting at memory address zero. The data segment is located right after the text segment, and it is used to store global variables. Next you will find the heap, which is used to support programming languages that allow the handling of memory dynamically. Finally, the stack, which begins at the highest memory address in the process address space and is used to control the calling and returning from subroutines and to save temporary space for local variables and parameters. Figure 9.2 shows an illustration of the process address space.

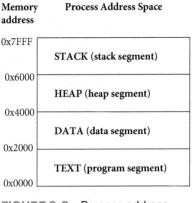

FIGURE 9.2 Process address space.

Process States

In a computer system, a **process state** describes the activity the process is engaged in. Interrupts can be considered events that tell the operating system when to move a process from one state to another. When we refer to interrupts, we mean traps, hardware interrupts, and system calls. Some of the states a process can be in are as follows:

- **Ready:** The process is waiting to get some CPU time.
- **Running:** The process is using the processor.
- **Waiting on I/O:** The process is waiting for the completion of an I/O operation.
- **Suspended:** The process is temporarily suspended because the OS needs to use the CPU.
- **End:** The process has just run to completion.
- **Abend:** Abnormal end due to program error or program malicious behavior.

If a process is in one of these states—ready, running, or waiting on I/O, or waiting for a page, we can say the process is active; otherwise, we consider it not active. Figure 9.3 depicts the process state diagram.

As you can see in the state diagram, states are connected by labeled arrows denoting the name of the events that move a process from one state to another. If you observe figure 9.3 carefully, you will find that the label names represent interrupts. For this reason, we define an operating system as an event-driven program. Below, we describe these transitions individually.

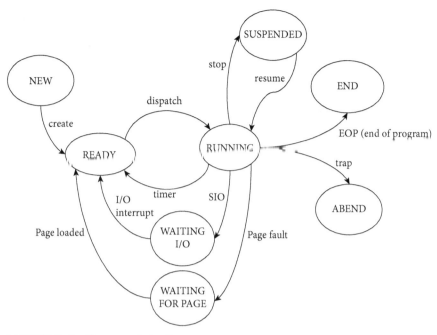

FIGURE 9.3 Process state diagram.

Current state	Interrupt	New state
Ready	Dispatch	Running
Running	SIO	Wait for I/O (to be completed)
Running	Timer	Ready
Running	EOP	End (run to completion)
Running	Trap	Abend (abnormal end)
Running	Stop	Suspended (Temporarily)
Suspended	Resume	Running
Wait for I/O	I/O interrupt	Ready

Dispatch: This means assigning the processor to a process by copying the context from its PCB into the CPU.

SIO: The system call SIO stands for start and I/O operation on a specific device.

Timer: This is an asynchronous hardware interrupt, which is triggered at fixed intervals, to allow the OS to recover control of the CPU.

EOP: End of program indicates that a program has run to completion properly.

Trap: Traps are mechanisms to detect malicious program behavior or program errors.

Stop: This is used by the operating system to suspend a program temporarily because the OS needs to handle an interrupt.

Resume: This allows the operating system to resume execution of a suspended process by bringing the process context back to the processor.

I/O interrupt: This is an asynchronous hardware interrupt, which alerts the operating system about the successful completion of an I/O operation. To handle it, the operating system needs to use the processor, and therefore it must temporarily suspend the running process.

There is another state in the diagram and one arrow, labeled **page fault**, connecting the running state with the **wait for page** state and another arrow, **page loaded**, connecting the wait for a page to the ready state. We include them here just to let readers get used to the idea of **explicit I/O** operations and **implicit I/O** operations. Explicit I/O is related to the input/output operations the programmer places in a program; for example, open a file, read, write, print, and so on. Implicit I/O operations are initiated by the system as a side effect of the execution of the user program. For example, in operating systems that support virtual memory, user programs are divided into blocks called **pages**. All the program pages reside in the hard disk. This allows the OS to load one or a few pages of the program into memory to initiate its execution, instead of the whole program. Then, if the program references a page that is not in memory, a page fault occurs, and the operating system changes the state of the running process to wait for a page and starts an implicit I/O operation to load the new page into memory. The user program is unaware of the number of additional implicit I/O operations executed by the operating system on behalf of the user program.

Transforming a Program into a Process

As you already know, a process is defined as a program in execution, and there is a substantial difference between a program and a process. An **executable program file** is a passive entity that sits idle in the hard drive. The file has a header and several sections. In the header you can find the program identification or name, entry points to each section in the file, and the length of each section. Concerning the sections, we will mention three of them for our example:

- Text section
- Data section
- Symbol table section

In the text section resides the program in executable form (binary), and the data section stores the static global variables. The text section will be loaded into the TEXT segment of the process address space, and the data section will be copied in the DATA segment. Then the operating system will define two other areas in the process address space, one for the stack and the other one for the heap. Along with the process address space, the operating system will create a PCB to store the process context. It is convenient to recall that in the PCB, the program counter is set up to point to the first instruction to be fetched, and the stack pointer will point to the stack. The PCB also contains the id, state, space to store the contents of some processor registers, mode, open files, and so on. This arrangement can be seen in figure 9.4.

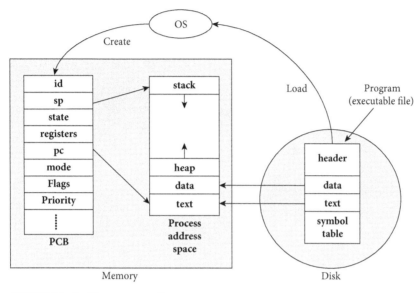

FIGURE 9.4 Process creation.

Thread Control Block

At the beginning of the chapter, we quoted some definitions of the process concept. One of them is quite interesting because it implicitly defines what we know nowadays as a **thread**. It is necessary to quote once again the definition of Dennis and Van Horn to analyze it in detail.

> *A process is a locus of control within an instruction sequence. That is, a process is that abstract entity which moves through the instructions of a procedure as the procedure is executed by a processor.*
> —Jack Dennis and Earl C. Van Horne, *Programming Semantics for Multiprogrammed Computations* (1966)

A thread is defined, in general, as the unit of execution of a process, and Dennis and Van Horn defined a process as the "locus of control within an instruction sequence," and that matches the former definition. Practically, both definitions are stating that each process has a thread of execution. By the way, it is worth mentioning that Jerome Saltzer has a footnote in his PhD thesis indicating that in the mid-1960s Victor Vyssotsky suggested the term *thread* as an alternative to the term *process*.

After this brief historical review of the term *thread*, we will define a thread as the **unit of execution of a process**, and it is manifested by a data structure called the **thread control block (TCB)**. A subset of the information contained in the process control block defines the TCB. You might notice that the thread control block is a lighter data structure compared to the amount information stored in the PCB. For this reason, threads are also known as **lightweight processes**. Figure 9.5 shows a single-threaded process highlighting the thread control block within the process control block.

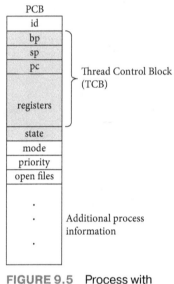

FIGURE 9.5 Process with one thread.

In the early days, when the process concept was implemented, there was only one thread per process, and the thread number and process number were the same. Currently, a process might contain more than one thread (**multithreading**), and therefore, each thread has its own thread id number, as depicted in figure 9.6. Multiple threads within the same process share all process resources, and taking a look back to the process address space in figure 9.6, you will see that there are two threads sharing the text segment. Data and heap segments are also shared by the threads, but each thread has its own stack.

On Threads and Multicores

The IBM/360 PL/1 and the Burroughs/B5000 ALGOL and COBOL programming languages in the late 1960s provided programming constructs for **multitasking**. This technique allowed the concurrent execution of several procedures (routines) within a program to run concurrently, sharing a processor (one core). Conceptually, there is a resemblance between this

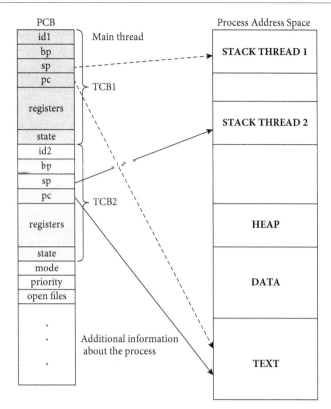

FIGURE 9.6 Process with two threads.

multitasking concept and multithreading as we know it nowadays. The main different is in the implementation aspects. Figure 9.7(a) shows this approach. With the advent of **multicores**, several threads from the same program could be placed in a processor by dispatching each thread in a different core, as illustrated in Figure 9.7(b). This new approach reduced context switching substantially.

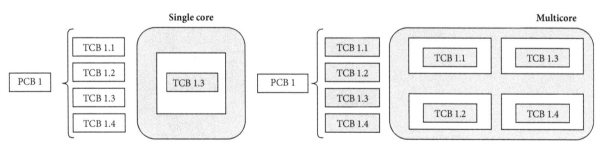

FIGURE 9.7a Four threads sharing a one-core processor.

FIGURE 9.7b Several threads from the same program running on a multicore.

Multicore processors also support the parallel execution of threads from different programs. The operating system is able to dispatch threads from different processes and place them in different cores, thereby allowing the parallel execution of two or more programs in the same processor. Figure 9.8 presents four threads belonging to two different processes executing in parallel in a multicore processor. From the forgoing examples we can infer that operating system threads (kernel threads) can run in parallel on multicores and share the cores with user threads. This is illustrated in figure 9.9.

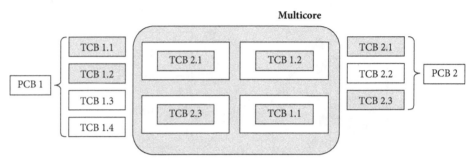

FIGURE 9.8 Two programs sharing a multicore processor.

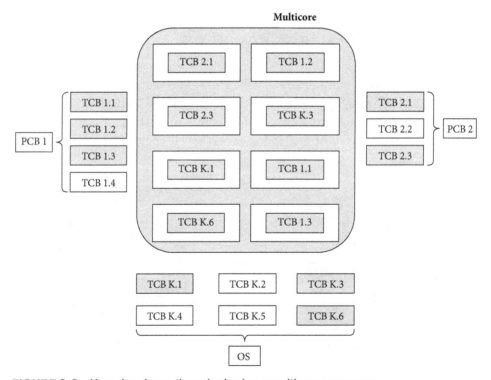

FIGURE 9.9 Kernel and user threads sharing a multicore processor.

SUMMARY

We began this chapter by presenting the process concept as a program in execution. Then a necessary review of the names task, thread, and process was given to clarify that those three names denote the execution of a program. Then we described the way the operating system transforms a passive entity called a program into an active entity called a process. We showed how, on process creation, the operating system assigns to the process a memory area called the process address space and a data structure called the process control block. We illustrated with a state diagram the different states a process can be in while the program associated with the process is running. In this regard, we also presented interrupts as the events that alert the operating system to change a process from one state to another. After presenting a process and its implementation, we moved on to introduce a unit of execution of a program or thread. We explained the difference between a single-threaded program and multithreading. Finally, we gave an overview of the way threads run on single-core processors and multicores.

EXERCISES

1. What is a process?
2. What is a thread?
3. What are the names of the four segments that compose the process address space?
4. What is the difference between the PCB and TCB?
5. Imagine you have five windows open on your computer. Three of them are running the same browser, and the other two run the same text editor. How many processes and how many threads are running?
6. What is the interrupt that moves a process from the ready state to the running state?
7. Draw a picture showing the PCB and process address space for a program with three threads.
8. When the operating system dispatches a process, what fields of the PCB are copied in the CPU?
9. What is the difference between multitasking and multithreading?
10. What does concurrent execution mean for you?
11. Could two threads belonging to the same program run simultaneously in a one-core processor?
12. Could two threads belonging to same program run simultaneously in a two-core processor?
13. What is context switching?
14. Could two threads belonging to two different programs run simultaneously in a two-core processor?

15. When a process is in the running state and an I/O interrupt occurs, what is the name of the state the process will be moved to?

16. When a running process initiates an I/O operation, an interrupt occurs. What is the name of the interrupt?

Bibliographical Notes

Since the early 1960s the terms *process*, *task*, and *thread* have been associated with the execution of a program in the context of operating systems. In 1962 the designers of the first time-sharing systems used the word *process*.[1] Some years later the designers of the MULTICS[2,3,4] and THE[5,6,7] operating systems used the concepts of process as we conceive it nowadays. According to a footnote found at the beginning of chapter 3 in Jerome Saltzer's doctor of science thesis, the term *thread* to refer to a process was suggested by Victor Vyssotsky circa 1962.[8] *Task* was the term used by IBM to refer to a program in execution.[9] Multitasking was the term used in the 1960s and 1970s to refer to a program able to execute several procedures from the same program to run concurrently. Elliot Organick gives a good description of multitasking on the BurroughsB5700/ B6700.[10] There are many good operating system books where you can read more about processes and threads.[11,12,13] A nice and detailed conceptual descriptions of single-threaded processes and multithreading can be found in Anderson and Dahlin.[14] Hansen is an excellent source to study the evolution of operating systems.[15]

Bibliography

1. F. J. Corbató, M. Merwin-Daggett, and R. C. Daley, "An Experimental Time-Sharing System," in Proceedings of the Spring Joint Computer Conference 21, New York: The American Federation of Information Processing Societies (*AFIPS*), 1962. pp. 335–344.
2. V. A. Vyssotsky, F. J. Corbato, and R. M. Graham, "Structure of the Multics Supervisor," in Fall Joint Computer Conference 27, Las Vegas, NV, 1965.
3. E. I. Organick, *The Multics System: An Examination of Its Structure*. Cambridge, MA: MIT Press, 1972.
4. J. Dennis and E. Van Horn, "Programming Semantics for Multiprogrammed Computation," *Communication of Association for Computing Machinery*, 9 (1966), pp. 143–155.
5. E. W. Dijkstra, *Cooperating Sequential Processes*. Eindhoven, Netherlands: Eindhoven University of Technology, 1965.
6. E. W. Dijkstra, "The Structure of 'THE' Multiprogramming System," *Communication of Association for Computing Machinery*, 11, no. 5 (1968), pp. 341–346.
7. A. N. Habermann, *Introduction to Operating System Design*. Chicago: Science Research Associates, 1976.
8. J. Saltzer, *Traffic Control in a Multiplexed Computer System*. Boston: Massachusetts Institute of Technology, 1966.
9. S. E. Madnick and J. J. Donovan, *Systems Operating*. New York: McGraw-Hill, 1974.
10. E. I. Organick, *Computer System Organization: The B5700/B6700 Series*. New York: Academic Press, 1973.
11. H. M. Deitel, P. Deitel, and D. R. Choffnes, *Operating Systems*. Upper Saddle River, NJ: Pearson-Prentice Hall, 2004.
12. A. S. Tanenbaum, *Modern Operating Systems*, 2nd ed. Englewood Cliffs, NJ: Prentice Hall, 2001.
13. A. Silberschatz, P. B. Galvin, and G. Gagne, *Operating System Concepts*. Hoboken, NJ: Wiley, 2013.
14. T. Anderson and M. Dahlin, *Operating Systems: Principles and Practice*. Recursive Books, 2014.
15. P. Brinch Hansen, *Classic Operating Systems: From Batch Processing to Distributed Systems*. New York: Springer-Verlag, 2001.

Chapter 10

Process Synchronization

The whole question of parallelism and concurrency has been pushed a little bit more into the domain, where it belongs: implementation.
—Edsger W. Dijkstra
  A Synthesis Emerging?

INTRODUCTION

When several sequential processes are being executed concurrently and are allowed to read or write from a shared resource, the critical section problem arises, and to maintain data consistency, the implementation of mutual exclusion is necessary to grant access to the shared resource one process at a time. Process synchronization encompasses the mechanism to lock and unlock the critical section to enforce mutual exclusion. This way, when a process is executing its critical section, other processes will not be allowed to execute theirs. The critical section is a set of machine language instructions in a program where a shared resource is accessed and data might be modified. By machine language instruction we mean an instruction executed in a CPU instruction cycle. Dijkstra gave a smart solution to the mutual exclusion problem for n processes in 1965.

We begin this chapter by presenting the concept of concurrent execution. Then we explain the critical section problem, mutual exclusion, and race conditions. Hardware and software solutions to enforce mutual exclusion in critical sections are described. Finally, we present solutions for the producer-consumer and readers-writers problems; two classical examples for teaching concurrency.

CHAPTER OBJECTIVES

- To understand concurrent execution of cooperating sequential programs.
- To understand the critical section problem.
- To explore different programming constructs to solve the critical section problem.
- To explore classical concurrent problems that require process synchronization.

VOCABULARY

This is a list of keywords that herald the concepts we will study in this chapter. They are organized in chronological order and will appear in the text in bold. We invite you to take a look at these keywords to find out which ones you are familiar with.

Concurrency	Atomic operation	Fatbar
Apparent concurrency	Disable interrupts	if...fi
True concurrency	Enable interrupts	do...od
Critical section	Producer-consumer	Guard
Race condition	Monitor	Guarded list
Mutual exclusion	Condition variable (CV)	Guarded command set
Lock	CV.wait	Alternative command
Unlock	CV.signal	Iterative command
Test-and-set	Waiting signalers	Communicating sequential processes (CSP)
Busy waiting	Readers-writers problem	
Semaphore	Guarded command	

ACTIVATING PRIOR KNOWLEDGE

In this section we will present a series of activities. In some of them you can choose one or more options. Sometimes, if you do not agree with the given answers to choose from, you will be allowed to give your own answer. By the way, this is not a test.

1. What is concurrent execution?

    Processor sharing ☐
    Parallelism ☐
    Interleaving instruction from two programs ☐

2. Mark the words denoting the same concept.

    Concurrent execution ☐   Processor sharing ☐   Multiprocessors ☐

3. Do you know any of these terms?

Instruction cycle	Yes ☐	No ☐
Fetch step	Yes ☐	No ☐
Execute step	Yes ☐	No ☐
Timer interrupt	Yes ☐	No ☐

4. Do you know any of these terms?

Test-and-set	Yes ☐	No
Semaphores	Yes ☐	No

Monitor	Yes ☐	No
Message passing	Yes ☐	No

5. Skim the chapter and pay attention to the words written in **bold**. Count how many of those words you are familiar with.

6. Which one of these problems are classical problems to study concurrency?

Producer-consumer	☐
Readers-writers	☐
Sleeping barber	☐

7. Do you know any of these programming languages?

ADA	Yes ☐	No ☐
OCCAM	Yes ☐	No ☐
Python	Yes ☐	No ☐
Go	Yes ☐	No ☐
Java	Yes ☐	No ☐
Mesa	Yes ☐	No ☐

Concurrent Execution

Concurrency is a word that we generally associate with simultaneity, and this could be the reason why people tend to define concurrency as "two programs running at the same time." However, if by running programs we mean executing instruction in a single-core CPU, this definition is misleading because a single-core CPU only executes one instruction at a time; therefore, it would be impossible to execute instructions from two different programs at the same time. To shed some light on the concurrency definition, we will look at concurrency from two different standpoints. We will introduce the concepts of apparent concurrency and true concurrency.

> **Apparent concurrency:** When two or more programs residing in memory at the same time share the CPU by interleaving instruction. This is commonly known as processor sharing.

- In this case, the operating system selects one of the programs stored in memory for execution and dispatches it (assigns the CPU). The selected program begins to execute instructions until an interrupt changes the program state from running to some other state. For example, a timer interrupt will allow the operating system to put the running program back into the ready state and assign the CPU to a different program. This happens so fast that in a couple of seconds the CPU interleaves the execution of instructions from several programs (one program at a time), which gives the illusion that several programs are running at the same time.

True concurrency: When two or more processes carry out different activities on different devices at the same time.

- In this regard, we can imagine a process running instructions in the CPU and another one executing an I/O operation or two different processes running instructions on two different CPUs. In this case we can talk of simultaneous execution.

According to Leslie Lamport, the field of concurrency in computer science started with Dijkstra's 1965 seminal paper, and we agree. In his 1965 paper, Dijkstra gave a solution to the critical section problem.

Critical Sections, Mutual Exclusion, and Race Condition

Imagine a multiprogramming system with two processes running instruction and sharing a common variable. We will focus in observing the side effects that might occur when interleaving instructions from both programs. This could be easy to visualize by keeping track of the system state after executing each instruction. The part of a program we are interested in is that part where a set of instructions accesses a shared variable. This set of instructions is called a **critical section**. If we allow two or more programs to be in their critical sections simultaneously, a race condition might arise. A **race condition** is an undesirable situation that occurs when two or more processes have access to a shared variable, and the final result depends on the order of execution of the instructions in their critical sections. To avoid race conditions, we must serialize the execution of a critical section with this simple rule: if a program is executing its critical section, other programs are not allowed to execute theirs. This is called **mutual exclusion**, and to implement it, we must create mechanisms to lock the critical section while a program is executing it. Let us study these concepts through an example. Figure 10.1 depicts the initial state of a system with two processes (process 1 and process 2) and a shared variable (x). Program 1's critical section are instructions 19, 20, and 21; similarly, program 2's critical section are instructions 54, 55, and 56.

For each process, we show the program and a tiny process control block (PCB) with two fields only: the program counter and space to save a register A. In PCB_P1 you can see the fields PC1 and A, and in PCB_P2 you will see PC2 and A as well. On the other hand, you can also see a CPU with two registers: the instruction register (IR), with question marks on all fields because we do not know which one was the last instruction executed, and the pair PC and register A. PC = 19 tells us that the next instruction to be executed is the one at address 19 in program 1 and A = 0. This means that process 1 is running, and in the next instruction cycle the following change of state will occur: In the fetch cycle, the instruction at memory address 19 is copied in the IR and the PC is incremented by one and points to instruction stored at location 20. In the execute cycle, the value of the shared variable located at address <x> is loaded in register A. This is shown in figure 10.2.

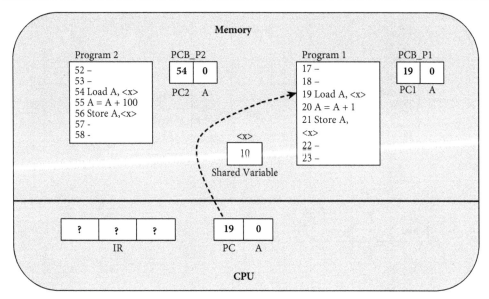

FIGURE 10.1 System state when the operating system assigns the CPU to process 1.

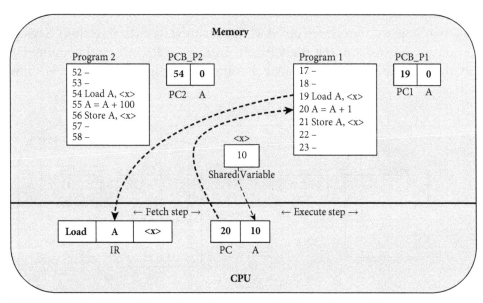

FIGURE 10.2 State of the system when process P1 is running and the process executes instruction at line 19.

Figure 10.3 illustrates the state of the system after fetching and executing instruction at line 20. Please observe all changes in the system state by comparing figures 10.2 and 10.3.

Now, let us assume that at this moment a timer interrupt occurs and the operating system must free the CPU, save process 1 context, and change the process state to ready (keep

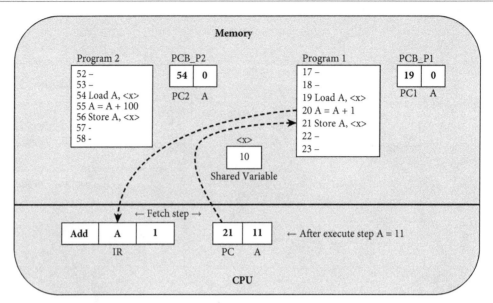

FIGURE 10.3 State of the system when process P1 is running and the process executes instruction at line 20.

in mind that program 1 was interrupted while executing its critical section). Saving process 1 context means copying the CPU.PC into PCB_P1.PC1 and copying CPU.A into PCB_P1.A. The system state after the timer interrupt was handled is shown in figure 10.4.

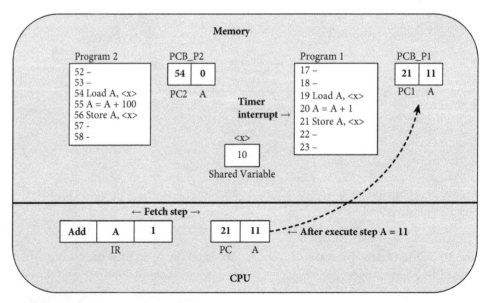

FIGURE 10.4 State of the system when a timer interrupt occurs and the context of P1 is saved in its PCB.

As the CPU is idle, the operating system can dispatch another process. Let us assume that the selected process to use the CPU is process 2. Then the context of process 2 is copied into the CPU, as shown below:

$$CPU.PC \leftarrow PCB\_P2.PC2$$
$$CPU.A \leftarrow PCB\_P2.A.$$

As you can see in figure 10.5, once the CPU is assigned to process 2, CPU.PC points to location 54 in program 2's critical section.

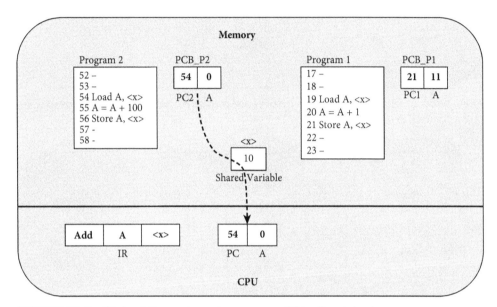

FIGURE 10.5 State of the system when process P2 is dispatched.

From now on, we will show the system state after executing each instruction. In the next instruction cycle, program 2 executes the instruction at memory location 54, and the system state changes, as shown in figure 10.6. The PC points to memory location 55, register A = 10, and the instruction that was executed resides in IR. **It is worth mentioning that both processes are currently in their critical sections.**

Figure 10.7 shows the system state after executing instruction at location 55. You can observe that CPU.PC is pointing to the last instruction in its critical section at memory location 56 and the CPU.A holds the value 110.

In the next instruction cycle, the CPU executes the last instruction at location 56 in program 2's critical section, and the changes in the system state are shown in figure 10.8. Observe that

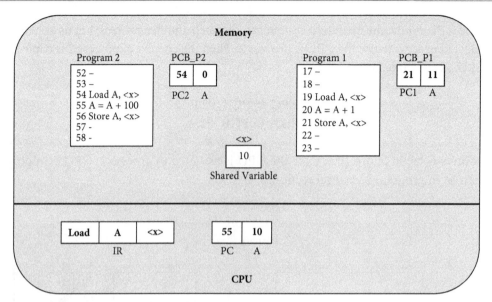

FIGURE 10.6 State of the system when process P2 is running and the process executes instruction at line 54.

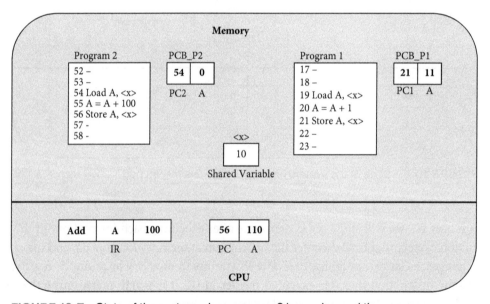

FIGURE 10.7 State of the system when process 2 is running and the process executes instruction at line 55.

the value stored in the shared variable <x> is 110. Let us assume now that after executing the instruction at location 56, there is a timer interrupt, as shown in figure 10.8.

The system state after a context switch is shown in figure 10.9. The context of process 1 is copied into the CPU, which means that CPU.PC points to instruction 21 in program 1 and the register A is restored with the value 11 from PCB_P1.A (CPU.A = 11).

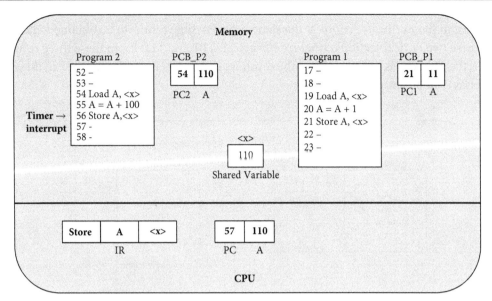

FIGURE 10.8 State of the system when process 2 is running and the process executes instruction at line 56 and then a timer interrupt occurs.

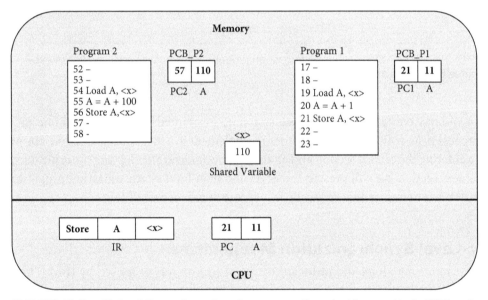

FIGURE 10.9 State of the system when the process 2 context is saved in its PCB and process 1 is dispatched (context switch).

In figure 10.10 you can see the system state after executing instruction at memory location 21. Taking a closer look at the figure, you will see that the value of the shared variable <x> was overwritten, and the final resulting value for variable <x> after the two updates is 11, which is wrong! This is a direct consequence of a race condition for allowing both processes to coexist in their critical sections at the same time. Possible results to be obtained after running these two critical sections concurrently are 11, 110, and 111. From these three resulting values, the right one is 111, and that is the result we should obtain each time we run these two processes concurrently.

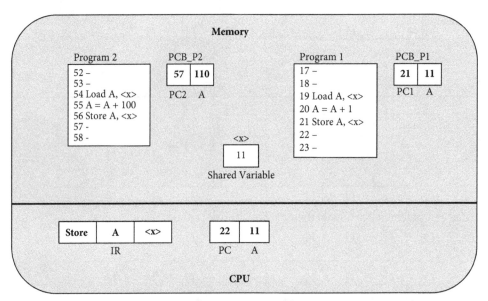

FIGURE 10.10 State of the system when process 1 is running and the process executes instruction at line 21.

To avoid race conditions, mutual exclusion must be granted in order to allow one and only one process in its critical section at a time. To implement it, a lock mechanism must be placed before entering the critical section and an unlock mechanism after leaving the critical section. In the next section, we will present low-level and high-level synchronization programming constructs to enforce mutual exclusion in order to avoid race conditions.

Low-Level Synchronization Mechanisms

The first solution to **lock** and **unlock** the critical section was proposed by IBM. The company created a solution at the hardware level by implementing an atomic instruction (executed in one instruction cycle). The instruction was called **test-and-set**, and it works this way:

1. There is a 1 bit variable, let us call it "s," whose initial value is zero.
2. The lock and unlock instructions are able to modify the variable value in one instruction cycle.

Below you will find the description of lock and unlock using test-and-set:

Lock   **Unlock**
loop: if s = 1 then go to loop;   s = 0;
      s = 1;

Let us see how test-and-set works using the same example we used to explain the race condition problem. Recall that initially, s = 0 and shared variable x = 10.

Program 2   Program 1

52 –   17 –

53 **Lock**   18 **Lock**

54 Load A, <x>   19 Load A, <x>

55 A = A + 100   20 A = A + 1

56 Store A, <x>   21 Store A, <x>

57 **Unlock**   22 **Unlock**

58 –   23 –

Using the same scenario, we assume that program 1 starts out executing instructions, and it executes lock. After executing lock, variable s becomes 1, and the critical section is therefore locked. Program 1 continues running, and the CPU executes instructions at lines 19 and 20. Once instruction 20 is executed, a timer interrupt occurs, and the state of process 1 is saved in PCB_P1. According to figure 10.4, CPU.PC = 21 and CPU.A = 11 are saved in PCB_1. The operating system then assigns the CPU to process 2, and program 2 starts out executing instructions. When program 2 executes lock (recall that s = 1), it will spend all the time assigned by the operating system engaged in a **busy waiting**, which means executing the lock instruction time and again. As you can see, program 2 is blocked at the entrance of its critical section and will remain there until a timer interrupt indicates to program 2 that its time is up. Once the timer interrupt is handled, process 2 context is saved in its PCB_2. Then let us say that the operating system gives the CPU back to process 1 (CPU.PC = 21 and CPU.A = 11), and program 1 resumes execution and executes instruction at line 21, saving the value 11 in shared variable <x>. Then after executing instruction at line 22, variable s becomes 0, and the critical section is freed. Now you can see that if the CPU is assigned again to process 2, it will execute instruction at line 53, but this time, variable s is equal to 0, and therefore program 2 gets out of the busy waiting, enters the critical section, and locks it. Instructions 54, 55, 56, and 57 are executed, and the final result will be x = 111, which is correct. Busy waiting is an undesirable situation in single-CPU systems because too many CPU cycles are wasted. Nevertheless, it is a good solution for multiprocessor systems.

In 1965 Dijkstra proposed a more interesting solution to the critical section problem that avoids busy waiting. His solution is based on semaphores. A **semaphore** is defined as a variable, but you can think of a semaphore as a data structure with two fields, an integer (the semaphore value) and a pointer to implement a queue where blocked processes have to wait to be awaken (this represents the state, waiting on a semaphore). There are two **atomic operations** that can be used on a semaphore P (aka wait) and V (aka signal). Below, you will find the description of these two instructions on a semaphore s, assuming the value of s is initially 1.

s = 1;

P(s)

s := s − 1;
if s < 0 **then**
    Blocks running process on semaphore queue.

V(s)

s := s + 1;
if s ≤ 0 **then**
    Take a process from the semaphore queue and change its state to ready.

Taking a closer look at P(s) and V(s), you will see that once these operations (you can see both of them as functions) are compiled, they generate several instructions in machine language (assembly language). Thus, the following questions arise: How can P and V be indivisible (atomic) operations if when called the CPU has to execute several machine instructions? Is there a potential race condition because s is a shared variable?

We will answer those questions by showing you how to implement P and V as indivisible operations. As you might recall, the instruction cycle is *fetch-execute-check interrupts,* but if interrupts are set up as disable, the instruction cycle is transformed into *fetch-execute*. Let us work with the timer interrupt, which can potentially be triggered at any time and detected after an instruction cycle has concluded. Operations P and V can be executed without the CPU accepting any timer interrupt if the timer interrupt is disabled. Once P or V has been executed, interrupts are enabled, and the CPU goes back to its *fetch-execute-check interrupts cycle*. This way P and V are implemented as software indivisible operations. Below, you will find the description of the implementation of P and V as atomic operations.

s = 1;

P(s)

Disable interrupts
s := s − 1;

if s < 0 **then**
    Block running process on semaphore queue.

Enable interrupts

V(s)

Disable interrupts
s := s + 1;

if s ≤ 0 **then**
    Take a process from semaphore queue and change its state to ready.

Enable interrupts

The P operation can be used to lock a critical section, and V to unlock it and awake one of the processes waiting on the semaphore queue. Using the former example, as shown below, and assuming s = 1, you can observe that if program 1 is running and executes P(s), then s becomes zero. Let us assume there is a timer interrupt after instruction A = A + 1 is executed; then program 1 goes back to the ready state, and as the CPU is now idle, the operating system dispatches program 2. When program 2 executes P(s), the value of s becomes negative, and program 2 is blocked before entering its critical section and the CPU becomes idle. As you can see, busy waiting is no longer an issue and as CPU is idle, the operating system will assign the CPU to another process. Using s = 1 implicitly tells us that only one process can be in its critical section at a time.

Program 2
52 –
53 **P(s)**
54 Load A, <x>
55 A = A + 100
56 Store A, <x>
57 **V(s)**
58 –

Program 1
17 –
18 **P(s)**
19 Load A, <x>
20 A = A + 1
21 Store A, <x>
22 **V(s)**
23 –

For solving other types of problems, semaphores can be initialized to values greater than one. For instance, if we need to keep track of the number of items we are inserting in an array of size five and be alerted when the array is full, s = 5 will be the initial value, and then if P(s) is executed several times, once s becomes negative that indicates the array is full. We will show you this semaphore usage in the next section, when we will describe the solution of a classical problem known as the bounded-buffer producer-consumer problem.

The Bounded-Buffer Producer-Consumer Problem

In the **producer-consumer** problem, there is a buffer and two processes. One of them is called the producer and the other the consumer. The producer produces items and inserts them into the buffer (one on each iteration). The consumer gets items from the buffer and consumes them one at a time. Both processes are sharing the buffer (let us called it B), and let us say that each one of them is engaged in an endless loop, as shown below.

Producer
49 k := 0;
50 **while**(true) **begin**
51 produce(item);

Consumer
14 i := 0;
15 **while**(true) **begin**
16 P(newitem_in_B);

```
52  P(empty_space);                                    17  P(mutex);
53  P(mutex);                shared buffer B           18  value := B[i];
54  B[k] := item;            [ | | | | ]               19  i = i + 1;
55  k := k+ 1;                                         20  if i = 5 then i := 0;
56  if k = 5 then k := 0;                              21  V(mutex);
57  V(mutex);                                          22  V(empty_space);
58  V(newitem_in_B);                                   23  consume(value)
59  endwhile                                           24  endwhile
```

In this example, produce (item) and consume (value) are auxiliary functions just to implement the actions of producing an item and consuming a value respectively. Taking a closer look, you can see the existence of three semaphores whose names are empty_space, mutex, and new_item_in_B. Their initial values and usage are:

Empty_space is used to control when the buffer is full. If the buffer is full, the producer is blocked on this semaphore when the process executes P(empty_space) and the semaphore value is less than zero. Its initial value is the buffer length, and therefore in our example empty_space = 5.

Mutex is used to lock the critical section, and its initial value is mutex = 1.

Newitem_in_B is used to detect whether the buffer is empty. If it is, the consumer process is blocked on this semaphore when the process executes P(newitem_in_B) and the semaphore value is less than zero. Its initial value is newitem_in_B = 0.

Let us explore this solution to the producer-consumer problem. Assuming the consumer is dispatched and starts executing instructions, once the instruction P(newitem_in_B) is executed, the consumer will be blocked because newitem_in_B < 0. On the contrary, if the producer is dispatched and starts running instruction, then a new item is inserted into the buffer on each iteration. Let us assume that the producer iterates five times, then empty_space = 0 and the state of the buffer will be full:

$$B = [item1 \mid item2 \mid item3 \mid item4 \mid item5]$$

It the producer intends another iteration, once P(empty_space) is executed, the semaphore value will be less than zero and the producer will be blocked. The mutex semaphore is used to implement mutual exclusion and avoid a race condition. Each time an item is produced and is inserted in buffer B, the instruction V(newitem_in_B) is executed and the semaphore "newitem_in_B" is incremented to tell the consumer process that there is a new item in the buffer. Eventually, the consumer will run in the CPU and will be able enter its critical section to get items from buffer B.

Monitors

Semaphores can be considered a low-level programming construct that leaves the burden of synchronization to be explicitly provided by the programmer. Fortunately, a high-level synchronization mechanism called **monitor** was proposed in the 1970s. Per Brinch Hansen proposed the monitor concept in 1973, and C. A. R. Hoare further explored this concept in his famous 1974 tutorial paper. A monitor is an abstract data type that encapsulates private data, one or more functions, and sets out some initial values, as shown below.

```
myfirstmonitor: monitor
   <declarations of data local to the monitor>
   procedure procname-1 (… formal parameters …);
     begin
     procedure body …

     end;

   procedure procname-2 (… formal parameters …);
     begin
     procedure body…

     end;

     -
     -
     -

   procedure procname-n (… formal parameters …);
     begin
     procedure body …
     end;

begin
<initialization of local data of the monitor>
end;
```

A monitor is a programming construct that allows safe and mutually exclusive access to shared data by providing a mechanism for blocking and waking up processes. You can think of a monitor as acting like a fence that protects shared data (private data) and procedures declared inside it to handle the private data. To clarify the monitor concept, we will give you a description of how it works.

- Each monitor procedure is an entry point to the monitor, and only the procedures declared inside the monitor have the right to manipulate the private data (shared data).
- To call a procedure local to the monitor, you have to give the monitor name followed by the procedure name. For example, to call procedure-2 in the monitor described above, we will write: ***myfirstmonitor.procedure-2(…actual parameters…)***.

- Many processes might request access to the monitor, but only one process at a time can be active within the monitor.
- There exists a data type denoted **condition variable (CV)**, and there is a queue associated with each condition variable.

Example: **var x: condition**;

There are two operations that can be applied to condition variables, and they are CV.wait and CV.signal. We will use the condition variable x declared above to show you how these operations work:

x.wait means that the running process inside the monitor is suspended in the queue associated to condition x, until another process executes an **x.signal** instruction.

x.signal means resume one of the suspended processes waiting in the queue associated with condition x. If the queue is empty, the signal operation has no effect.

There is also an internal queue called **waiting signalers**. Each process within the monitor that executes an x.signal instruction will be suspended in the waiting signalers queue. Each time a process leaves the monitor, it signals the signalers queue.

Let us give an intuitive view of a monitor in action. In figure 10.11 you can see a graphical view of a monitor. Observe that there is a process (F) inside using the monitor, and there is another process (D) waiting on condition queue c1. Three more processes (A, B, C) are requesting access to enter the monitor, but remember that only one process is allowed to be executing inside the monitor at a time. The dashed arrows indicate that process F executes a c1.signal to allow process D to reenter the monitor from c1 queue to resume execution. The c1.signal will move process F into the signalers queue. This is shown in figure 10.11.

Figure 10.12 shows process D executing procedure E1, process F waiting in the signalers queue, and processes A, B, and C waiting to enter the monitor. The dashed arrows indicate that process D finished up the execution of procedure E1 and left the monitor. When process D leaves the monitor, a signal is sent to the signalers queue to allow a process from that queue (process F) to regain control of the monitor. This is shown in figure 10.12.

Figure 10.13 shows that process F resumes execution of procedure E1 and will finish up the execution of that procedure. At that moment the actions to be taken are highlighted by the dashed lines. The dashed lines indicate that process F leaves the monitor after executing procedure E1, and the monitor decides whether to signal the signalers queue in case there were processes in that queue; otherwise, it will allow the entrance of one of the processes in the input queue into the monitor. In our example it will be process A, which enters the monitor to execute procedure E2.

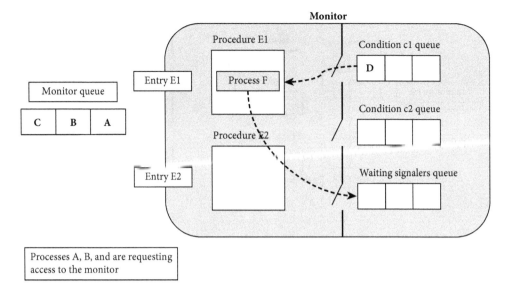

FIGURE 10.11 Process F is using the monitor procedure E1, and process D is waiting on c1 queue. Process F executes C1.signal.

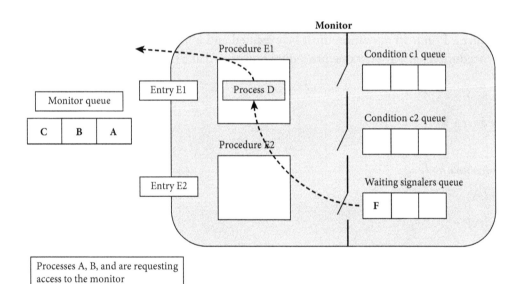

FIGURE 10.12 Process D is using the monitor procedure E1, and process F is waiting on signalers queue. Process D finishes up execution of procedure E1 and leaves the monitor. Then F resumes execution within procedure E1.

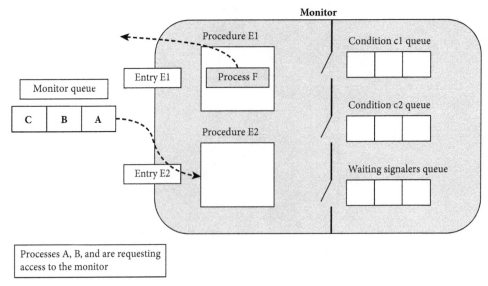

FIGURE 10.13 Process E1 finishes up execution of procedure E1 and leaves the monitor. Process A enters the monitor.

Now that we have an idea of how a monitor works, let us explore some implementation issues. We will use semaphores to explain how a monitor ensures mutual exclusion among all procedure. We need a *mutex* semaphore initialized to 1. Then at the beginning of each procedure a P(*mutex*) operation must be executed and a V(*mutex*) operation at the exit of the procedure. This way only one procedure is executed at a time.

P(*mutex*)

Procedure E1

$\{$ *Procedure body*

V(*mutex*)

P(*mutex*)

Procedure E2

$\{$ *Procedure body*

V(*mutex*)

In Figure 10.11 we explained that process F signals condition c1 to allow process D to resume execution, and process F is enforced to wait in the signalers queue until the process that regained access to the monitor (D) leaves the monitor and permits process F to reenter the monitor to resume execution at the point it left off. To explain this implementation, we will use pair of semaphores called *condsem1* associated to a condition variable and *signaler*, where signaler processes suspend themselves using the operation P(*signaler*), both initialized to 0. The c1.signal operation executed by process F while executing procedure E1 might be implemented as follows.

```
condition.signal operation.
signalers_count := signalers_count + 1;
if condition_count > 0 then {V(condsen1); P(signaler)};
signalers_count := signalers_count - 1;
```

The question now is, how did process D get into c1 queue? Inside procedure E1, process D executed the operation c1.**wait**. This can be clarified by explaining the steps followed by the operation condition.wait.

```
condition.wait operation
condition_count := condition_count + 1;
if signaler_count > 0 then V(signaler) else V(mutex);
P(condsen1)
condition_count := condition_count - 1;
```

The two operations described above have to be implemented for all condition variables declared within a monitor.

We have already discussed the bounded-buffer producer-consumer problem. Let us see an implementation of the producer-consumer using a monitor. The implementation is based on Hoare's 1974 paper.

```
//Monitor declaration

ProdCon: monitor
  buffer: array [0...N-1]
  noempty, nofull: condition;
  count, insert, take: integer;

procedure append (int item);
  begin
  if count = N then nofull.wait;
  buffer[insert] := item;
  insert := (insert + 1) mod N;
  count := count + 1;
  noempty.signal;
  end;
```

```
procedure remove (return y);
  begin
  if count = 0 then noempty.wait;
  y := buffer[take];
  take := (take + 1) mod N
  count := count - 1;
  nofull.signal;
end;

begin
  // initial values
  count:= 0;
  insert:= 0;
  take:= 0;
end; ProdCom

//producer
Loop forever
  produce(item);
  ProdCon.append(item);
end;

//consumer
Loop forever
  ProdCon.remove(item);
  consume(item)
end;
```

The second example shows a monitor for the **readers-writers** problem. This is a typical problem found whenever there is a database shared by two types of processes: processes that just read a record ("readers") or processes that modify a record ("writers"). Only reader processes may simultaneously access the same record. Writer processes must have exclusive access to records because they are updating them. Therefore, readers can access the database only when there are no writers. Writers can access the database only when there are neither readers nor another writer. Each reader executes the following actions.

Reader process
  Wait until no writers.
  Access database and read.
  When last reader leaves, it wakes up a waiting writer if any in writers queue.

Writer process
  Wait until no writers or readers.
  Access database and update record.

If readers waiting in condition queue, it wakes them up; otherwise, it wakes up writers if any.

We will describe a monitor to solve this problem. The monitor will need two condition variables named OKtoread and OKtowrite to place waiting readers and writers respectively. Also, there will be a Boolean variable called "busy" to indicate when a writer is accessing the database and another variable called "readcounter" to keep track of the number of readers that may simultaneously read the same record. Four procedures will be declared within the monitor:

- startread: used by readers to read
- endread: used by readers to indicate they finished reading
- startwrite: used by writers to initiate a modification of a record in the database
- endwrite: used by writers to indicate they finished writing

Initial values are:
readercount := 0;
busy := **false**;

Following, you will find the readers-writers monitor and the reader and writer procedures:

```
readers-writers : monitor;
begin
readercount : integer;
busy : boolean;
OKtoread, OKtowrite : condition;

procedure startread;
  begin
  if busy then OKtoread.wait;
  readercount := readercount + 1;
  OKtoread.signal;
  (*Once one reader can start, they all can*)
  end startread;

procedure endread;
  begin
  readercount := readercount - 1;
  if readercount = 0 then OKtowrite.signal;
  end endread;

procedure startwrite;
  begin
  if busy OR readercount != 0 then OKtowrite.wait;
  busy := true;
  end startwrite;
```

```
procedure endwrite;
  begin
  busy := false;
  if OKtoread.queue then OKtoread.signal
                    else OKtowrite.signal;
  end endwrite;

begin//Initial values
readercount := 0;
busy := false;
end;

end readers-writers;

procedure Reader;
  {
    while (TRUE)
    {
      ReadersWriters.StartRead;
      Read database      // read data
      ReadersWriters.EndRead;
    }
  }

procedure Writer;
  {
    while (TRUE)
    {
      Create data
      ReaderWriters.StartWrite();
      Write database     // update database
      ReadersWriters.EndWrite();
    }
  }
```

Guarded Commands

Sequencing, selection, and iteration are fundamental control structures found in most programming languages nowadays, and they are based on the early works developed by Corrado Böhn and Giuseppe Jacopini in 1966. These control structures are as follows:

Sequencing: statemen-1; statement-2; ... statement-n;
Selection: **if** condition **then** statement **else** statement;
Iteration: **for** loops or **while** loops or **repeat ... until**;

These control structures are deterministic, and to give you an example, let us take the selection statement. When we use an **if** ($w \leq 3$) **then** *statement-1* **else** *statement-2,* the condition is partitioning a set of values into two subsets, and this is telling us that the members of one subset will be handled differently than the members of the other subset. Practically, we are doing set partitioning, and this mean the members of the two subsets are mutually exclusive.

In 1975 Edsger Dijkstra proposed a new and quite different form of selection and loop control structures denoted **guarded commands**. He thought nondeterminism could be used on concurrent programs. These programing constructs have been implemented in CSP, Occam, Ada, and Haskell. We will give an introduction to nondeterministic control structures as proposed by Dijkstra. In the grammar below, you can observe the following.

a. The "**fatbar**" symbol ▯ is used to separate guarded commands.
b. Reserved words **fi** and **od** are closing reserved words for **if** and **do** respectively.
c. A **guard** is a Boolean expression.
d. A **guarded command** is a guard and its associated **guarded list**.
e. A **guarded list** is defined as either a single statement or a statement sequence.
f. A **guarded command set** is defined as either a single guarded command or a guarded command sequence.

The guarded command grammar is describe below.

```
<guarded command> ::= <guard> → <guard list>
<guard> ::= <boolean expession>
<guarded list> ::= <statement> {; <statement>}
<guarded command set> ::= <guarded command> {▯ <guarded command>}
<alternative construct> ::= if <guarded command set> fi
<repetitive construct> ::= do <guarded command set> od
<statement> ::= <alternative construct> | <repetitive construct> |
"other statements".
```

Note: The symbol "::=" can be read as "is defined as."

The **alternative command**:

```
if <boolean expression> → <statement>
▯  <boolean expression> → <statement>
▯  ...
▯  <boolean expression> → <statement>
fi
```

Semantics:

Each time the statement is reached for execution, all Boolean expressions are evaluated simultaneously.

If more than one of the Boolean expressions (guards) is true, one of them is chosen at random, and its corresponding statements are executed.

If none of the guards is true, a runtime error occurs that causes program termination.

The alternative command examples:

Example 1: Due to Sebesta:

```
if i = 0 → sum := sum + i
☐ i > j → sum := sum + j
☐ j > i → sum := sum + j
fi
```

If i = 0 and j > i the construct chooses nondeterministically between the first and the last statements.

If i = j and i != 0 a runtime error occurs.

Example 2: Find the largest of two numbers (due to Dijkstra):

```
if x ≥ y → max := x
☐ y ≥ x → max := y
fi
```

The iterative command:

```
do <boolean expression> → <statement>
☐  <boolean expression> → <statement>
☐  ...
☐  <boolean expression> → <statement>
od
```

Semantics:

All the Boolean expressions are evaluated each iteration.

If more than one of the Boolean expressions or guards are true, one of the corresponding statements is nondeterministically chosen for execution.

Once the statements are executed, the guards are evaluated again.

If all the guards are false, the loop terminates.

Example 3: Euclid's algorithm (Dijkstra EWD 398):

```
if A > 0 and B > 0 → a := A; b := B;
                    do a > b → a := a - b;
                    ☐  b > a → b := b - a;
                    od
                    print (a)
fi
```

In this example if the condition A > 0 and B > 0 is not satisfied, the program will be aborted. Otherwise the program gets out of the loop and prints the result when a = b.

Example 4: Sorting (due to Dijkstra):

```
q₁, q₂, q₃, q₄ := Q1, Q2, Q3, Q4;
do q₁ > q₂ → T := q1; q1 := q2; q2 := T;
 ▯ q₂ > q₃ → T := q2; q2 := q3; q3 := T;
 ▯ q₃ > q₄ → T := q3; q3 := q4; q4 := T;
od.
```

Initial values Q1, Q2, Q3, and Q4 are assigned simultaneously to variables q_1, q_2, q_3, and q_4. Let us assume that the values assigned are: q1 := 8, q2 := 6, q3 := 4, and q4 := 2. With these initial values you can see that all guards are true at the beginning of the program (true guards are highlighted). We will show this example step-by-step.

```
Initial values    q1   q2   q3   q4
                  8    6    4    2      q₁ > q₂   q₂ > q₃   q₃ > q₄
Guard selected
Step 1  q₂ > q₃   8    4    6    2      q₁ > q₂   q₂ > q₃   q₃ > q₄
Step 2  q₃ > q₄   8    4    2    6      q₁ > q₂   q₂ > q₃   q₃ > q₄
Step 3  q₁ > q₂   4    8    2    6      q₁ > q₂   q₂ > q₃   q₃ > q₄
Step 4  q₂ > q₃   4    2    8    6      q₁ > q₂   q₂ > q₃   q₃ > q₄
Step 5  q₁ > q₂   2    4    8    6      q₁ > q₂   q₂ > q₃   q₃ > q₄
Step 6  q₃ > q₄   2    4    6    8      q₁ > q₂   q₂ > q₃   q₃ > q₄
```

We have introduced the concept of guarded commands in this section for two reasons:

1. They can be used for controlling the sequential execution of nondeterministic programs.
2. They are an important component of CSP, a model of computation for implementing concurrent applications based on message passing. CSP will be the subject of the next section.

Message Passing

We introduced guarded commands in the preceding section because they are part of a new programming construct that expresses concurrency based on message passing. In 1978, C.A.R. Hoare published a seminal paper on **communicating sequential processes (CSP)**. Hoare's paper paved the way for the programming of distributed and parallel systems. CSP is a notational system or programming language for expressing concurrent and parallel execution of cooperating sequential processes. In this notational system, synchronous input-output operations are use as statements for process communication through message passing. We will give a brief introduction to the basic statements used in CSP, and then we will show a solution for the bounded-buffer producer-consumer problem. The basic statements are as follows.

```
Assignment:
  <variable> := <expression>  example: x := e;

Input (Receive)
  <source process> ? <variable>  example: B ? x  {variable x accepts
                                                   input from Process B}

Output (send)
  <Destination process> ! <expression>  example: A ! e  {Output the value e
                                                          to process A}

Alternative command:
  if <boolean expression> → <statement>
  ▯ <boolean expression> → <statement>
  ▯ ...
  ▯ <boolean expression> → <statement>
  fi

Iterative command
  do <boolean expression> → <statement>
  ▯ <boolean expression> → <statement>
  ▯ ...
  ▯ <boolean expression> → <statement>
  od
```

You can read the input statement B ? x as "**x** receives a value from Process **B**," and in the case of the output statements A ! e, this can be read as "expression **e** is sent to process **A**". Figure 10.14 shows an example of the usage of the input and output statements for synchronizing two processes. Be aware that there are no buffers in CSP, and therefore communication between two processes is synchronous. There is no communication to send a message until both processes are ready to execute a send-receive handshake. No matter what process arrives first to one of the input/output statements involved in the computation, the first one to arrive has to wait for the other process.

You can observe in figure 10.14 that variable x in process A is initialized to zero and variable y becomes 5 in process B. Both processes are executing instructions concurrently, and let us assume that process A reaches line 54; there is an input command (B ? x) indicating that variable x in process A is waiting to accept a value sent by process B. On the other hand, process B is executing instructions and eventually reaches line 22, where the output command (A ! y + 1) indicates that process B will send the expression "y + 1" to process A. What these two processes are doing once the two statements synchronously execute is "x := y + 1." Recall that the two processes could be running in the same machine or in different computers.

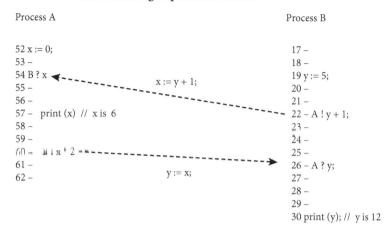

FIGURE 10.14 Synchronizing processes A and B using message passing.

The notation for sequential execution and repetition in CSP will be illustrated with two examples:

For sequential execution, you have to use square brackets → [C ? x; y := x +2;].
For repetition, you have to use square brackets preceded by "*" → *[C ? x; y := x +2;].

Now we will present the bounder-buffer producer-consumer using CSP. As there are no buffers in CSP, in addition to the producer and consumer processes, a third process is needed to play the role of a buffer. Processes are declared in CSP using "::" which means "is defined as." For example, to declare a process called X we have to use: "X ::" and then the variables and statements describing the process behavior.

Figure 10.15 shows a solution to the producer-consumer problem in CSP. You can assume producer and consumer processes are iterating. The producer process is sending values to the B (buffer process). The consumer uses the command "B ! more ( )" to send a signal to request an item, and if the request is granted, the consumer uses the command "B ? p" to receive an item. We must focus now on the guarded command in process B. The first line in the guarded command says that if the in < out + 10 and "producer ? buffer(in mod 10)" is true because the buffer has received an item from the producer, then "in" is incremented by one. The second line says that if out < in and a signal has been received from the consumer requesting an item, process B will output an item from the buffer to the consumer, and "out" is incremented by one. Recall that if the buffer is full, the first guard is false, and if the buffer is empty, the second guard will be false. But if there are some items in the buffer, both guards are true and one of them is selected randomly for execution. In case in = out, all guards are false and the *[...] command terminates. Recall that guarded commands are evaluated in each

Producer/Consumer

```
producer ::
    B ! p;           (send p to B)
```

```
consumer ::
    B ! more ( ) ;   (request value)
    B ? p;           (read value)
```

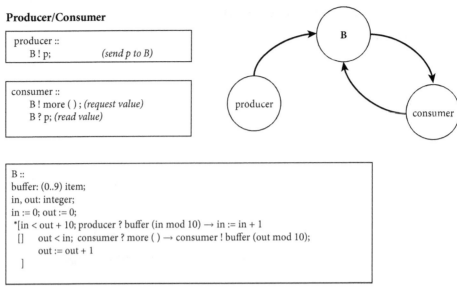

```
B ::
buffer: (0..9) item;
in, out: integer;
in := 0; out := 0;
*[in < out + 10; producer ? buffer (in mod 10) → in := in + 1
 []  out < in; consumer ? more ( ) → consumer ! buffer (out mod 10);
     out := out + 1
 ]
```

FIGURE 10.15 Bounded-buffer producer-consumer in CSP.

iteration. It is worth mentioning that the language Go whose popularity is rapidly growing uses CSP like message passing to support concurrency.

SUMMARY

We began this chapter by reviewing the concurrency definition and observing how the critical section problem arises when two or more cooperating sequential processes share a resource. Hardware and software mechanisms were presented to enforce mutual exclusion and thus avoid race conditions. We showed the usage of test-and-set and semaphores to solve the critical section problem and also showed a solution for the bounded-buffer producer-consumer problem using semaphores. A high-level synchronization mechanism called monitor was presented, and its usage for solving the bounded-buffer producer-consumer and the readers-writers problem was described. An introduction to sequential control structures for nondeterministic programs was given as a preamble to another synchronization mechanism based on message passing. This mechanism called communicating sequential processes (CSP) uses input/output instructions as synchronization primitives to implement message passing. Finally, a solution to the bounded-buffer producer-consumer using CSP is presented to be compared with the previous solution given to this problem using semaphores and monitors.

EXERCISES

1. What is busy waiting?
2. Define critical section, race condition, and mutual exclusion.
3. Explain how test-and-set works.
4. Using pseudocode, write down the algorithm for P and V.
5. What does the term atomic instruction mean?
6. Is it possible to interrupt the execution of a P operation on a semaphore?
7. Is a timer interrupt synchronous or asynchronous?
8. Define concurrent execution?
9. What is context switching?
10. What is a monitor?
11. Could two threads belonging to the same program run simultaneously in a one-core processor?
12. In the monitor procedure "endwrite" described below, when a writer ends writing, the readers have priority over the writers to reenter the monitor. Modify the procedure to work this way: Each time an endwrite is executed, it will alternate the priorities. This means that one-time readers will have priority over writers, and the next time the writers will have priority over the readers, and then readers have priority, and so on.

```
procedure endwrite;
  begin
  busy := false;
  if OKtoread.queue then OKtoread.signal
  else OKtowrite.signal;
  end endwrite;
```

13. What does it happen if, in an if ... fi statement, all guards are false?
14. Solve the bounded-buffer producer-consumer problem using CSP. But this time, there are two producers, one buffer, and one consumer.
15. Name two programming languages that had implemented CSP.
16. Is it possible to use monitors in a Java program?
17. Research question: Find out what message passing interface (MPI) is.
18. Is concurrent execution equal to parallel execution?
19. Go is an open-source programming language. Download the compiler and write a program to implement the bounded-buffer producer-consumer using message passing.

Bibliographical Notes

Test-and-set was implemented in the mid-1960s in the IBM System/360 Model 65.[1] The first correct solution to the critical section problem for two processes was given by T. J. Dekker in 1962.[2] Dijkstra gave the first efficient solution to the critical section problem for *n* processes in 1965[3] and also in the same year proposed synchronization primitives for concurrent programming. The monitor concept as a high-level synchronizing mechanism for concurrent programing was proposed by Brinch-Hansen in 1973,[4] and it was further explored by C.A.R. Hoare in his 1974 tutorial paper.[5] Corrado Böhn and Giuseppe Jacopini[6] proposed selection and iteration as control structures to describe how to construct structured flow charts. Nowadays, all procedural languages use Böhn-Jacopini's approach to control the sequential execution of programs. Guarded commands and nondeterministic control structures were proposed by Dijkstra in 1975 as sequential control structures for nondeterminism.[7] Using Dijkstra's guarded commands and input/output operations as primitive for process synchronization, in 1978 C.A.R. Hoare proposed communicating sequential processes (CSP).[8] With this paper, Hoare paved the way for the development of distributed and parallel computing using message passing. Good sources of the origin of concurrency are the works of Lesley Lamport[9,10] and Per Brinch Hansen.[11]

Bibliography

1. D. Gifford and A. Spector, "IBM's System/360-370 Architecture," *Communications of ACM* 30, no. 4 (1987), pp. 292–307.
2. E. W. Dijkstra, *Cooperating Sequential Processes*. Eindhoven, Netherlands: Eindhoven University of Technology, 1965.
3. E. W. Dijkstra, "Solution of a Problem in Concurrent Programming Control," *Communication of the Association for Computing Machinery*, 8, no. 9 (1965), p. 569.
4. P. Brinch-Hansen, *Operating System Principles*. Englewood Cliffs, NJ: Prentice Hall, 1973.
5. C. A. R. Hoare, "Monitor: An Operating System Structuring Concept," *Communications of the Association for Computing Machinery*, 17, no. 10 (1974), pp. 549–557.
6. C. Böhn and G. Jacopini, "Flow Diagrams, Turing Machines and Languages with Only Two Formation Rules," *Communication of the Association for Computing Machinery*, 9, no. 5 (1966), pp. 366–371.
7. E. W. Dijkstra, "Guarded Commands, Nondeterminacy and Formal Derivation of Programs," *Communications of the Association for Computing Machinery*, 18, no. 8 (1975), pp. 453–457.
8. C. A. R. Hoare, "Communicating Sequential Processes," *Communications of the Association for Computing Machinery*, 21, no. 8 (1978), pp. 666–677.
9. L. Lamport, "Turing Lecture: The Computer Science of Concurrency: The Early Years," *Communications of the Association for Computing Machinery*, 58, no. 6 (2015), pp. 71–76.
10. L. Lamport, *Concurrency: the Works of Leslie Lamport*, ed. D. Malkhi, New York: *Association for Computing Machinery*, 2019.
11. P. Brinch-Hansen, *The Origin of Concurrent Programming: From Semaphores to Remote Procedure Calls*, ed. P. Brinch-Hansen, New York: Springer-Verlag, 2002.

CPSIA information can be obtained
at www.ICGtesting.com
Printed in the USA
BVHW020903190123
656605BV00014B/659